"With a sophisticated grasp of the 'psy' disciplines across global contexts, Khan and Schwebach have curated an incisive and generative critique of the psychiatrization of trauma and the construction of 'mental health' that should be taken quite seriously. Collectively, the contributions have profound implications both for how we understand the history of psychology and for how we might imagine help, healing, and justice less rooted in structures and epistemologies of violence."

Patrick R. Grzanka, *Professor of Psychology, The University of Tennessee, Knoxville*

"An exciting and very thoughtful volume, which elegantly rethinks the trauma word, its meanings and practices on wide, global, American and intimate scales. This book's finely rendered cases will be taught and taught again."

Nancy Rose Hunt, Ph.D., *Professor of History, The University of Florida, author of* A Nervous State (2016) *and* A Colonial Lexicon (1999)

GLOBALIZATION, DISPLACEMENT, AND PSYCHIATRY

This book explores diasporic identities and lived experiences that emerge in global patterns of oppression and considers the consequences of treatment and cure when patients experience mental illness due to war, displacement and surveillance. Going beyond psychiatric institutions and conventional psychiatric knowledge by focusing on informal networks, socially contingent value systems, and cultural sites of healing, this book considers how communities utilize trauma productively for healing. The chapters in this volume consider the detection of mental illness and its treatment through claims to citizenship and belonging as well as denials of social identity and psychic experiences by institutions of the state. A multidisciplinary team of contributors and international range of case studies explore topics such as colonial trauma, feminized trauma, reproductive violence, military mental health and more.

This book is an essential resource for psychologists, psychiatrists, political scientists, sociologists and anthropologists, as well as scholars and those involved in policymaking and practice.

Sanaullah Khan is an incoming lecturer at Brandeis University where he will teach medical anthropology after the completion of his PhD in anthropology at Johns Hopkins University. He is currently also an adjunct professor in medical anthropology at the University of Delaware.

Elliott Schwebach (PhD, political science, Johns Hopkins University) is currently working as a DEI Consultant for Dr. Valaida Wise Consulting and teaching at Central New Mexico Community College.

International Perspectives on Forensic Mental Health

Edited by Patricia Zapf
Palo Alto University

A Routledge Book Series

The goal of this series is to improve the quality of health care services in forensic and correctional settings by providing a forum for discussing issues and disseminating resources related to policy, administration, clinical practice, and research. The series addresses topics such as mental health law; the organization and administration of forensic and/or correctional services for persons with mental disorders; the development, implementation and evaluation of treatment programs and interventions for individuals in civil and criminal justice settings; the assessment and management of violence risk, including risk for sexual violence and family violence; and staff selection, training, and development in forensic and/or correctional systems.

Published Titles

Diversity and Marginalisation in Forensic Mental Health Care
Edited by Jack Tomlin and Birgit Vollm

Safeguarding the Quality of Forensic Assessment in Sentencing
A Review Across Western Nations
Edited by Michiel van der Wolf

Globalization, Displacement, and Psychiatry
Global Histories of Trauma
Edited by Sanaullah Khan and Elliott Schwebach

For more information about this series, please visit www.routledge.com

GLOBALIZATION, DISPLACEMENT, AND PSYCHIATRY

Global Histories of Trauma

Edited by Sanaullah Khan
and Elliott Schwebach

Routledge
Taylor & Francis Group

NEW YORK AND LONDON

Designed cover image: © Getty Images

First published 2024
by Routledge
605 Third Avenue, New York, NY 10158

and by Routledge
4 Park Square, Milton Park, Abingdon, Oxon, OX14 4RN

Routledge is an imprint of the Taylor & Francis Group, an informa business

ISBN: 978-1-032-27557-4 (hbk)
ISBN: 978-1-032-27555-0 (pbk)
ISBN: 978-1-003-31184-3 (ebk)

DOI: 10.4324/9781003311843

Typeset in Bembo
by Apex CoVantage, LLC

CONTENTS

CONTRIBUTORS

Neil Krishan Aggarwal is a cultural psychiatrist and social scientist at Columbia University who specializes in the psychology of cross-cultural conflicts and negotiation. After medical school, he completed a residency in psychiatry, a graduate degree in South Asian Studies, and a post-doctoral fellowship in clinically applied medical anthropology. His areas of professional interest include cultural psychiatry, cultural psychology, and psychiatric anthropology. His books include Mental Health in the War on Terror (2015), The Taliban's Virtual Emirate (2016), Media Persuasion in the Islamic State (2019), Militant Leadership (2023), and a forthcoming book on the psychology of war and peacemaking with the former spychiefs of India and Pakistan's foreign intelligence agencies.

Roberto Beneduce, PhD, MD, anthropologist and psychiatrist, is full professor of Medical and Psychological Anthropology at the University of Turin, and founder of the Frantz Fanon Center (Turin, 1996), a center devoted to research and clinical intervention in the area of migration and asylum seekers. His research engages various intellectual terrains and fields (history of ethnopsychiatry; anthropology of memory and violence; racism and alienation; epistemic and environmental injustice; religious imaginaries and changes in local healing knowledge (Cameroon, Mali, Mozambique, and Senegal)). He has published in different international journals (Politique africaine, Medical Anthropology, Transcultural Psychiatry, Social Compass, Cahiers d'études africaines, Anthropos, etc.); among his works, he authored the following books: *Archeologie del trauma. Un'antropologia del sottosuolo* (Rome 2010), *Un lugar en el mundo. Senderos de la migración entre violencia, memoria y deseo* (Ciudad de México 2015); *L'histoire au corps. Mémoires indociles et* *archives du désordre dans les cultes de possession en Afrique* (Fribourg 2016) and, with N. Gibson, *Frantz Fanon, Psychiatry and Politics* (New York 2017).

Nora Berenstain is Professor of Philosophy and core faculty in Women's, Gender, and Sexuality Studies at the University of Tennessee, Knoxville. Her research spans topics in social & political philosophy, metaphysics of science, feminist epistemology and critical philosophy of race. Her current research explores non-accidental patterns of relations among structures of oppression and how such structures mediate knowledge production. Her work has appeared in *Hypatia, Synthese, Ergo, Mind, Contemporary Political Theory,* and collections with Oxford University Press. Dr. Berenstain co-directs the University of Tennessee's Intersectionality Community of Scholars, an interdisciplinary group of researchers oriented toward transformative social change.

Shinnyi Chou is a child, adolescent and adult psychiatrist based in Pittsburgh, Pennsylvania, USA. In addition to clinical care of patients, she conducts basic neuroscience research focused on understanding the intersection between cannabis and psychosis.

Crystal Han is currently a staff psychiatrist at the Harvard University Counseling and Mental Health Services and at the Massachusetts General Hospital Yawkey Center for Outpatient Child and Adolescent Psychiatry Department. She completed her BA at Cornell University and received her MD at the University at Buffalo School of Medicine. She completed her adult psychiatry residency and child and adolescent psychiatry fellowship at the University of Maryland/ Sheppard Pratt program. Her academic interests include cultural psychiatry, the Asian American transitional aged youth population and psychotherapy. She is a recipient of the American Psychiatric Association SAMHSA Minority Fellowship. She also completed the Washington Baltimore Psychoanalytic Center's Psychoanalytic Studies Program.

Sanaullah Khan is currently an adjunct professor of medical anthropology at the University of Delaware. He has been a junior fellow at the American Institute of Pakistan Studies and has received advanced training in global health, anthropology and history of medicine from Johns Hopkins University. He is also an incoming lecturer in medical anthropology at Brandeis University. In the past, his research on militarization and psychiatric care has appeared in *Critical Military Studies, Asian Anthropology, Journal of South Asian Studies, Medical History, South Asian Development* and *City & Society.*

Nerli Paredes-Ruvalcaba is a Chicana mother (raised in Mexico and the United States) and PhD candidate in the Department of Anthropology at Michigan State

University. Her research investigates issues related to reproductive and infant health, constellating across Indigenous Studies, Women and Gender Studies, Anthropology, and Public Health while using mixed methods to interface the confluences of varying sociocultural factors that influence infant feeding practices, health and development. Her academic training informs both the critical purview of her research scope and the interdisciplinary approaches she uses as a community-engaged scholar to tackle systemic issues and their underlying problems. Core to her academic practice is establishing crucial relationships that facilitate research and service while supporting non-traditional, first-generation, and traditionally underserved populations.

Elena Ruíz is Associate Professor at Michigan State University. Her research focuses on structural responses to gender-based violence and on structural justice advocacy frameworks for survivors of sexual violence.

Elliott Schwebach received his PhD in Political Science (Political Theory) at Johns Hopkins University, where he applied Freudian and Fanonian political psychology to questions regarding the nature and ethics of private property. During his doctoral work, he also attended the Washington Baltimore Center for Psychoanalysis as a student of their Psychoanalytic Studies Program. Elliott is currently teaching Political Science at Central New Mexico Community College, in a city and state that he loves.

Alyson K. Spurgas is Associate Professor of Sociology and affiliated faculty in the Women's, Gender, & Sexuality Studies Program at Trinity College in Hartford, Connecticut, United States. Spurgas researches, writes and teaches about sociologies of trauma, politics of desire and technologies of care from an interdisciplinary and intersectional feminist perspective. They are the author of *Diagnosing Desire: Biopolitics and Femininity into the Twenty-First Century* (The Ohio State University Press, 2020), which won the 2021 Cultural Studies Association First Book Prize, and *Decolonize Self-Care* (forthcoming on OR Book in 2023). Check out www.alysonkspurgas. com for info about Alyson's writing, teaching, speaking events and more.

Saiba Varma is Associate Professor of Anthropology at the University of California, San Diego. As a medical and cultural anthropologist, her work examines questions of violence, medicine, psychiatry, and politics as they pertain to Indian-controlled Kashmir and South Asia more generally. Her first book, *The Occupied Clinic: Militarism and Care in Kashmir*, was published by Duke University Press in 2020. She has also written for public venues such as *Salon, Economic and Political Weekly, The Nation,* and *Al Jazeera.*

Christopher M. Webb is a cultural anthropologist who studies violence, war, trauma and healing. His work investigates how local social/cultural values mediate the holistic experience of violence. As a medical anthropologist, Dr. Webb focuses on the social world of biomedical mental health categories, emphasizing the diagnosis of post-traumatic stress disorder. Dr. Webb has conducted fieldwork with Native American healers who conduct purification and healing rituals for war veterans. Dr. Webb is a North Americanist with a deep scholarly interest in the mythologies of North America. His diverse work considers contemporary veteran culture, biomedicine, North American Indigenous diaspora, American Northern Plains religion, warrior culture formations, healing rituals, U.S. military history and Appalachia. Dr. Webb is a veteran of the United States Army and recipient of the Purple Heart Medal.

Jie Yang is Professor of Anthropology at Simon Fraser University. She was trained in linguistic anthropology. Her current research focuses on critical studies of mental health and Indigenous and non-Indigenous psychology in China. She is editor of *the Political Economy of Affect and Emotion in East Asia* (2014, Routledge) and author of two monographs: *Unknotting the Heart: Unemployment and Therapeutic Governance* (2015, Cornell University Press; 2016 winner of Francis Hsu Book Prize) and *Mental Health in China: Change, Tradition, and Therapeutic Governance* (2018, Polity Press). Currently, she is working on two projects: one delineates troubling double binds and widespread distress among Chinese officials in the context of anti-corruption campaigns (she is completing a new monograph on the phenomenon of *guan xinbing* temporarily entitled *Officials' Heart Distress: Bureaucracy, Inner Friction, and Psychopolitics in China*); the other project delves into Chinese classics of philosophy, literature and medicine to investigate psychological systems and classifications of mental distress and their associated modes of treatment imbricated in these classic texts as well as their implications for contemporary psychological practice.

Xiaowen Zhang is a PhD student in anthropology at Simon Fraser University. Zhang's research interests lie in grief counseling, mental health and death rituals. Her PhD project specifically focuses on death that occurred during the COVID-19 pandemic in China, and how its aftermath in terms of survivors' mental health is being dealt with under the therapeutic ethos.

ACKNOWLEDGMENTS

Sanaullah Khan: This volume would not have been possible without the hard work of my co-editor, Elliott Schwebach. Our shared passion to understand the relations between political structures, globalization and psychiatric discourses kept us motivated. As an anthropologist in training, I learned a great deal from Elliott's appreciation of political theory and deep commitment to de-colonial frameworks and epistemology. Elliott's deep appreciation of global logics of inequality seemed to be too grand a scale at first, given my training in anthropology as well as the discipline's commitments to studying people's mundane and everyday realities. Yet the friendship and shared passion in global mental health that Elliott and I discovered and nurtured through our stimulating conversations led me to consider interesting ways to think about the macro and micro and the individual and the structural as part of the same story. This book is a testament to our friendship and collaboration, but more importantly, my own journey and training, thanks to Elliott, in a vision of scholarship inspired by social justice and ethics of care, kindness, empathy, transparency and responsibility.

Over the past few years, I have learned a great deal from the works of various psychiatric and psychological anthropologists as well as historians – I have yet to meet all of them in person, but their works have continued to shape my thinking. I want to specifically thank two of these people: Mark S. Micale, whose writing on the global history of trauma first inspired the idea of a project in which Elliott and I could start the story of trauma, for once, from outside the "West" instead of taking Western psychiatry, its histories of trauma and diagnostics as our benchmark for how people do or do not express distress. Second, I want to thank Tanya Luhrmann, whose work and guidance opened my eyes to what culture does to the workings of the psyche. My ideas of human subjectivity, disembodiment and agency in contexts of healing were shaped by the works of Rebecca Lester as well as the generous feedback on my broader work by Kamran Asdar Ali on various occasions, but most notably at the American Institute of Pakistan Studies Emerging Scholars symposium in 2022, which encouraged me to go beyond ideas of the "self" based on singularity and autonomy in my understanding of trauma, illness and treatment.

Elliott Schwebach: Firstly, thank you to Sanaullah for reaching out to me with this fantastic idea for a project, and for inviting me so graciously to participate as an editor. A warm thank-you to Sarah Rae, Patricia Zapf, and Katya Porter at Routledge for bringing this project to life. To the extent that this volume bears the influence of my devout psychoanalytic commitments, I owe a great deal to the Washington Baltimore Center for Psychoanalysis, and especially to my cherished classmates and friends from my time there. Finally, I am proud to acknowledge those in my life who helped sustain me, through care, support and counsel, as this book was being written. A special thanks to Noreen Honeycutt for helping me unpack my own losses and traumas, to the wittiness, warmth and wisdom of Benjamin Tellie, Julie Liebenguth, José Durán, Mohammad Murtuza, Claude Nganzeu, Chris Hewitt, Ian Schmid, Cliff Allington and Ryanne Fujita-Conrads, and to the love of my parents.

INTRODUCTION

Conceptualizing the Global

Sanaullah Khan and Elliott Schwebach

It is by now a truism bordering on cliché that we live within an increasingly globalized world. Flows of people, capital and ideas follow both liberalization and war, reproducing historical patterns of colonial power and generating staggering levels of forced displacement, as communication technology becomes progressively digitized, altogether embedding cultural exchange (and cultural conflict) deeper within social relations worldwide. Global power dynamics emerge as "threats" for authoritarian regimes opposing (neo)liberal growth, notwithstanding the global cultural influences and communication networks shaping the lives of many of their citizens; and conversely, yet under similar auspices of fear of intrusion of unwanted global forces and forms, the apparatuses of state surveillance and control stretch ever further into the social fabrics of liberal democracies. The landscape of global inequality is expanding under conditions of flexible labor regimes or the entry of workers into the gig economy. Medical systems are becoming increasingly digitized, disrupting patient–physician relations, and the possibility of environmental catastrophes, such as floods, heatwaves and disease outbreaks, remains an ever-present global threat. And patterns of oppression contingent to modern relations of power, such as racism, continue to make their mark in social policies, knowledge regimes, worldviews and language, reaching far into the unconscious to do so (see, e.g., Fanon, 1952/1994; Parker, 2019; Dennis, 2021), allowing long-standing psychic legacies of European colonial expansion to suffuse and continually reconstruct lived experiences into the present.

Coinciding with these realities is the global enlargement of psychiatric knowledge and praxis, developed and deployed across clinical, medical, legal, nonstate and extralegal contexts. It would therefore stand to reason that

DOI: 10.4324/9781003311843-1

psychiatry, alleging to describe the shape and nature of mental and behavioral (un)health, would be generally self-reflexive about its capacity to trace the relationships of the production and treatment of traumas to the manifold, dynamic global forces within which they are embedded. However, concerningly, this is largely not the case. Invocations of the global within "psy-"fields, despite some sincere but patchy attempts at institutionalizing self-reflexivity within training, often remain universalistic and "fraught with implicit monolithic principles from the Euro-centric intellectual traditions" (O'Byrne, n.d.; see also Mills, 2014), particularly insofar as they attempt to "multiculturally" expand an existing scientific edifice through a recognition of cultural differences superficially associated with broad ethnic or racial categories. And ideas of Western "exceptionalism" continue to pervade the politics of mental health and shape regimes of care and policing.

This collection represents an attempt to expose, chart and carefully unpack the global as it manifests, in its various forms, across psychological domains and sociopolitical subjectivities. More specifically, these chapters explore the production, conceptual nature, management and lived experience of traumas as they relate to what may be identified as *global or globalizing logics of power* within and across particular historical contexts. Thus, this volume examines mental health concerns as they become variously incorporated by modern disciplinary regimes, modes of psychiatric knowledge as they interface with overlapping cultural and political contingencies, and narratives of trauma, resistance and healing that emerge from global patterns of governance, migration and oppression.

Importantly, this collection aims to interrogate such global or globalizing logics as they emerge psychologically or psychiatrically at manifold *scales* as well as locales and forms: including the scale of the clinic but also those of the family, community, nation, state and international world. In addition, the volume targets conflicts and challenges of psychiatric inquiry beyond those merely at a methodological level. How does the global bear upon epistemologies of trauma and traumatogenesis? Among different spheres of psychiatric interaction, what do value differences and cultural conflicts reveal to us about epistemological or ontological occlusion, incorporation, violation or transformation with respect to diverse understandings of subjectivity and health? And how can an attunement to the global help psychiatry revise long-standing onto-images of the conscious and unconscious mind, and of the mind's relationship to the body and the wider social sphere, in a manner more befitting the complexities of psychic reality and treatment?

As editors, from the position of our commitments in the fields of anthropology and political theory, we have aimed to foster inquiry that might suggest relationships between the development of traumas and their broader global realities to be multidirectional, multidimensional and causally nonreductive. Our own work, which has combined an academic attention to power relations and societal context with interdisciplinary engagements with psychiatric scholars and practitioners, compels us to believe that trauma never appears in isolation from the contingencies of the social environment. In the same vein, we know that traumas (and how traumas are disciplined) further shape subjectivities and societal relations across scales, from familial to international, conditioning the operation of power and global political outcomes.

We therefore hope that the chapters that follow, as they register the societal feedbacks, causal ambiguities, constructions and deconstructions of trauma within particular, placed histories, can allow the reader a sense of the blurriness and unpredictability that accompanies multidirectional, recursive and fluctuating lines of influence. This is not to suggest that such lines are not causal or real; only that they are non-static, convoluted, and when it comes to the relation of the global to the local, often enigmatic. Through the semblance of global psychological dynamics that can be glimpsed, in snapshot form, from the mosaic of these chapters, we encourage readers to think psychiatrically *as well as* to dwell within the complexities and challenges that an attention to the global can bring. We hope that such an attitude, in fact, can further ambitions for a more mindful, honest and healing psychiatry.

Above all, we remain heedful of the fact that the research within this collection claims to reflect the traumatic histories of real people, and often of highly vulnerable populations. In addition, much of this knowledge has been constructed through field research, interviews or other "on the ground" interactions with psychiatric subjects and marginalized communities, or else through direct (e.g., clinical) cases between doctor and patient. We not only avow the paramount ethical importance of bearing witness and responsibility to the people that we represent in academic scholarship, but we believe that doing so well – particularly within situations where, as a function of trauma, psychic ambiguities proliferate – obliges a similar approach of humility and uncertainty in the face of complex realities. It also requires an active acknowledgment and consistent reappraisal of one's positionality and value commitments, and an alignment of those commitments toward ends that, to the best of one's knowledge and ability, do not work to deny or repress the agency of the oppressed.

We learn from the postcolonial psychology of Bonnie and Eduardo Duran, of Opelousas/Coushatta and Apache/Tewa heritage, respectively, that psychological research genuinely committed to global healing must keep as its foundation "knowledge . . . derived from within the community itself, because who can care more about the community and its survival than the members of the community?" (Duran and Duran, 1995, p. 208). And we agree with Eduardo Duran when he writes, with reference to the context of Native American counseling but drawing a conclusion with global significance, that both

> treatment and a new narrative [can emerge] with non-Native providers. However, the non-Native providers also must be able to make a serious analysis of their own history and take responsibility for that history. In this manner, the providers are involved in a narrative therapy of their own, and in this honest historical vessel the wounding itself can be healed.
>
> *(Duran, 2006, p. 28)*

We believe that this holds equally true for academic scholars (not just providers) working to better understand the traumas and treatment of oppressed subject populations. We therefore direct the research and intended use of this volume also to these ambitions.

Healing Global Mental Health

On a global scale, major western psychiatric institutes export biases, conceal imperial violence under the garb of scientific knowledge, deploy stereotypical assumptions about cultural values or identities and privilege only specific ways of expressing distress. One question in front of us is about how we understand trauma, on the one hand, and how it is expressed and concealed in people's political and social vocabularies, on the other. Another related question is about how psychiatric discourses are internationalized, or how western diagnoses overlap with or depart from local categories and symptomatology. This interaction begs sociological, philosophical and anthropological questions about the constitution of personhood and its variations between different cultures. These questions have implications for whether the brain, the body or interpersonal relations are treated as the cause of illness, and whether culturally specific interpretations of illness are treated as a problem of superstition and ignorance or recognized for their role in the provision of care. The internationalization of psychiatric discourses also compels questions of foundational importance for social science, namely those of *social difference*, the shape of global structural violence, and (through different forms of expert knowledge) the separation of the *medical* from the *social*.

By interrogating global histories of trauma, including as they are insufficiently attended to within psychiatric discourse, and as the violence underpinning them is masked by false, uncomplicated, objectivizing and essentializing invocations of global identities and interactions, this volume attends to the commanding question of global futurities and healing. We follow China Mills who asks, with her monograph *Decolonizing Global Mental Health*, "whether mental health can, or should, be global" (Mills, 2014). In the context of this study, we are led to ask a similar question: if the global is violent and traumatic, can these aspects of global relationality as they manifest psychiatrically be rectified? And if an affirmative answer can be found, can the decolonization of approaches toward mental health treatment reciprocally enhance global efforts at sociopolitical liberation? By posing them here, we wish for these questions to echo throughout the chapters that follow, even when they are not explicitly addressed or answered in great detail. Regarding psychiatry's capacities for unsnarling its complicities with global forms of oppression, and potentially expanding and more radically positioning the roles it can play for healing, the chapters in this collection present a diverse set of points of reference and inference. Taken together, they may allow the reader to form preliminary understandings that can guide further study and thought.

If global logics of power have not only traumatized and displaced but also shaped and forged contemporary subjectivities at least partly in their fashion, it seems sensible to pose at the outset the assumption that liberatory global futures, however they might be encouraged and created, would entail neither a surgical excision of present-day global relations nor a simple reversal or return to any imagined pre-colonial or pre-imperial past. It may be possible to resurrect minoritarian global concepts and approaches from within dominant traditions and employ them for decolonial ends: such as, for example, conceptualizations of foreignness in Sophistic Greek thought which oppose the Platonic/Aristotelean hierarchy separating Greek and non-Greek by measure of "civilization" (a hierarchy that would, in later centuries, morph into Euro-centrism and underpin patterns of colonial and neoliberal expansion). It is ever important to decenter the aspects of dominant power regimes that marginalize, invisibilize and other, and to correspondingly center the voices, values and knowledge thus affected. And global liberatory praxis may be vitalized by political strategies of reparation and/or repatriation, strategies which must nonetheless be met with a level of mindfulness commensurate to the incredible complexities and challenges presented by intersecting and overlapping histories of genocide and injustice.[1]

However, insofar as traumas, unconscious defenses and attachments, and pre-liberatory subjective identifications persist, the crucial strategies invoked earlier will be insufficient in themselves. The psychiatric legacy of Frantz Fanon helps us to bear in mind not only the necessities of *healing* for decolonial work, but also the importance of *globality*, and the revolution of global relations at manifold scales, for *healing itself*. Even Fanon's anti-colonial militantism was infused with a globality that transcended the immediate objectives of sovereign self-determination and statehood:

Frantz Fanon . . . being immersed in political struggle, observed and articulated the scope and reach of collective political action that was pitched beyond the nation-state and the continent. To put it another way, he understood and articulated the dynamic tension between two logics of sovereignty – the transcendent sovereignty of the imperial nation-states that is expansionist, divisive, and repressive; and the immanent sovereignty of colonized peoples, which destabilized and overthrew imperial structures of power.

(Bose, 2019, p. 673)

Or, in Fanon's own language: "The colonized, underdeveloped man is today a political creature in the most global sense of the term" (Fanon, 1961/2004, p. 40).

This presents us with the provocative possibility that decolonization and other efforts at redressing violent structures, including as these structures levy and pervade psychiatry and psychotherapeutic treatment, prompts not a *de*-globalization or a "de-globification," but rather a *re*-globalization or re-globification: a radical reshaping of how we conceptualize, experience and imagine the global. The "hows" of this question, and of psychiatry's role within it, remain subjects for careful deliberation and far exceed the confines of this book. Yet if psychiatric reflexivity, violence reduction and ethical and effective treatment are desired ambitions, it is imperative to heed Fanon's counsel and to carefully reflect upon the conceivable contours of liberatory global ideals.

Discipline and Psychiatry

Globally, an estimated 264 million people are affected by depression. We are currently living in an age where mental illness in some ways has become "normalized" as new aspirations and disappointments are fueled by the global economy (Chua, 2014). In some ways, everyone struggles with mental illness, either by experiencing acute symptoms or through mild symptoms that are vernacularized in different ways around the world (Estroff et al., 1991). In other words, mental illness no longer evokes the same stigma as it used to in the context of European mental asylums of the 20th century, where those with illness were separated from broader society. Psychotherapy sessions are now available in schools and universities. Students and adults with exceptional needs or challenges are no longer the only ones to receive psychotherapy. In today's world, personal psychotherapists are expected to help individuals navigate the stresses of life, even connecting with their clients through online Zoom calls if they are separated by geographic distances and time zones.

While in recent years, mental health treatment has been made more accessible in so-called developing countries, this is a moment to reflect on the place of psychiatry in global humanitarianism, which authorizes social suffering with the help of its claims to expert knowledge. Social conditions are now legitimated and made increasingly visible with the help of psychiatric discourses, as Didier Fassin (2012) writes in the context of France: "Suffering only became an efficacious notion in the definition of public policy at the point when it was addressed by psychiatrists and set in a legitimate institutional framework" (p. 33). In other words, social problems, including urban poverty and turns to violence, are now increasingly "psychiatrized." One ramification of this move has been to overdiagnose populations without addressing deep-rooted social problems. In the case of France, the use of psychiatric discourses was used, according to Fassin, to represent the weight of social suffering. However, in many other cases, psychiatric care is marked by a move to conceal the relationship between mental illness and social conditions by health experts (Scheper-Hughes, 1993). Public health in many counties now increasingly incorporates mental health, but often public health initiatives, due to their emphasis on population health and disease eradication, continue to neglect the psychological effects of disease outbreaks and attempts by states to maintain "healthy" populations, even when this means separating loved ones and divorcing the vulnerable from much-needed networks of care and emotional support. When health systems do engage with mental health of the vulnerable, the relations between punishment and care often result in stigmatizing mental health, as is demonstrated in the case studies of postcolonial India and Pakistan in this volume.

A fundamental problem of postcolonial psychiatry raised by Franz Fanon is that maladies in social relations are treated as personal problems rather than as pathologies caused by conditions of colonialism. These social forces are now operating at global scales in the form of pandemics, conflicts and displacements. Thus, even as mental health screening has been made increasingly accessible, the increase in psychiatric disorders requires us to consider a parallel story: namely about the globalizing forces of displacement. Conditions of scarcity create new pressures on human sociality and result in new disorders. These disorders are social in nature, structural mainly, but also interpersonal, as wider economic and social shifts are experienced in intimate relations (as in, perhaps, a child's disobedience and violence toward their parents, treated as a sign of illness rather than a demoralization created by conditions of extreme poverty) (Das, 2006). These disorders range from problems of addiction to mental illness and give voice to structural pathologies, albeit in ways that do not respect the standard template of a medical complaint.

There are also many ways in which structural forces have the effect of numbing the human mind, or "dissociation," to borrow a psychoanalytic term: to distract oneself from precarious job markets, retrenching welfare states and the ever-present threat of conflict and violence (Khan, 2017). The category of "accident" (market crash, flood, etc.), as Virilio (2007) reminds us, is used by states to further garner psychopolitical complicity. The overall numbing effect is a product of the intensification of trauma and the experience of trauma as routine and repetitive, with victims and perpetrators brought into the vortex of state violence: the former inflicting torture and creating conditions of death, and the latter shouldering the unconscious burden of bearing witness to these horrors. Numbing as well as anxiety-inducing, today's globalizing forces also create new psychiatric subjects and technologies of control. These new psychiatric subjects (ranging from the migrant to the refugee seeker to the internally displaced) are exposed to new forms of policing and carcerality that create the very conditions of madness or irrationality that states paradoxically also arduously try to eradicate. Thus, the psychiatric effects of state-led violence are continuously erased in torture cells and prisons, just as force is used to correct pathologies and shape bodies.

While the problems are novel, the rich intellectual tradition of postcolonial psychiatry offers some insights. Fanon shows how colonialism creates problems of identity which prompt the colonized to constantly ask, "In reality who am I?" In fact, Fanon also wrote about the relevance of the social for clinical practice, especially when he suggested that "in some circumstances the socius is more important than the individual" (Fanon, 1961/2004, p. 105). At another point, he stated, "we are driven from the individual back to the social structure. If there is a taint, it lies not in the 'soul' of the individual but rather in that of the environment" (Ibid., p. 213). Just as colonial authorities around the world pathologized resistance to power structures, the figure of Fanon highlighted the potential for a different, more radical kind of psychiatry: one that is attuned to mundane and everyday forms of suffering. In his exploration of the effect of colonialism on conjugality, he argued that war "deepens relations between husband and wife and cements their union. There is a simultaneous and effervescent emergence of the citizen, the patriot, and the modern spouse" (1965, p. 114). At other points, he suggested that colonization leaves deep fractures in social relations. The reason why postcolonial psychiatry requires a grounding in Fanon is that Fanon helps us understand how psychiatric care can result both in giving agency to patients to decide the terms of their treatment, by painstakingly recovering the mundane pathologies that erupt in everyday experiences due to conditions of social violence, but also in undoing state-led violence itself.

Despite the headway made by global psychiatric institutions in making psychiatric care accessible to populations, we are now experiencing ever-increasing risks of what Deleuze and Guattari (1977) have detected in Freud's fascination with the Oedipus complex as a cause for neurosis. Deleuze and Guattari (1977) argue that the "daddy-mommy-child" triad privileges and universalizes a specific family structure, which is far more inflected with historical and cultural contingency than Freud's model acknowledges, and which fails to reflexively capture the possible tightening or social reproduction of the family unit by psychoanalysis itself. Posing the figure of the schizophrenic against the oedipalized child, Deleuze and Guattari (1977) write, "Freud never went beyond this narrow and limited conception of the ego. And what prevented him from doing so was his own tripartite formula – the Oedipal, neurotic one: daddy-mommy-me" (p. 23). Referring to this as a type of analytic imperialism, they note,

> the small child lives with his family around the clock; but within the bosom of this family, and from the very first days of his life, he immediately begins having an amazing nonfamilial experience that psychoanalysis has completely failed to take into account.

Posing schizo-analysis as an alternative, they write that this approach "sets out to explore a transcendental unconscious, rather than a metaphysical one; an unconscious that is material rather than ideological; schizophrenia rather than Oedipal; nonfigurative rather than imaginary; real rather than symbolic" (pp. 109–110). Can we return to Deleuze and Guattari's insight to guard against contemporary psychiatric excesses? There are several contemporary iterations of similar critiques about how humanitarian psychiatry views specific cultural relations as inherently pathological, without explicating the multiplicity of relations in combination with adverse political situations that are generative of mental illness. In creating caricatures, states create new justifications to expand political violence. Thus, in today's world, in which psychiatric regimes are exported abroad (employing normative assumptions as universals, increasing distrust toward psychiatry and unintentionally stigmatizing various forms of mental illness), a schizo-framework acquires a new salience. The question becomes: how we can recover the specificity and uniqueness of psychiatric experiences?

Symptoms of Reality

According to the DSM-V and previous iterations, traumatic experiences and responses involve intrusion and avoidance symptoms, where exposure to traumatic conditions creates stress and specific avoidance mechanisms. Avoidance mechanisms entail avoiding experiences that recall traumatic events. The critique that has been leveled onto the use of the DSMs to understand mental illness globally has been its emphasis on specific symptoms which may or may not be experienced universally, such as flashbacks (Jones et al., 2003). It is also worth questioning whether trauma necessarily follows a temporality of initial trauma, recurrence and avoidance (Khan, 2016, 2017). Meanwhile, symptoms of psychosis are viewed as necessarily bearing a disconnect with reality and are often treated with pharmaceuticals alone. Psychosis is often treated strictly as a neurochemical problem instead of (at least partly) a social one, despite the prevalence of experiences of psychosis being interpreted through or laden with particular cultural values (Sadowsky, 2020). The question of whether they represent normal or pathological experience continues to be debated, but how patients, their families and physicians employ different social interpretations or explanatory models for illness is still a relevant question (Farmer, 2010). When illness and symptoms of psychosis continue to be treated from a strictly medical framework, the solution too remains largely medical, and not sensitive to the social and political experiences that surround the illness.

Foucault historicizes and complicates the philosophy of psychiatric treatment in *Psychiatric Power*. For Foucault (2008), an earlier modality of psychiatric power represented in the works of Pinel and Esquirol entails the psychiatrist playing up to the imaginations of the patient, where treatment is based on maintaining the patient's as-if structures. The psychiatrist accepts the reality of the illness imposed by the patient and in that way works toward its recovery. This began to change, however, as psychiatrists, by the turn of the 20th century, began to impose their own meanings of the real on the patient. In other words, the psychiatrists' understanding of the real is final, and the patient's recovery is dependent upon coming to terms with this reality, which now means that the patient will go through a range of infra-penalties every time their version of the "real" is suggested. One question that we can ask, borrowing from Foucault, is: how do patients, physicians and their families debate what constitutes the real? Is it only the psychiatrist who can impose a definition of the real?

Instead of simply suggesting that psychiatrists alone create definitions of the pathological, this volume considers the multiplicity of ways cultures and people define pathologies, while reflecting on how pathologies are situated not just within individuals but also their broader social structures. While patients may refer to the cause of illness as resulting from precarious situations, we also know from existing evidence (such as from studies of patients experiencing problems of addiction) that structural causes of illness are often ignored in medical treatment, placing the blame for illness disproportionately on the constitutions or subjectivities of patients (Bourgois, 2009).

While madness may represent a disjuncture from reality, does that mean that its symptoms bear no relationship to the social or political context? We contend, by contrast, that treating symptoms and delusions as bearing no relationship with the real is itself a political act, one that is shaped by the impulse to discredit the relationship between trauma and oppression. When a patient refers to the social structure as the cause of illness, both their registering of a personal reality and their expression of a political protest are likely to be disregarded. Altogether, this forecloses the traumatic depths of specific political events.

In line with the complicated trajectory of Freudian thought, some psychodynamic and adaptational postulations from psychiatrists such as Adolf Meyer, Abram Kardiner and Henry Stack Sullivan in the US context and Vladimir Myasishchev in the Soviet Union considered mental illness as a response to (or conflict with) specific social milieus, shifting from earlier theories that relied solely on hereditary factors. Yet in many contexts, the language patients used to describe their mental illness continued to be either ignored or treated as strictly medical, denying their symptoms socially etiological significance. Skultans (1998), for example, observes how Latvian subjects described their symptoms in terms of being "short of air" or having one's heart "on strike" as forms of political resistance, given a history of psychiatric discourses being used for subjugation (where even small acts of disobedience could be met with a psychiatric response). This example encourages us to think about the life of psychiatric discourses, which can humanize but also brutalize the subjects of illness, sometimes both at once.

Psychiatric diagnoses also have a life as they move globally and acquire new salience to make suffering legible or to conceal it. While, on the one hand, the movement of psychiatric classification invokes the need to be receptive toward culturally specific ways of expressing illness, these symptoms in most cases carry with them signs of the broader social worlds, with symptoms, such as delusions and psychoses, being buffered, magnified or channelized through specific cultural experiences of senses and psyche, absorption and porosity (Luhrmann, 2012). Illness narratives offer a political critique as much as they illuminate personal injury. While psychiatric institutions may become the voice of the state, a different, more radical psychiatry may challenge the assumptions about what the symptoms represent by siding with patients to turn symptoms into critique, even as the state tries to depoliticize symptoms by enforcing a distinction between symptoms and political reality.

Finally, a more radical psychiatry might interrogate assumptions about what constitutes the subject of treatment. Mental illness can invite us to consider non-human ontologies and temporalities that are ignored as part of the liberal subjectivity in which agency is considered as firmly rooted within an individual (Asad, 2003). For instance, within Islamic contexts, patients refer to their afflictions and seizures as examples of demonic possessions, where healing presents a site for the recovery of not only the individual but the social relation causing the illness. The psyche is thus difficult to disentangle from histories, spaces and relations. However, for many reasons (including its complicities with Eurocentric, colonial and racist assumption sets), we hesitate to look straight to the archetypal logic that dominates Jungian psychiatry to acknowledge the psyche's global relatedness. For us, what globalizing logics prompt us to think about is how knotted experiences present themselves as symptoms where neither a simple beginning can be privileged, nor where there is a straightforward resolution through abreaction. Modern experiences of trauma blur distinctions between the mind and the body, the self and the other, and the human and the non-human. Thus, a question of central importance is how the idea of the self or the causes of illness are contested within clinical contexts. How are histories of trauma erased or subsumed in specific ways that privilege or make trauma "intelligible" to specific communities?

The Globalization of Trauma: An Outline

Conventionally, trauma is represented in terms of traumatic experiences, their re-experience and mechanisms of avoidance. With this volume, we seek to understand trauma not merely as the symptoms that come to represent it, but also as a political concept: it is a marker of political violence, as it represents the maddening impacts of wars, nationalism, local and global hierarchies, family disorders, and ethnic provincialism (etc.) lived out in varied contexts and expressed in myriad ways. To understand the healing of trauma caused by various levels and intensities of oppression and subordination, we do not disregard the psychiatric clinic (we find it rather crucially important), but we are also interested in investigating the intersections between clinics and other spaces: such as nonclinical sites of healing, domestic spaces, etc.

With this volume, we therefore hope to explore five important aspects about trauma and the globalizing forces that shape it:

Temporality: What are the temporalities of traumatogenesis and the forces of displacement as global conflicts become more routinized?

Expression: How do expressions of trauma vary cross-culturally, and how do traumatic experiences find expression in sites outside of the clinic?

Ontology: How is the experience of trauma related to questions of personhood? How might the experience of mental illness challenge Cartesian dualisms? And how might patients and healers negotiate between multiple selves: both human and non-human?

Intimacy: How might taking seriously the fluid, relational and intersectional construction of identity help us better analyze the capacities and challenges of psychotherapeutic intervention?

Psychosis: How might psychotic symptoms, if related to political oppression and displacement, represent psychic attempts for relief from the maddening effects of structural violence?

This volume does not provide the first account of the limits of western diagnoses, nor of the differences between western or global and nonwestern or local models of trauma. Nor is the volume unique in posing questions about the confluences and intersections between psychological and physiological conditions, of course, as this has been a persistent feature of Freud-inspired psychiatric study. We hope to supplement existing approaches along these lines with a heightened emphasis on globalization and global political structures, logics and scale, examining how they manifest within an array of local contexts and cases and bringing a diversity of theoretical perspectives and voices to bear.

To do so, we order the volume into four parts. In Part 1, "Trauma, Globality and Death," Roberto Beneduce levies the psychiatric case studies of Frantz Fanon to ask what contemporary patterns of migration, including migrant and immigrant death, reveal about the hidden articulations and implications of trauma. Following Roberto's chapter, a chapter by Xiaowen Zhang and Jie Yang explores the intrusive uses of public health for political control, the production of death through the medical triaging of patients, medical neglect toward non-COVID patients to keep the health system intact, and the isolation of patients with COVID-19 from the wider society. These elements, according to the authors, served a thanatopolitical function in the Chinese city of Wuhan during the outbreak of the coronavirus-2019 pandemic. Zhang and Yang argue that long-standing traditions focusing on the responsibility to the nation were mobilized to favor collective over personal interests to an extent that conditions for death were produced to "ensure stability of the social and medical order."

In Part 2, "Global Surveillance and Trauma," we situate a chapter by Neil Krishan Aggarwal, which explains how manipulating thresholds or definitions of torture allows the US state to erase or underplay the effects of its violence upon Guantanamo detainees, where a discourse of American exceptionalism is used to justify this violence, but is also, paradoxically, used by prisoners to make a case for justice. We position this chapter alongside a study of psychiatric care and public health in Kashmir by Saiba Varma, who advances the concept of "social impunity" to give voice to patient experiences and resistances under state occupation and sociomedical control.

In Part 3, "Culture, Displacement and Healing," we present two chapters that each unpack the complexities of non-clinical care and cross-cultural values. Christopher M. Webb, a medical anthropologist and combat veteran, explores Indigenous ritual treatments of combat trauma for both Native and non-Native military veterans alongside a dominant discourse of "warriordom" as it reinforces white settler violence. Then, in a study about the religious (Islamic) treatment of mental illness in Pakistan, Sanaullah Khan demonstrates how effective care in this context entails a cultivation of sensitivities to both spiritual ethics and nonhuman agents.

There are three chapters in Part 4. In "Global Bodies, Logics and Clinics," interdisciplinary social theorists Alyson K. Spurgas and Elliott Schwebach begin with a dialogue about psychological assumptions and psychotherapeutic practices as they become complicit with structural patterns of oppression, including gender-based violence and sexual control. In the following chapter, Elena Ruíz, Nora Berenstain and Nerli Paredes-Ruvalcaba bear witness to gender-based forms of administrative violence and control, including reproductive violence (such as reproductive rights rollbacks in the United States), as they emerge from and support settler colonial statecraft. Finally, in a chapter that offers direct, practical takeaways for psychiatrists and psychotherapists, Crystal Han and Shinnyi Chou demonstrate the centrality of colonial power relations for the development and experience of trauma for AAPI populations (Asian Americans and Pacific Islanders). Crystal and Shinnyi present a diverse array of case studies to show not only how the global political dimension is reflected in traumatic symptomatology, but also how it is often insufficiently accounted for in psychiatric treatment.

Altogether, we hope that this volume will help to explicate the patterns of global power that permeate psychiatric knowledge and care, and to make global psychiatry's conventional ontological and cultural assumptions a little more strange. We also hope to encourage the reader to continue evaluating the methodological and epistemological frameworks that render trauma visible or invisible, and in so doing, we hope to make suffering both more complex and more mean-ingful. It is from this basis, we believe, that better care can follow.

Note

1 Within the burgeoning literature on these complexities and challenges, which is by now too vast to comprehensively cite, we wish to draw attention to a remarkable literature review by Olivia Klutse entitled "Repatriation and Reparations: Land-Based Indig-enous and Black Futurity," recognized for an undergraduate research award in 2018.

References

Asad, T. (2003). *Formations of the Secular: Christianity, Islam, Modernity*. Redwood City: Stanford University Press.

Bose, A. (2019). Frantz Fanon and the politicization of the third world as a collective sub-ject. *Interventions* 21:671–689.

Bourgois, P. (2009). *Righteous Dopefiend*. Berkeley: University of California Press.

Chua, J. (2014). *In Pursuit of the Good Life: Aspiration and Suicide in Globalizing South India*. Berkeley: University of California Press.

Das, V. (2006). *Life and Words: Violence and the Descent Into the Ordinary*. Berkeley: University of California Press.

Deleuze, G. & Guattari, F. (1977). *Anti-Oedipus: Capitalism and Schizophrenia*. New York: Viking Press.

Dennis, E. (2021). The paranoid-schizoid position and envious attacks on the Black other. *Psychoanalysis, Self and Context* 17(2):141–153. Advance online publication.

Duran, E. (2006). *Healing the Soul Wound: Counseling With American Indians and Other Native Peoples*. New York: Teachers College Press.

Duran, E. & Duran, B. (1995). *Native American Postcolonial Psychology*. Albany: State University of New York Press.

Estroff, S.E., Lachicotte, W.S., Illingworth, L.C. & Johnston, A. (1991). Everybody's got a little mental illness: accounts of illness and self among people with severe, persistent mental illnesses. *Medical Anthropology Quarterly* 5:331–369.

Fanon, F. (1965). *A Dying Colonialism*. New York: Monthly Review Press.

Fanon, F. (1994). *Black Skin, White Masks* (R. Philcox, Trans.). New York: Grove Press. (Original work published 1952).

Fanon, F. (2004). *The Wretched of the Earth* (R. Philcox, Trans.). New York: Grove Press. (Original work published 1961).

Farmer, P. (2010). *Partner to the Poor: A Paul Farmer Reader*. Berkeley: University of California Press.

Fassin, D. (2012). *Humanitarian Reason: A Moral History of the Present*. Berkeley: University of California Press.

Foucault, M. (2008). *Psychiatric Power: Lectures at the College de France, 1973–1974*. London: Picador.

Jones, E., Vermaas, R.H., McCartney, H., Beech, C., Palmer, I., Hyams, K. & Wessely, S. (2003). Flashbacks and post-traumatic stress disorder: the genesis of a 20th-century diagnosis. *The British Journal of Psychiatry: The Journal of Mental Science* 182:158–163.

Khan, N. (2016). *Mental Disorder: Anthropological Insights*. Toronto: University of Toronto Press.

Khan, N. (2017). *Cityscapes of Violence in Karachi: Publics and Counterpublics*. Oxford: Oxford University Press.

Klutse, O. (2018). *Repatriation and Reparations: Land-Based Indigenous and Black Futurity*. Published online by Seattle University. https://scholarworks.seattleu.edu/cgi/view-content.cgi?article=1008&context=ura.

Luhrmann, T.M. (2012). *When God Talks Back: Understanding the American Evangelical Relationship With God*. New York: Alfred A. Knopf.

Mills, C. (2014). *Decolonizing Global Mental Health: The Psychiatrization of the Majority World*. Hove, UK: Routledge.

O'Byrne, M. (n.d.). Appendix F1: a review of cross-cultural training in mental health. In *Report on the Evaluation of a Cultural Consultation Service in Mental Health*. McGill University. www.mcgill.ca/culturalconsultation/report/appendices/review.

Parker, R.N. (2019). Slavery in the White psyche. *Psychoanalytic Social Work* 26:84–103.

Sadowsky, J. (2020). *The Empire of Depression: A New History*. Cambridge, UK: Polity.

Scheper-Hughes, N. (1993). *Death Without Weeping: The Violence of Everyday Life in Brazil*. Berkeley: University of California Press.

Skultans, V. (1998). *The Testimony of Lives: Narrative and Memory in Post-Soviet Latvia*. London: Routledge.

Virilio, P. (2007). *The Original Accident*. Cambridge, UK: Polity.

PART 1

Trauma, Globality and Death

1

WHERE PSYCHE, HISTORY AND POLITICS MERGE

Decolonizing PTSD and Traumatic Memory With Fanon

Roberto Beneduce
Translated from Italian into English by Richard Bates

Archives of Pain and New Necro-Geographies

To understand the hidden text in the narratives of so many asylum-seekers and immigrants, to measure the violence their scars and tales recount, we need to achieve a reading similar to that which Althusser defined as "symptomatic," remembering that it is not what we *do not* see that is the problem, but what is imposed on our senses so clearly (pain, death, violence) to make us forget what allows or feeds that pain, those deaths, those tragedies. It is the *opacity of the immediate*, writes Althusser, taking up a formula of Spinoza, that needs to be questioned.[1] A historical and political opacity, certainly, but also epistemological, which the images and news of recent years also reveal in the metaphors used by the media and by governments.

What are the forgotten pages of this dark narrative? What is the origin of this opacity, which, in the face of the new maps of dominion and our present-day *necro-geographies*,[2] leaves us grasping only a few fleeting images of despair and the faded text of some clinical diagnoses? How do we grasp the meanings and the borders of "trauma" within contemporary diasporic narratives? It may be useful to look again at some of these images of death and indifference.

Thirty-nine bodies of Asian citizens,[3] found in a lorry (cargo truck) not far from London, horrified public opinion. On June 20, 2000, in Dover, England, there was a similar episode: the lifeless bodies of 58 Chinese citizens were found in a lorry, in which they had hidden to enter the UK, an uninterrupted series of grim events, about which we have developed a singular form of "cultural anesthesia" (Feldman, 1994).[4] In June 2022, more than 50 bodies of Mexicans,

DOI: 10.4324/9781003311843-3

Guatemalans and Hondurans were found without life in a lorry in the town of San Antonio, in the US state of Texas.

Dying frozen, dehydrated or suffocated in an attempt to cross borders has simply become another possible way of death in the contemporary world: a side effect of modern *teichopolitics* – policies of border control through the proliferation of walls, barbed wire, barriers of every kind and highly technological surveillance systems whose aim is to prevent illegal immigration (Ballif and Rosière, 2009; Rosière and Jones, 2012).

According to the authors who coined this neologism, *teichopolitics* (drawn from a Greek word for a fortified wall) are a recent development of biopolitics for the control of peoples and the subjection of bodies. In the age of late-capitalist and neo-liberal brutalism (Mbembe, 2020), the value of human life seems to waver furiously between that of a useful body, reduced to a mere work force, that of disposable bodies/objects, and that of a humanitarian lament that questions the hypocritical silence of governments and institutions.

The control of mobility (*kinetocracy* is a term suggested by Benedetta Rossi) (2015, p. 152), initially effected under colonization, is not just about nation-state making, national borders, airports or checkpoints: we find new expressions of it within our cities, where new spaces of detention isolate illegal immigrants and invisible confines separate rich from poor areas, and where any *suspicious* gesture can legitimize the most brutal violence: as happened in March 2018 in Sacramento in the US state of California, where Stephon Clark, a 22-year-old Black man, was shot and killed by the police because his cell-phone was mistaken for a pistol.

The centrality of the racial – and postcolonial – question in the episodes just mentioned is expressed particularly clearly in the case of Yaguine Koita and Fodd Tounkara, two adolescents from Conakry, Guinea, found frozen to death in the undercarriage of a Sabena airplane in Brussels. With their story, the two young Africans were to foster a serious debate and add another chapter to the painful archive on migration, because Yaguibe and Fodd had a letter with them, written with "*grande confiance*" to the European heads of state. I quote some passages from it as it occupies a unique place in our present-day narratives of diaspora:

> Your Excellencies, members, and officials of Europe,
>
> It is a distinctive honor and privilege to write this letter to talk to you about the aim of our trip and our suffering – we the children and the youth of Africa. We put our trust in you.
>
> First of all, we bring you our greetings – the sweetest, the most adorable and respectful greetings of life. To this end, please be our support and help, we the people of Africa. Otherwise whom shall we turn to for help?
>
> We beseech you, come to our rescue. Think of your love for your beautiful continent, your people, your family, above all the love of your children

that you love so dearly like life. Moreover, think of the love and kindness of the creator, "God," the Almighty, who has given you the good experiences, wealth, and power to construct and organize your continent so well that it has become the most beautiful and admirable of them all. . . .

Finally, we beseech you to forgive us for daring to write such a letter to you important people whom we truly respect. Do not forget that it is to you that we must plead [?] the weakness of our strength in Africa.[5]

In discussing the letter, De Boeck and Honwana (2005, p. 8) wonder: "Why are these young Africans so powerfully attracted to the west? What is their vision of a good life? What is their cultural politics, and in what geographies, ecologies, and subjectivities is it located and imagined?" With a "symptomatic reading," however, a deeper truth emerges. It is *the style in which this letter is written* that gives us pause. Alluding to Bhabha's analysis of (post)colonial strategies of "mimicry," Ferguson (2002, p. 552) notes that, reading this text, it is impossible not to feel "a specific sort of embarrassment, as well as a stark horror. . . . It is the embarrassment of encountering Africans – in postcolonial era – who humbly beg Europeans to come to their bluntly ask for help 'to become like you.'"

The letter of Yaguibe and Fodd lays bare the hypocrisies of those who govern us with a power of the dead and the oppressed. Their words are the writing of *another* disaster (Blanchot, 1980/1995), the staging of the obscenity of so-called "illegal" migration (De Genova, 2013). But another kind of obscenity should be recognized: that of the categories that ever more often claim to define neutrally the range of human experiences and crises, as in the case of post-traumatic stress disorder, or PTSD.

As part of the transformation of disciplined societies into controlling societies (Deleuze, 1995, pp. 177–182), systems of governance now introduce a tragic asymmetry that is once again developing along the *line of color*, to use the words of du Bois, understood here broadly to consider the racial violence that is now grafted onto migration policies or is unleashed as a homicidal symptom on city streets. In Italy: the case of Moussa Balde, a citizen from Conakry in Guinea who was savagely attacked by men in Ventimiglia in 2021, then taken to a detention center in Turin, where he killed himself; the strangling of Alika Ogorchukwu, a disabled Nigerian citizen, in Civitanova Marche in plain sight; the murder of a homeless young Moroccan, Youns El Boussetaoui, by a League member of the town council of Voghera. These episodes recall the expression of a violence that we do not wish to recognize and an anguish that results, but for which there seems to be no adequate diagnosis.[6]

In recent decades, the literature on the notion of "trauma" has developed dizzyingly, and not only in clinical circles. Fed by literary studies, postcolonial novels and studies that have sought to investigate the politics of memory or the consequences of historical dramas, trauma has more and more frequently ended up questioning the disciplines that had first defined it (i.e., psychoanalysis and war psychiatry).[7] The reflections that follow draw above all on such contributions for its ideas, as a critical approach to trauma is able to recount what clinical sources often ignore: the historical genealogy of our diagnostic categories, in the palimpsest of the symptom (Beneduce, 2016a; Kienzler, 2022; Mianji and Kirmayer, 2022).[8]

The perspective suggested here takes its cue from what Caruth wrote on the success of PTSD. In her words,

> the more we satisfactorily locate and classify the symptoms of PTSD, the more we seem to have dislocated the boundaries of our modes of understanding. . . . The phenomenon of trauma has seemed to become all-inclusive, but it has done so precisely because it brings us to the limits of our understanding.
>
> *(Caruth, 1995, pp. 3–4)*

This is undoubtedly true. Yet, I do not believe that the "limits of our understanding" explored by psychoanalysis can be considered in the same way as ontological limits of the human condition or intrinsic to traumatic experience. The limits that Freud drew attention to do not just reveal the functioning of the unconscious, but also derive from other processes: the politics of memory, the phenomena of institutional concealment, the registers of verification and falsification (Foucault, 2014). My aim in these notes is to uncover some of the areas of epistemic and political opacity that characterize the diagnosis of PTSD, which might contribute to its decolonization. In doing this, I will be helped by the epistemic break introduced by Fanon, and in particular by Chapter Five of his *The Wretched of the Earth*, a chapter that may represent the high water mark of Fanon's blending of the political and the psychic (Beneduce, 2011, 2016b; Gibson and Beneduce, 2017; Jabr, 2019; Lazali, 2021; Sibertin-Blanc, 2014). Before summoning Fanon, however, we need to examine another dossier.

Globalizing Trauma or Decolonizing Memory? The Shadows of a Disputed History

Why did the trauma clinic become the locus where so many of the essential threads of our modernity ended up meeting almost naturally? What made the diagnosis of PTSD so fundamental as to extensively saturate common language, the social imaginary and even the dialogue of some cartoons?[9] And why does their amalgam of the political, the clinical and the historical now take on a special importance? To answer these questions, we must describe some features of the setting in which these themes took form.

In the late 19th century, no fewer than three contexts defined the social and epistemological contours of the idea of trauma, all interlinked as in an extraordinary diorama. The first was the various changes brought about by the processes of production, with the increased number of mishaps caused by the appearance of new means of transport (e.g., Erichsen's disease or "railway spine") or by the rhythms of factory work. Gramsci would note in 1934 that the production of "machine-like behavior" ("atteggiamenti macchinali") in the human body was an explicit aim of Taylorism (Gramsci, 1970, p. 2165). Bodies were trying to *resist* the accelerated tempo of modernity by struggling to adapt or by letting new ailments emerge.[10]

The second context consisted of the theories that were distinguishing between various kinds of neurosis, which debated whether observed symptoms were caused only by psychic reactions or if their appearance necessarily connoted a neurological lesion too. Here the background was Freud's theory of child seduction as a cause of hysteria, which would be followed, after 1897, by the idea that the patients' accounts of their symptoms were laden with fantasy, and that fantasy always bore a primary connection to the Oedipus Complex. With the introduction of the idea of "belatedness" or "afterthought" (*Nachträglichkeit*), which Lacan would claim to have extracted from Freud's work, suggesting "après-coup" in French, a new and decisive element entered the *narrative of trauma*: one of temporality. This allows us to understand how traumatic events in the past encounter a significance only *a posteriori* (in Freud's model, after the "latency period"). This is an idea of which the epistemological, clinical and political potential may not yet have been wholly explored, particularly insofar as the notion of latency can be extended to historical traumas (genocides, mass atrocities, mass migrations, slavery). We can ask the question: how long can the latency of a collective trauma be before *symptoms* arise? And what form will these symptoms take?

The third context is that of the Great War, or First World War, with the hell of the trenches and the grenades: it led Ferenczi to say in 1917 that only cinematic images could adequately represent the singular and, until then, unknown symptoms observed in soldiers who had returned from the front (muscular spasms, awkward bearing and gait, tics, language disturbances, etc.) (Ferenczi, 1994, pp. 124–141). Here Ferenczi seems to suggest that ordinary clinical categories and concepts encounter a limit in describing and understanding the reality of suffering brought about by a new technology of death.

As Young (1997) has shown, the category of post-traumatic stress disorder (PTSD) seems to forget the complex history that preceded its birth. Mixing symptoms and diagnostic categories already present in previous classifications, PTSD would reformulate trauma treatment and continue to expand in the years following the context of the diagnosis' emergence (the Vietnam War) to include ailments caused by *any kind* of traumatic event (natural disasters, rapes, wars, looting, migration, etc.), irrespective of the sociocultural situation, place and role of the subjects involved. The rapid tectonic movement of PTSD diagnoses shook up psychiatry in the late 20th century, redefining its classificatory axes and the very idea of trauma, but at the same time encouraging a new (mechanical) model of memory (Young, 1997, pp. 270–279) and a singular ontologizing of human experience itself.[11]

If clinicians make a serious mistake when they ignore the historical matrices of their categories, the risks multiply when the socio-cultural maps in which they take form and significance are ignored. The case of the Wolfman is perhaps one of the best known.[12] More recently, analyzing the case of Daniel Paul Schreber, a German judge who suffered from schizophrenia, Santner (1996) has highlighted the hidden links between Schreber's illness and the prevalent anxieties of his time surrounding the role of the nation-state and the gradual assertion of antisemitism in German society.

But there is also another context that should be evoked in the reconstruction of the genealogy of trauma and, later, that of PTSD: that of the colonial space and the racial apparatus, where the violence and seduction that were its plot and wrote its "little secret" (Mbembe, 2006) were accompanied by a particular anxiety – that of suspicion. It was this last context that offered perhaps the most decisive (and still underexplored) *conjunction* between medico-psychological theories, strategies of subjection, epistemic anxieties and the success of some diagnostic categories. If the analogy between criminal, woman, neurotic and "primitive" was well known, suspicion of the working class or *lumpenproletariat*, and then of the colonized, would be the common denominator of the systems designed to inspect, control and classify these masses regarded as threatening, a logic that was arguably extended from regimes of control over slaves (Genovese, 1972). This humanity of uncertain and threatening appearance, and modes of suffering that would generate diagnostic doubt, were later accompanied by asylum seekers, whose tales and experiences would be subjected to increasingly detailed examination and control (Beneduce, 2015; Beneduce, 2018). The clinical gaze fostered this ideology of suspicion, coining innumerable diagnoses (from that of "sinistrosis," alleging a propensity to overexaggerate the harms suffered by minor accidents, to the more recent "factitious disorder" and "malingering," referring to alleged tendencies to feign or deliberately produce illness)[13] that were directed mainly at the socially marginalized groups: subordinates, the working class, members of ethnic and racial minorities or immigrants.

During the First World War, suspicion did not spare soldiers who manifested symptoms of the terror experienced in the trenches (shell shock syndrome). What is striking, once again, is the relation between suspicion, the social class of patients, and diagnosis: while officers and higher ranks usually received diagnoses such as neurasthenia or depression, the lowers ranks would be accused of simulating their symptoms for their own advantage (to avoid returning to the front). The military psychiatrist Julius Wagner-Jauregg, a future Nobel Prize winner, for the treatment of syphilis, entertained doubts as to patients' suffering, and, to counteract what seemed to him simply chicanery or cowardice, prescribed electric shock treatment for them. The tragic consequence was that some of them ended up committing suicide, leading to polemics and a legal case in which Freud himself testified.[14]

To understand how the diagnosis of PTSD met with such success, it is thus important to set out a *genealogy of suspicion* with a *critical genealogy* of the idea of trauma and the category of PTSD (Beneduce, 2010; Fassin and Rechtman, 2009; Young, 1997). Doing so will show the colonial/racial setting as its place of origin and its chosen image.

Colonial psychiatry had already launched a peculiar form of globalization of the unconscious. Henry Aubin, a distinguished figure in French colonial psychiatry and the psychiatric school directed by Antoine Porot in Algiers, and influenced by psychoanalysis (particularly in its Jungian form), may be one of the most eloquent examples of this desire. According to Bullard, by interpreting magic thought or other religious practices as the expression of "denial" in the psychoanalytic sense of the term, and perceiving the symptoms of Africans as similar to those of European patients, Aubin contributed to the construction of a "global unconscious."[15] And, unlike other psychiatrists of the period, he dismantled the barrier of cultural difference that other psychiatrists had erected in approaching Indigenous madness, as they described the role of superstitions and beliefs in the ravings of Africans.[16] This perspective, Bullard continues, canceled other differences too: ideas about magic or witchcraft, for example, had been "disarmed" of their specific metaphysical and ontological value, and the *global unconscious* had inexorably bent temporalities, experiences and autonomous narrative registers within the hegemonic interpretive code of western psychoanalysis and psychiatry. As Anderson et al. (2011) observe:

> Cultural globalization assumes a universal and cosmopolitan subject as prerequisite for its possibility. Globalization's aqueous metaphors (flows of information, the fluidity of capital exchange, floods of refugees) tap the same well as Freud's oceanic self, as does the republican universalism that overwhelms difference or anchors it within a civic teleology. Although these discourses allow room for particularism, they do so only to the extent that such differences are assimilable into a single model of the subject that conceals real difference in favor of a uniform possibility of transformation and fluid exchange.
>
> *(p. 2)*

Thirty years later, the category of PTSD would carry out a similar strategy, massively and even more effectively universalizing the significance of traumatic experience and its clinical effects, but also the temporality typical of traumatic memory and its treatment. Through a complex epistemic and political torsion, the trauma of American veterans in Vietnam perpetuated that secret impulse to *globalize* the significance of symptoms, experiences and treatments that psychiatry had already tried to achieve in the colonial period. To ensure its influence, however, the diagnosis of PTSD once again had to silence other conflicts and contradictions, concealing in particular the racial nature of the violence and suffering associated with the war in Vietnam. Contempt for an enemy, hated, derided, racialized and animalized, was necessary to perpetrate violence and atrocities even against civilians. The zoological language that Fanon had described in detail in the colonial context once again took center-stage in the history of the US military. And as often happens, it was often language that preserved, like splinters of wood embedded in flesh, the (racial) meaning of abuse, atrocity and destruction. Consider the case of the racial slur designating the Vietnamese, "g★★k," a term already used by US soldiers against Asian people during other colonial wars (in Korea, and still earlier in the Philippines) and employed also against Black Haitians in the early 20th century.[17] The history of the term is exemplary for the function it played to dehumanize the enemy, and further to placate any sense of guilt, moral crisis and anguish for American soldiers. A perverse competition developed around the number of Vietnamese killed or Vietnamese women raped, who, after all, were no longer men or women, but simply "g★★ks."[18] The idea of a *g★★k syndrome*, a concept coined by Lifton (1969/1970), recalls one of the most important pages in the history of PTSD:

> The men who fought the long Vietnam ground war were drawn into what I shall call the "g★★k syndrome." The scapegoated victims of American soldier-survivors of the ground war in Vietnam were not the North Vietnamese or the NLF guerrillas, or even South Vietnamese civilians and soldiers. Rather, they were the "g★★ks". . . . So predominant was the g★★k syndrome that trying to avoid it made one "abnormal," and even those who consciously fought its dehumanization were inevitably drawn into it. . . . Despite everything, however, more humane feelings toward Vietnamese did persist. Such feelings could be kept alive by involvements with families or by various encounters with the suffering of individual Vietnamese. Children could play a particularly great part in resensitizing experiences. Veterans recalled their shock at seeing American trucks barreling through villages and running over children in the road. These are what I call images of ultimate transgression, of ultimate "mismatch" – the helpless young, whom adults are supposed to nurture and protect, cruelly destroyed by all-powerful but totally unfeeling American machines.
>
> *(pp. 70–71)*

Combining the *cultural genealogy of suspicion* with the analysis of a diagnostic category, relating the scene of *racial violence* examined by Fanon with colonial psychiatry's "denial" (Taïeb, Aubin, Mannoni, Carothers)[19] and the moral and political questions left in the background by the diagnosis of PTSD, I adopt a perspective not far removed from the approach of Laura Briggs (2002), Selma James

(1974/2012) and other feminist scholars who trace the connections between colonialism, sex, race and social class to structurally analyze the dominant global forms of exploitation. In my analysis, I work to distill a symptomatic understanding of trauma from these premises.

Colony: Another Kind of Trauma; or, When the Waves of the Political Break on the Banks of the Psychic

The fifth and final chapter of *The Wretched of the Earth* can rightly be regarded as the piece of thinking that fully asserts the project of a *decolonial clinical practice* that, once any Eurocentric residue in the diagnosis has been dealt with and a socio-genesis of mental disturbances has begun, can turn to consider the psychic scars inflicted on the colonized, on the "wretched of the earth," who (as Fanon's life work avows) embody a particular historical consciousness of the disaster and lived experience (or *Erlebnis*) of domination. As in *Black Skin, White Masks*, Fanon shows in Chapter 5 of *Wretched* that sociogeny and alienation do not spare the colonizers and French society, either. Reflecting the Manicheism of colonialism famously discussed in the first chapter of *Wretched*, Chapter 5 demonstrates how (though the costs and symptoms are radically different) alienation penetrates and pervades both sides of the colonial world.

Fanon begins by wondering if a chapter on mental disturbances might not seem "untimely" in "a book like this." Its inclusion comes from the awareness that the colonial period was a twisted one, where political and psychopathological oppression were structurally knotted together: "The truth is that *colonization, in its very essence, already appeared to be a great purveyor of psychiatric hospitals*" (emphasis added). Returning to clinical material in the midst of an analysis of national culture or anti-colonial struggle is therefore necessary for Fanon. But Chapter 5 is a complex chapter. The previous assertion is followed by others that sound almost paradoxical: that anti-colonial resistance struggle, while necessary to uproot from colonized minds the "seeds of rottenness" planted by oppression (Fanon, 1963, p. 181)[20] *also generates mental disturbances*; and that mental unhealth (including as it is wrought by decolonial resistance) is impossible to treat within the colony.[21]

Like a mournful echo, mental disturbances accompany the various phases of occupation, dominion and resistance. While they continue to inhabit the space of psychopathology, we can still recognize their "infrapolitical" value (Scott, 1990, pp. 183–201), which lends a more than metaphorical significance to the idea of "defense mechanism." There are few authors before Deleuze's and Guattari's method of "schizoanalysis" who have so effectively tied the symptom to the political, the unconscious to history. What interests me here is how the work enabled Fanon to imagine another narrative for these mental disturbances that had arisen in the context of violence and colonial war. In his texts, and especially the climactic Chapter 5 of *Wretched*, Fanon succeeds in setting out an original theory of trauma, whose structure is radically different from the one characterizing the idea of PTSD.

His first step was to consider suffering *both* in the colonizers *and* in the colonized. The cases in the first group of patients ("Series A – Five cases have been collected here, all involving Algerians or Europeans who had clearly defined symptoms of severe reactive disorders"; Fanon, 1963, p. 185) document, for example, the symptoms of two colonial police officers (cases 4 and 5). Later we read of a French woman, the daughter of a civilian, responsible for violence against Algerians and "obsessed" with hunting them down. Though Fanon acknowledges the psychic wounds of French occupiers and even of those responsible for torture, he does not neglect the differences between those who try to question their role (case 4) and those who ask only to be able to continue to torture without suffering (case 5), nor does he neglect the differences between mental disturbances for aggressors and for victims. If one of the police officers displays a state of depression and a panic attack after accidentally meeting someone he had subjected to torture, the victim, who had also recognized his tormentor and feared he had come after him even in hospital to continue his work, has a much more serious reaction: he attempts suicide. The conclusion is that *there is no natural way in which trauma takes its course*. The trauma's position within the sociopolitical fabric will impose different prognoses and fates upon its differently positioned subjects. This is what I have previously called Fanon's "political semiotics" (Beneduce, 2011; Gibson and Beneduce, 2017).

There is a second step by which Fanon sets forth his original theory of trauma that is closely connected to the first. The question with which Fanon had begun his reflections on racial alienation 20 years earlier ("What does a man want? What does the black man want?"; Fanon, 1986, p. 10) became – after bearing witness to the accounts of the tortured, treating their wounds, listening to the silence of the raped women – the terrible enigma of the colonized: "Who am I in reality?" In the colony, dehumanization, humiliation and "thingification" generate radical demands on one's own status. This question signifies a new page in Fanon's phenomenology, where he insists that the violence inflicted on colonial territories and the occupation of colonized bodies is coextensive, where he sketches a *political and clinical ecology* that lays out on the same canvas the "wounds inflicted on the colonized during a single day under a colonial regime" and the pain of places, expropriated lands and evacuated villages:

In Algeria there is not simply domination but the decision, literally, *to occupy nothing else but a territory*. The Algerians, the women dressed in *haiks*, the palm groves, and the camels form a landscape, the natural backdrop for the French presence.

(Fanon, 1963, p. 182)

Bodies, memories, lands, goods: the colony makes no distinctions in what it appropriates, and everything will be forcibly *alienated* in the legal (as well as psychological) sense of the term. This is another of the aspects forgotten by PTSD as a diagnosis, which ignores the broader destruction of symbols and places that is bound up within colonial suffering, and the *territorial anguish* that it generates.[22]

Fanon begins his reflections in Chapter 5 by declaring he wants to avoid "any semiological, nosological, or therapeutic discussion." However, the pages that follow introduce new perspectives in these areas. This represents the third step in Fanon's establishment of an original theory of trauma. While psychiatry settled for describing colonial symptoms as benign "psychotic reactions" (184), circumscribing and banalizing their causes, Fanon insisted on the fact that they emerge from "a bloody, pitiless atmosphere" (183). This indicates that psychic suffering is the inevitable response to a world that is collapsing, to an "atmospheric violence."[23] If colonialism takes on the characteristics of genocide, it is no wonder that its symptoms appear differently than conventional approaches in psychiatry might imagine: "Another well-established notion that deserves in our opinion to be reevaluated is that these psychotic reactions are relatively benign . . . *We believe on the contrary that the pathological processes tend as a rule to be frequently malignant*" (Fanon, 1963, p. 183; my italics).

Fanon attempted to make use of psychoanalytic interpretive models to read the symptom of those who became impotent on learning their wife had been raped by the French (were these incestuous ghosts?),[24] or the night-time ravings of a man who felt persecuted during the night by the image of an old woman.[25] In both cases, the interpretations proved unsatisfactory, however. Unlike what Aubin has suggested by drawing on the notion of denial, or Mannoni, who had interpreted the nightmares of Madagascan children as reflecting castration fears (Mannoni, 1956), Fanon lifted another curtain: instead of trying to globalize the unconscious of the colonized, or pathologize their reactions, he sought to recognize how far the violence of war had colonized emotions, words and imaginaries. His insistence on the "dislocated personality" of victims of torture, and his prognostic pessimism ("In all evidence the future of these patients is compromised"), are the clinical counterpoints of his political and anthropological thinking. In addition, continuing a development he set forth in *Black Skin, White Masks*, Fanon lifted the veil that prevented psychiatrists and psychoanalysts of the time from naming the experience of terror wrought by the voice of the colonist or the racial gaze, or the drama of those who lived their lives as a daily apocalypse.

The violence Fanon witnessed in Algeria was the painful, infected suture between colonial domination and racial alienation, the very one that the trauma treatment emerging in the context of the Vietnam war would symptomatically mask.[26] But it is perhaps Fanon's fourth step that is decisive in our critique of PTSD.

In Chapter Five of *Wretched*, Fanon accommodates a recognition that colonial violence evacuates, for its subjects, a sense of moral standing or orientation, surrounding the colonial situation with a feeling of moral vertigo. For torture survivors, for example, Fanon observes that a sense of justice is felt to be lost and that there remains an "indifference to any moral argument," an ethico-affective position that others have gleaned from the stunned experience of some survivors of Nazi concentration camps. Fanon therefore troubles the easy moral narrative that may too easily be read into the traumas of victimhood: including by those who would read Fanon himself as espousing a moral certitude within colonial resistance. Simultaneously, Fanon avoids the pitfalls of failing to attend to moral considerations at all, a tendency that is highly prevalent within PTSD diagnoses.

By probing morality for a myriad of actors, from subjects to participants, within the colonial scene, Fanon also examines the moral orientation of two young Algerians who were responsible for the murder of one of their companions: an adolescent like them, but who was French. "Are you sorry you killed someone?" Fanon asks the first. "But that's no reason for killing your friend," he replies to the second. In response: silence. This silence, the young Algerians' seeming indifference, is eloquent. They reveal an abyss that colonial violence has gouged out of experience. It is the colonial machine that Fanon wants us to recognize through the symptom of this silence, a symptom that covers the deeply felt emptiness of moral exhaustion.

The historian Caroline Elkins (2005, 2022) has shown how the atrocities committed by the British Empire, not unlike those carried out in Indochina, Madagascar or Algeria by France, were systematically silenced, concealed or justified as exceptions due to alleged emergency conditions; only in 2021, 60 years later, for example, did France admit to the torture and murder of the young mathematician Maurice Audin. The case of the *Migrated Files*[27] may be the most recent example of the desire to conceal, at whatever cost, the sleepless traces of colonial violence, silencing the untimely voice of colonial survivors, and even managing to discredit the research of historians.[28] The "pathogenic secret" of the bourgeois family (Freud), from which the theory of trauma arose, has a no less dark chapter in colonial history (and in the history of the nation-state). But the *symptoms* that originated from colonial trauma would be equally stubborn, equally painful, as is shown by the macabre violence of the civil war in the 1990s and the mysterious disappearance of hundreds of minors in present-day Algeria (Lazali, 2021).

Untimeliness: Remembering the Past, Reclaiming the Future, or Rethinking "True History" With *The Wretched of the Earth*

In 1957 in Kenya, as in other colonies, arrest and torture without trial was the norm (see also Fanon, 1964, p. 66). Eric Griffith-Jones, attorney-general of the

British administration at the time, suggested precise techniques for beating the Mau Mau detainees in the concentration camps. What interests me here is his insistence on the need to maintain absolute emotional detachment and complete discretion upon performing these practices: "vulnerable parts of the body should not be struck, particularly the spleen, liver or kidneys. . . . Those who administer violence . . . *should remain collected, balanced and dispassionate*. . . . If we are going to sin, *we must sin quietly*" (my italic).[29]

This appeal to keep the "sin" a secret is useful for examining the psychic consequences of state-sanctioned violence. Is it reasonable to wonder if the onset of PTSD symptoms, perhaps especially flashbacks, among Vietnam veterans is connected with the United States' military pedagogy of violence and the imposition of secrecy upon practices of torture, abuse and humiliation?[30]

A comparative analysis of violence within colonial periods and within the recent wars that have seen the rampant development of PTSD diagnoses (Vietnam, Iraq, Afghanistan) enables us to recognize similar mechanisms of racialization across both contexts, as in the case of Abu Ghraib (Adams et al., 2006; Green, cited in Améry, 1966/1980, pp. 22–23), yet it also lays bare new developments in, and questions about, the modern expressions of trauma.

The images of drowned persons in the Mediterranean, and of children separated from their families along the Mexican border during the Trump administration, stand alongside those of children belonging to minorities (Indigenous Natives, Black Americans) who were subjected to procedures of forced adoption in the United States (Briggs, 2020), Europe (Taliani, 2018) or institutionalization in Canada or Australia, or to the images of unauthorized drug-testing in prisons or colonies (Anderson, 2006; Eschadely, 2014; Lachenal, 2014). The clinical literature has had little to say about the effects of this state-sanctioned violence, about the burden they place on those who suffered them and has never asked *how* the oppressed and dispossessed *remember*. These images, which speak of *state traumas*, also challenge the clinical literature to question how clinical institutions may bear some responsibility for their emergence (Niezen, 2016).

My question, then, becomes: how should we name and treat these forms of racial violence and trauma that are structurally connected to the institutions of the nation-state?[31] It is this space that gives rise to a recognition that it is by virtue of their *spectral* nature (Gordon, 2008) that both a linear historical reconstruction and the use of a generic diagnostic category for persistent effects of trauma become impossible. The broken phrases and nightmares of asylum-seekers recall this, particularly in their invocations of slavery, in their arrests for being found without documents, in the racist insults hurled against them in the street, or when memories of the traumas suffered during voyages toward Europe or America mix with those of forced admissions to a psychiatric ward. Pondering what she calls "epidemics of trauma" in Kashmir, Saiba Varma reaches similar conclusions, showing that the chronic atmosphere of uncertainty and violence in which many are forced to live rebels against the idea that suffering and disturbances can be "localized" and named within a diagnostic category such as that of PTSD: a category proposed by the health facilities of the very governments responsible for the violence and terror exercised against the daily lives of these patient populations (Varma, 2020).[32]

It is within this horizon that we can at last recognize that the pain and suffering filed as PTSD are the palimpsests not only of *one* traumatic event but of a much broader space-time within which generations, places, ties and epochs may *legitimately* merge to contest any linear reconstruction, or any banalizing medicalization. And when clinical theories or political analyses mark out only an arid desert, it is literature that sets thought moving again and announces the possible decolonization of traumatic memory (Erickson, 2009; Jarvis, 2021; Morrison, 1987, 1988).

I find within this contradictory and heterological territory, fed by critical theory and literary studies, the possibility of combining Fanon's question about the "*untimely*" with the notion of *untimeliness*, interpreted by Wendy Brown as the will to reclaim a present, and – I may add– a dis-alienated future.

I would like to conclude with a final connection, one between the notion of trauma and the notion of nostalgia. The latter, too, has, after all, its own genealogy in contexts of war, migration and violence (Naqvi, 2007). Nostalgia, racial melancholia,[33] diasporic and postcolonial melancholia (Gilroy, 2005) also demand to be freed from their fate of pathologization and medicalization which has often been their connotation. They affirm, on the contrary, as the work of recent decades has repeatedly shown, the stubborn will not to forget, not to allow the memory of violence and the accompanying infinite loss to be swept away. Racial and postcolonial suffering often does this through other languages, other imaginaries, other epistemologies, which often disturbs the ordered framework of diagnostic categories, their grammar, and through this act asserts itself as an authentic form of resistance and counter-memory (Lipsitz, 1990; Segato, 1998). In describing "diasporic melancholia as a response to the social and physical genocide of African chattel slavery" (2007, p. 512),[34] Clarke Kaplan recalls Nora's view that "true history" is above all that of the "Jews of the diaspora, peasant culture, and ethnic minorities." May we add to this list immigrants and asylum-seekers? Can we claim the racism which continues to target them is theirs, a trauma experienced every day, and such as to make us ask, as Baldwin did (2017), by what miracle they are not all prey to a "raging paranoia"? These, too, are questions that can contribute to eroding the empire of trauma, just like the arrogance of diagnostic compulsion that insists on hushing the significance of the insidious "insurrection" of its symptoms.

Notes

1 The idea of "lecture symptômale" (*symptomatic reading*) was suggested by Althusser. In taking up Marx's criticism of Smith for not seeing what was in front of him – the difference between constant and variable capital, Althusser reads Marx and *Capital* using a similar critical perspective. The concept arises from the awareness of how what is visible can often, paradoxically, escape the observer (Althusser, 2015).

2 I use this term not in the usual sense of the geographical study of funeral practices and places of death, but rather, taking my cue from the idea of "necropolitics" (Mbembe, 2019), to designate, to adopt Klemperer's expression, a "geography of the hell of universal history" (Klemperer, 1996, p. 120), and index those place and city names (San Antonio, Dover, Calais, Lampedusa, Moria, Kufra, Melilla, Ventimiglia, Balesur-e) marked on the migratory maps of those who try to cross borders. These are the names – laden with a baleful sonority– that measure out our present knowledge of the world.

3 They were first described as Chinese until they were found to be Vietnamese. Often these bodies long remain nameless, identified only on the basis of their somatic features, supposed nationality and a geographical area: no different from how the "shapeless masses" of the colonized were in the past described by the colonial psychiatry of Antoine Porot.

4 Feldman suggests this expression in his comment on Rodney King's trial. Concerning the paradoxical interpretation made by the defense attorneys for the policemen of the policemen's violence against Rodney King, Judith Butler writes:

> That it *was* achieved is not the consequence of ignoring the video, but, rather, of reproducing the video within *a racially saturated field of visibility*. If racism pervades white perception, structuring what can and cannot appear within the horizon of white perception, then to what extent does it interpret in advance "visual evidence"?
>
> *(Butler, 1993, pp. 15–16; emphasis added)*

5 The passage cited and the translation, including the question mark to indicate translation uncertainties, can be found in Ferguson (2002, pp. 551–552).

6 Whenever I have the opportunity, I recall the names of the victims of racial violence in our present as part of a counter-history designed to cure the threatening amnesia that does not even spare the social sciences.

7 For example, consider the works of Jennifer Cole in Madagascar; Michael Taussig in Colombia; Kimberly Theidon in Peru and Michael Lambeck in Mayotte; See Connerton (1989).

8 Broch-Due and Bertelsen suggest a similar opinion when they claim:

> The expansion of trauma into all walks of life, and its new psychological mooring in the mind, would be impossible without a western modernity, not only intellectually but also technologically and politically. Trauma-writ-large complements the *industrialization of violence, and they are both characterized by a speedy and spectacular visibility.* These blown-up versions, however, sidetrack the slower modes of atrocities and suffering seeping *through marginalized spaces, which typically remain out of sight of global attention.* This empirical diversity in the forms of violence and trauma powerfully reveals the limits of universalizing axiomatic language and interpretative frames . . . Whilst these modern renditions of trauma and memory are *ahistorical, abstracting and atomizing devices, they also remove agency* from those afflicted along with the specificity of their suffering.
>
> *(Broch-Due and Bertelsen, 2016, p. IX; my italics)*

9 I refer here to *Antz*, of 1998.

10 Beard wrote his treatise on *Neurasthenia* in 1880, to be followed a year later by that on *American Nervousness*.

11 This process was particularly visible starting with the success of a therapeutic model such as eye movement desensitization and reprocessing (EMDR), which, given the dizzying expansion of its army of experts and the promise of effective treatment in a few sessions and in any context (from 11 September to earthquakes, to the case of traumas that mark the daily life of the Palestinian people), weakened the narrative paradigm inaugurated by psychoanalysis.

12 This limit has been brought out by Deleuze and Guattari:

> The fundamental problem about these texts is the following: must we see, in all these *sexual-social* investments of the libido and these object choices, mere dependences of a familial Oedipus? Must we save Oedipus at all costs by interpreting these investments and object choices as defenses against incest? . . . Must these be understood as compromises and substitutes for incest?
>
> *(Deleuze and Guattari, 1983, pp. 353–354)*

Historical and philological criticism has been expressed more recently by Ginzburg (2012).

13 The most recent example of the structural connection between suspicion and medical-psychiatric diagnosis is without a doubt that of "resignation syndrome" in Sweden, where the serious symptoms noted in the children of asylum-seekers had long been interpreted as an attempt to obtain the benefit of international humanitarian protection. But the history of medical suspicion and pathologization of political issues is a long one. In 1851 Cartwright had interpreted the recurrent attempts of slaves to escape the plantations in Haiti as the symptom of an overwhelming, pathological impulse, "drapetomania." In colonial Kenya, Carothers (1955, p. 4) interpreted the Mau Mau struggle as the expression of a "forest psychology," in need of rehabilitation . . . Beyond the criticism initiated by Fanon (1986; Fanon and Lacaton, 1955), this criticism has been developed further with regard to the immigrant population (Bennani, 1980; Lipsedge and Littlewood, 1989; Sayad, 2004). Psychiatric diagnosis, racism, gender (Morrison, 1992) and dominion are fields of action that often overlap.

14 In a short piece of 1920, Freud intervened on the case that saw Dr. Julius Wagner-Jauregg on trial: called on to give his opinion, without expressing himself explicitly on the choice of using electric shock treatment on patients affected by neuroses from war (a therapy that Ferenczi had criticized for his part), he seized the opportunity to assert the primacy of psychoanalysis and in fact deny that there is an autonomous diagnostic entity of "war neurosis." See Danto (2016) and Jasna (2020). We should recognize that PTSD may have been the first diagnosis of the effects of traumatic experiences that assigned them a status of truth, though a posteriori – that is to say, starting from the diagnosis given by an expert (*if* symptoms of PTSD are present, *then* the patient has been exposed – no matter whether as victim, witness, or perpetrator – to a trauma) (Young, 1995).

15 See Bullard (2011). Years earlier, Crewe had suggested a similar interpretation regarding the work of Wulff Sachs in South Africa: "Sachs tries to inscribe the South African native subject in the *colonial global imaginary of 1930s psychoanalysis*" (Crewe, 2001, p. 418; my italics).

16 An example is Suzanne Taïeb, who, unlike Aubin, concentrated on the role of magical-religious ideas in the Maghreb to interpret the ravings of women and men encountered in the psychiatric hospital of Blida (Taïeb, 1939). But Taïeb's approach ended up as just another case of denial. She seemingly ignored all the daily violence her patients were victims of, forgetting the rapes, humiliations and the atmosphere of threats and coercion in which they were forced to live. In this sense, by a singular mechanism, the unconscious "denial" of the colonized, so similar to the denial of the colonizers and

westerners, in Aubin's view, would be at bottom the veil behind which to conceal another denial: that of the psychiatrists themselves in the face of obscure forms of colonial domination. See also Beneduce (in press). Another interpretation of "denial" among the colonized was offered by Fanon and Lacaton concerning the Algerians accused of crimes, whose attitude was characterized by the denial of any kind of responsibility for the criminal act they committed. This refusal, Fanon and Lacaton affirm, depends on the absence of a true integration and recognition in the colonial world:

> For the criminal to recognize his act before a judge is to deplore it, to legitimize the irruption of the public into the private. By denying, by retracting, does the North African not refuse just this? What we probably see manifested in this way is the full separation between two social groups that co-exist – alas, tragically! – but where the integration of one by the other has not begun. The accused Muslim's refusal to authenticate, by confessing his act, the social contract proposed to him, means that his often-profound submission to the constituted powers . . ., which we have noted, cannot be confounded with an acceptance of this power.
>
> *(1955, p. 660)*

Here, according to Fanon and Lacaton, the symptom, the "defense mechanism," bears the meaning of true political acts.

17 Some authors claim that the slur originated in the use made by American troops in Haiti. Works published in the journal *Vietnam Generation* effectively analyze the racist and sexist imaginary at work in the US military and the psychic consequences of this experience on those African American soldiers (or from other minorities), who, despite having themselves direct, painful experience of racism in the United States, found themselves exercising forms of perverse racial violence toward the enemy. See Beavers (1989) and Shatan (1989) among others.

18 Editors' note: we have opted to censor this slur, including in Lifton's usage, because neither we nor Lifton identify with the oppressed groups that the term is used to attack. Our position is that it is important for racially oppressed groups to have ownership over such slurs.

19 I'm suggesting here that the "denial" of colonial violence and its alienating power in colonial psychiatry was a specific form of what Mills calls "white ignorance" (Mills, 2007), and more particularly a typical effect of the "racial contract." In fact, according to Mills,

> on matters related to race, the Racial Contract prescribes for its signatories an inverted epistemology, an epistemology of ignorance, a particular pattern of localized and global cognitive dysfunctions (which are psychologically and socially functional), producing the ironic outcome that whites will in general be *unable to understand the world they themselves have made.*
>
> *(Mills, 1997, p. 18; emphasis added)*

20 My translation. Philcox translates the phrase *"germes de pourriture"* as "seeds of decay."

21 Fanon had already asserted this theme in his letter of resignation from his psychiatric post in Algeria: "If psychiatry is the medical technique that aims to enable man no longer to be a stranger to his environment, I owe it to myself to affirm that the Arab, permanently an alien in his own country, lives in a state of absolute depersonalization" (Fanon, 1964, p. 53). Now Fanon insists on "the difficulty of 'curing' a colonized subject correctly, in other words making him thoroughly fit into a social environment of the colonial type" (Fanon, 1963, p. 181). It is no surprise that these considerations have inspired in recent years reflections on the psychopathology of the Palestinian people (see, e.g., Sheehi and Sheehi, 2022).

22 "Territorial anguish" is a concept proposed by Ernesto de Martino. A similar issue was partially explored by Eisenbruch (1991) with the idea of "cultural bereavement." Starting

from the need to recognize how places have a memory (see, e.g., Basso, 1996), some scholars most recently investigated this aspect in relation to Mozambique (Igreja, 2003).

23 This is the term Fanon often uses, both in recalling the anti-colonial struggles, from Indochina to Congo and Algeria, and in speaking of colonial repression. It is a key concept in his lexicon, the space-time *par excellence* that recalls the lived experience of the colony and colonial wars. The same term has been used recently by Eliad Weizman referring to Palestine and the Israeli colony (https://forensic-architecture.org/programme/events/atmospheric-violence-eyal-weizman) to suggest a specific aspect of the causality of violence in the contexts of the colony: where there are often no traces or evident "causes," and everything is invaded by the toxic cloud of violence, control and alienation. From the centrality in PTSD of the idea of "cause" and "traumatic event" we can guess how much Fanon's (and Weizman's) "atmospheric violence" is a decisive concept for emerging from the mechanism of a diagnostic category and imagining a very different structure of traumatic experience. See below.

24 "Case No. 1 -Impotence in an Algerian following the rape of his wife" (Fanon, 1963, pp. 185–189).

25

> The question was then of knowing whether we were in the presence of an unconscious guilt complex after his mother's death, as Freud describes in his "Mourning and Melancholia." We asked him to tell us more about this woman since he knew her so well and was supposed to have killed her.
>
> *(Ibid., pp. 192–193)*

26 Richard Wright and Ralph Ellison had described racial alienation in America in their novels: Fanon often refers to their texts. Years later, James Baldwin would describe this inferno brilliantly, drawing partly on Fanon. Baldwin's speech in Rome in 1956, *Princes and Powers*, at the same conference at which Fanon had taken part, presenting his famous text *Racism and Culture*, was undoubtedly one of the decisive chapters in the decolonial counter-archive in those years.

27 The expression "Migrated Files" refers to the 8000 files that remained confidential after being brought to Britain, concerning among other things the violence of the colonial period, whose existence at Hanslope Park was only acknowledged in 2011 in all its dark recesses. Of them, around 1300 (294 boxes) concern Kenya and the atrocities committed against the Kikuyu and members of the armed militia of Mau Mau (rapes, mutilations, torture, cases of persons burnt alive, etc.). The other files concern Cyprus, Singapore, Malaysia and Malta.

28 The most embarrassing example is James Pascal Imperato's virulent criticism (2005) of the work of Caroline Elkins (and of another book, that of David Anderson, *Histories of the Hanged*), whose historical truth was questioned, claiming that it was an arbitrary reconstruction, and the expression of history as practiced by the new left in the spirit of deconstructionism and its "hermeneutics of suspicion." Today the reader can only see in this analysis another example of denial.

29 I. Cobain & R. Norton-Taylor (2012, April 18). *Sins of Colonialists Lay Concealed for Decades in Secret Archive*. www.theguardian.com/uk/2012/apr/18/sins-colonialists-concealed-secret-archive.

30 Alongside the "g★★k syndrome," Lifton also analyzed the consequences of a new kind of war:

> The essence of numbed warfare, then, is the near total separation of the act of killing from the *idea* of killing. As such, numbed warfare is perhaps the most malignant expression of the broad cultural gap between our technology and our feelings.
>
> *(1969/1970, p. 70)*

What is the role of the new military technologies in the onset of PTSD?

31 Yet the profound historical, social, cultural and economic differences between the contexts evoked do not cancel that common denominator that in Benjamin's words sounded like a sinister historical diagnosis: "The tradition of the oppressed teaches us that the 'state of emergence' in which we live is not the exception but the rule" (Benjamin, 1969, p. 257).

32 Among other things, Varma remembers how trauma's international vocabulary suppresses or ignores the local and more pertinent idioms for expressing the feeling of distress, despair and dispossession.

33 Drawing on the idea of "structures of feeling" (Williams, 1977) and, simultaneously, on that of "racial melancholia," Eng and Han read this condition not in individual terms but as a collective experience: as *an index of racial identification* useful for understanding "the historical processes of immigration, assimilation, and racialization underpinning the formation of Asian American subjectivity" (Eng and Han, 2018, p. 35). Another issue, not analyzed here, concerns the intertwining relationships between contemporary subjectivities, religious imagination, migration and psychosis in the Arab world (Pandolfo, 2007).

34 The author notes the risk of an identification that might foster new forms of "imperial cooptation." I share her concern and the need to avoid slipping into allegorical fantasies that end up forgetting what is at stake in these expressions of resistance and counter-memory.

References

Adams, G.B., Balfour, D.L. & Reed, G.E. (2006). Abu Ghraib, administrative evil, and moral inversion: the value of 'putting cruelty first'. *Public Administration Review* 66(5):680–693.

Althusser, L. (2015). *Reading Capital: The Complete Edition*. London: Verso.

Améry, J. (1980). *At the Limits of the Mind: Contemplation of a Survivor on Auschwitz and Its Realities*. Bloomington: Indiana University Press. (Original work published 1966).

Anderson, W. (2006). *Colonial Pathologies: American Tropical Medicine, Race, and Hygiene in the Philippines*. Durham: Duke University Press.

Anderson, W., Jenson, D. & Keller, J. (Eds.). (2011). *Unconscious Dominions: Psychoanalysis, Colonial Trauma, and Global Sovereignties*. Durham: Duke University Press.

Baldwin, J. (2017). *I Am Not Your Negro* (Adapted for film) (R. Peck, Director). Velvet Film.

Ballif, F. & Rosière, R. (2009). Le défi des 'teichopolitiques': analyser la fermeture contemporaine des territoires. *L'Espace géographique* 38(3):193–206.

Basso, K.H. (1996). *Wisdom Sits in Places: Landscape and Language Among the Western Apache*. Albuquerque: University of New Mexico Press.

Beavers, H. (1989). Contemporary Afro-American studies and the study of the Vietnam war. *Vietnam Generation* 1(2):6–13.

Beneduce, R. (2010). *Archeologie del Trauma: Un'Antropologia del Sottosuolo*. Bari: Laterza.

Beneduce, R. (Ed.). (2011). *Decolonizzare la Follia. Frantz Fanon: Scritti Sulla Psichiatria Coloniale*. Verona: Ombre Corte.

Beneduce, R. (2015). The moral economy of lying: subjectcraft, narrative capital, and uncertainty in the politics of asylum. *Medical Anthropology: Cross-Cultural Studies in Health and Healing* 34(6):551–571.

Beneduce, R. (2016a). Traumatic pasts and the historical imagination: symptoms of loss, postcolonial suffering, and counter-memories. *Transcultural Psychiatry* 53(3):1–25.

Beneduce, R. (2016b). L'Archive Fanon, politique Africaine l'archive Fanon: clés de lecture pour le présent. *Politique Africaine* 143(3):7–34.

Beneduce, R. (2018). Une nouvelle bataille de vérité: discours sorcellaires, cicatrices corporelles et régimes de crédibilité dans les droits d'asile. *Cahiers d'Études Africaines* LVIII(3–4), 231–232(3):763–792.

Beneduce, R. (2023, in press). Les couleurs d'Œdipe. In L. Boni & S. Mendelshon (Eds.), *Psychoanalyse du reste du monde: Histoire d'une subversion*. Paris: La Découverte.

Benjamin, W. (1969). *Illuminations*. New York: Schoken Books.

Bennani, J. (1980). *Le Corps Suspect: Le Migrant, son Corps et les Institutions Soignantes*. Paris: Galilée.

Blanchot, M. (1995). *The Writing of the Disaster*. Lincoln: University of Nebraska Press. (Original work published 1980).

Briggs, L. (2002). *Reproducing Empire: Race, Sex, Science and U.S. Imperialism in Puerto Rico*. Berkeley: University of California Press.

Briggs, L. (2020). *Taking Children: A History of American Terror*. Oakland: University of California Press.

Broch-Due, V. & Bertelsen, B.E. (2016). *Violent Reverberations: Global Modalities of Trauma*. London: Palgrave Macmillan.

Bullard, A. (2011). Denial, la crypte, and magic: contribution to the global unconscious from late Colonial French West African psychiatry. In A. Warwick, S. Jenson & R. Keller (Eds.), *Unconscious Dominions: Psychoanalysis, Colonial Trauma, and Global Sovereignties* (pp. 43–74). Durham: Duke University Press.

Butler, J. (1993). Endangered/endangering: schematic racism and white paranoia. In R. Gooding-Williams (Ed.), *Reading Rodney King/Reading Urban Uprising* (pp. 15–22). London: Routledge.

Carothers, J.C.D. (1955). *The Psychology of Mau Mau*. Nairobi: Government Printer.

Caruth, C. (Ed.). (1995). *Trauma: Explorations in Memory*. Baltimore: The John Hopkins University Press.

Connerton, P. (1989). *How Societies Remember*. Cambridge: Cambridge University Press.

Crewe, J. (2001). Black Hamlet: psychoanalysis on trial in South Africa. *Poetics Today* 22(2):413–433.

Danto, E.A. (2016). Trauma and the state with Sigmund Freud as witness. *International Journal of Law and Psychiatry* 48:50–56.

De Boeck, F. & Honwana, A. (2005). *Makers & Breakers: Children & Youth in Postcolonial Africa*. New York: James Currey.

De Genova, N. (2013). Spectacles of migrant 'illegality': the scene of exclusion, the obscene of inclusion. *Ethnic and Racial Studies* 36(7):1180–1198.

Deleuze, G. (1995). *Negotiations, 1972–1990*. New York: Columbia University Press.

Deleuze, G. & Guattari, F. (1983). *Anti-Oedipus: Capitalism and Schizophrenia*. Minneapolis: The University of Minnesota Press.

Eisenbruch, M. (1991). From post-traumatic stress disorder to cultural bereavement: diagnosis of Southeast Asian refugees. *Social Science & Medicine* 33(6):673–680.

Elkins, C. (2005). *Imperial Reckoning: The Untold Story of Britain's Gulag in Kenya*. New York: Henry Holt and Company.

Elkins, C. (2022). *Legacy of Violence: A History of the British Empire*. New York: Alfred A. Knopf.

Eng, D.L. & Han, S. (2018). *Racial Melancholia, Racial Dissociation: On the Social and Psychic Lives of Asian Americans*. Durham: Duke University Press.

Erickson, D. (2009). *Ghosts, Metaphor, and History in Toni Morrison's Beloved and Gabriel Garcia Marquez's One Hundred Years of Solitude*. New York: Palgrave Macmillan.

Eschadely, H. (2014). *De l'ombre vers la lumière: Le combat du docteur Salem Esch-Chadely*. Tunis: Institut Superieur de l'Histoire du Mouvement National.

Fanon, F. (1963). *The Wretched of the Earth* (R. Philcox, Trans.). New York: Grove Press.

Fanon, F. (1964). *A Dying Colonialism* (C.L. Markmann, Trans.). New York: Grove Press.

Fanon, F. (1986). *Black Skin, White Masks* (H. Chevalier, Trans.). New York: Pluto Press.

Fanon, F. & Lacaton, R. (1955). Les conduites de confession en Nord-Afrique. Nice: Congrès de Psychiatrie et de Neurologie de langue française, LIIIe session. *L'information Psychiatrique* 51(10):57–660.

Fassin, D. & Rechtman, R. (2009). *The Empire of Trauma: An Inquiry Into the Condition of Victimhood*. Princeton, NJ: Princeton University Press.

Feldman, A. (1994). On cultural anesthesia: from desert storm to Rodney King. *American Ethnologist* 21(2):404–418.

Ferenczi, S. (1994). *Further Contributions to the Theory and Technique of Psychoanalysis*. London: Karnac.

Ferguson, G.J. (2002). Of mimicry and membership: Africans and the new world society. *Cultural Anthropology* 17(4):551–569.

Foucault, M. (2014). *Wrong-Doing, Truth-Telling: The Funtion of Avowal in Justice*. Chicago: University of Chicago Press.

Genovese, E.D. (1972). *Roll, Jordan Roll: The World the Slaves Made*. New York: Vintage Books.

Gibson, N. & Beneduce, R. (2017). *Frantz Fanon, Psychiatry and Politics*. New York: Rowman & Littlefield.

Ginzburg, C. (2012). *Threads and Traces: True False Fictive*. Berkeley: University of California Press.

Gilroy, P. (2005). *Postcolonial Melancholia*. New York: Columbia University Press.

Gordon, A.F. (2008). *Ghostly Matters: Haunting and Sociological Imagination*. Minneapolis: University of Minnesota Press.

Gramsci, A. (1970). *Quaderni del carcere* (Tomo III, Quaderni 12–29). Torino: Einaudi.

Igreja, V. (2003). Why are there so many drums playing until dawn? Exploring the role of Gamba spirits and healers in the post-war recovery period in Gorongosa, Central Mozambique. *Transcultural Psychiatry* 40(4):459–487.

Imperato, P.J. (2005). Differing perspectives on Mau Mau. *African Studies Review* 48(3):147–154.

Jabr, S. (2019). *Dietro I fronti: Cronache di Una Psichiatra Psicoterapeuta Palestinese Sotto Occupazione*. Roma: Sensibili alle foglie.

James, S. (2012). *Sex, Race, and Class: The Perspective of Winning. A Selection of Writings 1952–2011*. Oakland: PM Press. (Original work published 1974).

Jarvis, J. (2021). *Decolonizing Memory: Algeria and the Politics of Testimony*. Durham: Duke University Press.

Jasna, K. (2020). Freud on the first world war (part 2). *European Journal of Humanities and Social Sciences* 1(3):45–60.

Kalpan, S.C. (2007). Souls at the crossroads, Africans on the water: the politics of diasporic melancholia. *Callaloo* 30(2):511–526.

Kienzler, H. (2022). SymptomSpeak: women's struggle for history and health in Kosovo. *Culture, Medicine & Psychiatry* 46:739–760.

Klemperer, V. (1996). *LTI. La langue du IIIe Reich: Carnet d'un philologue*. Paris: Albin Michel.

Lachenal, G. (2014). *Le Médicament Qui Devait Sauver l'Afrique: Un Scandale Pharmaceutique Aux Colonies*. Paris: La Découverte.

Lazali, K. (2021). *Colonial Trauma: A Study of the Psychic and Political Consequences of Colonial Oppression*. New York: Polity Press.

Lifton, R.J. (1969/1970). The 'gook syndrome' and the 'numbed warfare'. *The Saturday Review* 18:66–72.

Lipsedge, M. & Littlewood, R. (1989). *Aliens and Alienists: Ethnic Minorities and Psychiatry*. London: Unwin Hyman.

Lipsitz, G. (1990). *Time Passages: Collective Memory and American Popular Culture*. Minneapolis: Minnesota University Press.

Mannoni, O. (1956). *Prospero and Caliban: The Psychology of Colonization*. New York: Praeger.

Mbembe, A. (2006). La colonie, son petit secret et sa part Maudite. *Politique Africaine* 102:101–127.

Mbembe, A. (2019). *Necropolitics*. Durham: Duke University Press.

Mbembe, A. (2020). *Brutalisme*. Paris: La Découverte.

Mianji, F. & Kirmayer, L.J. (2022). 'Women as troublemakers': the hard sociopolitical context of soft bipolar disorder in Iran. *Culture, Medicine & Psychiatry* 46(4):864–888.

Mills, C. (1997). *The Racial Contract*. New York: Cornell University Press.

Mills, C. (2007). White ignorance. In S. Sullivan & N. Tuana (Eds.), *Race and Epistemologies of Ignorance* (pp. 11–38). Albany: State University of New York Press.

Morrison, T. (1987). The site of memory. In W. Zinsser (Ed.), *Inventing the Truth: The Art and Craft of Memoir* (pp. 103–124). Boston: Houghton Mifflin Company.

Morrison, T. (1988). *Beloved*. London: Pan Books.

Morrison, T. (Ed.). (1992). *Race-ing Justice, En-Gendering Power: Essays on Anita Hill, Clarence Thomas, and the Construction of Social Reality*. New York: Pantheon Books.

Naqvi, N. (2007). *The Nostalgic Subject: A Genealogy of the 'Critique of Nostalgia'*. Working Paper 23. CIRSDIG. Messina: The University of Messina.

Niezen, R. (2016). Templates and exclusions: victim centrism in Canada's truth and reconciliation commission on Indian residential schools. *The Journal of the Royal Anthropological Institute* 22(4):920–938.

Pandolfo, S. (2007). Finitude and the politico-theological imagination of illegal migration. *Anthropological Theory* 7(3):329–363.

Rosière, S. & Jones, R. (2012). Teichopolitics: re-considering globalisation through the role of walls and fences. *Geopolitics* 17(1):217–234.

Rossi, B. (2015). Kinetocracy: the government of mobility at the desert's edge. In D. Vigneswaran & J. Quirk (Eds.), *Mobility Makes States: Migration and Power in Africa* (pp. 149–169). Philadelphia: University of Pennsylvania Press.

Santner, E.L. (1996). *My Own Private Germany: Daniel Paul Schreber's Secret History of Modernity*. Princeton: Princeton University Press.

Sayad, A. (2004). *The Suffering of the Immigrant*. Cambridge: Polity.

Scott, J. (1990). *Domination and the Arts of Resistance: Hidden Transcripts*. New Haven: Yale University Press.

Segato, R.L. (1998). The color-blind subject of myth; or where to find Africa in the nation. *Annual Review of Anthropology* 27:129–151.

Shatan, C.F. (1989). Happiness is a warm gun: militarized mourning and ceremonial vengeance. *Vietnam Generation* 1(3):69–122.

Sheehi, L. & Sheehi, S. (2022). *Psychoanalysis Under Occupation: Practicing Resistance in Palestine*. New York: Routledge.

Sibertin-Blanc, G. (2014). Décolonisation du sujet et résistance du symptôme: clinique et politique dans les Damnés de la terre. *Cahiers philosophiques* 138(3):47–66.

Taïeb, S. (1939). *Les idées d'influence dans la Pathologie mentale de l'indigène Nord-Africain: Le rôle des superstitions*. Thèse pour le Doctorat en Médecine présentée et soutenue publiquement le 24 juin 1939. Alger: Ancienne Imprimerie Victor Heintz.

Taliani, S. (2018). Sometimes I feel like a motherless child: Nigerian migration, race memories and the decolonization of motherhood. In C. Gualtieri (Ed.), *Migration and the Contemporary Mediterranean: Shifting Cultures in 21st-Century Europe* (pp. 111–130). Lausanne: Peter Lang.

Varma, S. (2020). *The Occupied Clinic: Militarism and Care in Kashmir*. Durham: Duke University Press.

Williams, R. (1977). *Marxism and Literature*. Oxford: Oxford University Press.

Young, A. (1995). Reasons and causes for post-traumatic stress disorder. *Transcultural Psychiatry* 32(3):287–298.

Young, A. (1997). *The Harmony of Illusions: Inventing Post-Traumatic Stress Disorder*. Princeton: Princeton University Press.

2

OBLIGATORY DEATH IN WUHAN

The Power to Decide Who Died, and Therapies for Those Who Survived

Xiaowen Zhang and Jie Yang

Introduction

Early February 2020, in a short video clip which became viral and received widespread comments online, a girl cries as she follows an ambulance that is slowly driving away (Xingshipin, 2020). Another clip posted in late February 2020 shows a middle-aged woman in a protective suit chasing a running ambulance, crying (Suzhou Release, 2020). Actually, the ambulances in both videos are heading to the crematorium, in which bodies of the women's loved ones – a mother in the first case, a husband in the second – were placed. They had just died from pneumonia and were taken from the hospital directly to be cremated without being appropriately accompanied by family members. This was not uncommon during the first half of 2020. The Chinese government implemented lockdowns in various cities. Hundreds of thousands of people died nationwide, either directly from the novel coronavirus or from other causes. All were taken immediately to be cremated.

Anthropologists and sociologists have generally studied death as a social, cultural and political event (Huntington and Metcalf, 1979; Rosaldo, 2004; Stepputat, 2014; Simpson, 2018; Kipnis, 2021). This is due to the close entanglement of life with regimes of governance and authority, including what Michel Foucault (2003) and Achille Mbembe (2003) call "sovereign power," the ultimate or overriding form of authority in premodern times (see also Foucault, 1990; Agamben, 1998; Rose, 2007). Compared to sovereign power and its "right of seizure" (Foucault, 1990, p. 136), power in the modern era focuses on preserving and generating life. The right of death is therefore redefined under the framework of

DOI: 10.4324/9781003311843-4

"life-administering" power or "biopower" (Foucault, 1990, p. 136). The connection between life and death is usually discussed in favor of the former: life must be ensured, while death becomes the unwilling result of all life-saving efforts. Modern society tends to deny, silence or even ignore death (Stepputat, 2014).

This dilemma came to the fore when COVID-19 first exploded in Wuhan, China, in 2019. According to one official document released by the Operation Center of COVID-19 Pandemic Prevention and Containment of Wuhan Municipal Government (武汉新冠肺炎疫情防控指挥), cumulative mortality for confirmed cases reached 3,869 by April 16, 2020 (Xinhua News, 2020), but this death toll covers only cases confirmed by positive nucleic acid testing results. Death caused directly and indirectly by COVID pneumonia during this period would amount to a much greater number. Uncalculated cases of death also include those resulting from unconfirmed COVID cases, noncommunicable diseases (such as diabetes, heart disease and cancer), and suicide. This fact is supported by another research on mortality of all causes in Wuhan from January to March 2020 (J. Liu et al., 2021). Their statistics show that, in this period, the mortality rate was 33% higher compared with that of the same period in 2019. The same research also reveals that of these excess deaths, pneumonia-caused cases occurred both inside and outside of hospital, while for deaths from causes other than pneumonia, there were "significant reductions in hospital deaths and significant increases in non-hospital deaths" (Liu et al., 2021) in 2020 compared with 2019. This change in numbers implies that, early in this epidemic, numerous patients died at home who might have been denied access to hospitals, receiving no treatment at all for whatever ailed them. If this is the case, then death itself became a site of contestation.

According to Foucault, the intention of biopower is to ensure and sustain life (Foucault, 1990). Why, then, a contradiction? The Chinese response appears to contradict biopolitical reality and permits actual death. These deaths were tacitly enabled, if not directly produced, to avoid the total breakdown of the local medical system by putting more burden than it could take. Yet this act that leads to death for the sake of national interest is somehow supported by the duty-bound traditions of the Chinese culture. For example, Confucianism and Daoism situate understandings of the self within interpersonal connections (Dien, 1983), and this interdependency between self and other is secured by mutual obligations, which extend even to a sense of "indebtedness" between one's family and nation. According to Lung-kee Sun, a person is already in debt to her family and nation before her birth for being "raised and nurtured" (Sun, 1991, p. 31) by them. Therefore, one should always prioritize social obligation over personal interest. This logic explains that people in Wuhan fulfilled social obligations defined by emergency policies and regulations, sacrificing self-interest for a collective good, including the freedom of movement, income and even their lives.

Many may tend to explain the contradiction between biopolitical reality and the Chinese pandemic response by recourse to what Achille Mbembe (2003) calls "necropolitics," or the racialized sanctioning of terror and death ordering the experiences of the living. We take a different approach. We follow the approach taken by Roberto Esposito (2008) and Stuart Murray (2006) with their discussion of "thanatopolitics," referring to the forces by which death *generates* certain conditions of life. Acknowledging the particular role of cultural values that appear within the Chinese context, we offer the term "obligatory death" to refer to most of the deaths that happened during the first lockdown in Wuhan from January 23 to April 8, 2020. Conditions for the death of local people during this period were created to ensure stability of the social and medical order.

We use the concept of obligatory death to answer questions emanating from personal stories of those people who lost their loved ones due to the COVID outbreak in Wuhan between 2019 and 2020. These tragedies include but are not limited to people like Kai Chang, aged 55, Wuhanese, who died of pneumonia in 17 days with his whole family including his parents, elder sister and himself, failing to make it to the hospital (Shenghuo Newspaper, 2020). Li Liu, aged 77, Wuhanese, was under a similar condition. The whole family was infected, his wife and granddaughter survived, while he and his daughter died due to limited medical resources (Liu, 2020). On Weibo (微博), a Chinese microblogging service, under the hashtag "COVID patients seeking help" (肺炎患者求助), there were more than 700 posts from that period, each telling a heart-breaking story of desperate patients failing to get medical assistance (Weibo, 2020). These stories bring about many questions including: How was death facilitated against the mainstream biopolitical ethos of "make live" (Foucault, 2003, p. 241)? What unique or even novel forms of power might this reveal? Deaths during the pandemic are not specific to China, but how might the Chinese case differ?

Our research suggests that obligatory death includes three major concerns. First, from the perspective of death, it reveals the fact that sovereign power remains, as reigning powers retain the capability to produce death and this is not confined to capital punishment. However, with biopower playing a central role as well, the power over death is exercised within certain temporal and spatial boundaries. Second, the sovereign wields the power over death based on the understanding that an individual's life does not belong to herself or himself, but is shared by her "significant others" (Sun, 1991, p. 40) (including family, community and the state). Third, obligatory death constitutes a "bad death" (不得善终) in the Chinese cultural context, as it deprives the dead of family care or medical assistance, and the living of proper mourning through death rituals. The supposedly "natural" or biological process of death has been intervened or interfered by social, political and economic forces

We position obligatory death within the framework of thanatopolitics offered by Esposito (2008) and Murray (2006). We adopt this approach because it refers specifically to a dynamic force within biopolitics generated by a reversal of death and life. It sees death function as a modus operandi within a biopolitical space. In Wuhan, as COVID-19 swept the city in early 2020, the government prioritized protecting the medical system and the social and political stability, which led to deaths in order to protect other lives. It is for this biopolitical purpose that thanatopolitics comes into effect, permitting or even encouraging deaths. Moreover, the sovereign power of the Chinese state temporarily turned the city of Wuhan into a "state of exception" (Agamben, 1998, p. 38) by the lockdown policy, allowing thanatopower to be directly exercised upon "bare life" (Agamben, 1998, p. 11) – bodies deprived of political rights – by community staff and medical authorities. However, attempting to understand obligatory death solely under the thanatopolitical framework may result in oversimplification. In China, we must consider Chinese cultural and philosophical tradition, which prioritizes the collective over the individual and emphasizes one's identity based on one's value for society. Valuing an "interdependent self" and interpersonal connections and as social obligations, advocating selfless and collective values (e.g., filial piety, loyalty, community), and following a sense of communal indebtedness all contribute to the rationale of obligatory death in Wuhan.

This chapter also seeks to go beyond a simple notion of death. Returning to the two video clips at the beginning of this chapter, cases of death were followed by bereavement among thousands of heart-broken survivors. More than an emotional state that is socially and culturally produced, grief in the face of obligatory deaths during the lockdown in Wuhan was unique. For one, while the quality of death mainly "lies in the eyes" (Van der Geest, 2004, p. 909) of the living, bad death in the Chinese context is more frustrating and devastating for beholders than good death. For another, the unavailability of death rituals adds on to the crippling effects of such deaths. Chinese death rituals contain important cultural beliefs that bring comfort to the bereaved, including a sense of closure and beliefs that the deceased matter the most (死者为大), and that the deceased will rest in peace after burial (入土为安). What's more, death rituals remain an important way of expressing filial piety (孝顺), a core moral value in Chinese culture which has been renewed and even written into the Chinese constitution in 2013 (see Yang, 2022). So, the cessation of this practice is agonizing to live with (see also Rosaldo, 2004). What's worse, due to the quarantine and city lockdown, the ever-important interpersonal connections and social bonding were hindered as well, leaving survivors by themselves to deal with bereavement and alienation intensified by the aforementioned factors.

In what follows, from analyzing the thanatopolitical rationale and techniques of governing the Chinese pandemic-era deaths, we explore how the distinct elements of obligatory deaths contribute to grief in China and what therapeutic measures have been taken in response to such grief.

Thanatopower and Obligatory Death

We can start by disentangling the concept of obligatory death from the power that lies behind it – the power of death. Following Foucault and Giorgio Agamben, Mbembe (2003) focuses his work on control over mortality and the right to kill wielded by modern governments: what he terms as necropolitics. Challenging Foucault's biopolitical perspective, Mbembe examines the exercise of necropolitics through cases such as Nazi concentration camps, slavery, colonial occupation and contemporary wars. In so doing, Mbembe argues that biopower is not enough to explain contemporary forms of governing life. We must also understand necropolitics, which explains both the killing of individuals and the creation of a "death world" (Mbembe, 2003, p. 40), where devalued people (such as people of color) experience slow death and incomplete existence. Jaime Alves (2018) shows how Foucault's concept of biopower is Eurocentric, ignoring how colonial history and racism justify the existence of anti-Black terror fostered by police violence. Both Mbembe and Alves suggest that necropolitics act as the dominant power regime in some spaces of sovereign exception, enabling genocide to strengthen or achieve more control.

Thanatopolitics takes a different perspective, in which death functions as something more generative. In Murray's (2006) study on suicide bombers who commit terrorist attacks, their deaths are understood to contribute to existential uncertainty, haunting the space of everyday biopolitical life. Thanatopolitics is thus described as a form of "death-in-life" (Murray, 2006, p. 207). This concept is further developed by Esposito (2008), who argues that for strengthening life, death is often cultivated. His study of concentration camps in Nazi Germany suggests that they function to engender a "therapeutic attitude under the thanatological frame" (Esposito, 2008, p. 115).

Based on the mutually inclusive relation between life and death as indicated by thanatopolitics, we have a preliminary understanding of obligatory death as generative. Its fundamental logic seems to be: by permitting the death of some, the state actually tries to save or secure others' chance to live. On this basis, obligatory death in Wuhan bears certain resemblances with the above cases. The first one lies in the created space of exception (Agamben, 1998). In the state of exception, the law is suspended and political rights for citizens are annulled. People living within the state of exception are reduced to biological existence, or "bare life"; anything carried out against them goes unpunished.

In Wuhan, this state of exception was created upon the implementation of the city lockdown policy. In the early morning of January 23, 2020, the Operation Center of COVID-19 Pandemic Prevention and Containment of Wuhan Municipal Government (武汉疫情防控指挥部) issued notice No.1, which stated that, from 10:00 am onwards, departure channels from Wuhan, including airport and railway stations, would temporarily close (Beijing News, 2020). Lockdown remained in place until April 8. Seventy-six days of isolation meant separation from the rest of the nation, with no public transportation, creating a temporal and spatial state of exception. At the same time, people living in Wuhan were temporarily excluded from the rest of political community, and they lost many previously held rights. The decision to restrict or even ban freedom of action and immediate access to medical resources exposed everyone – elderly, sick and disabled people in particular – to thanatopower. Death was cultivated among the most fragile individuals, including COVID patients, people struck by sudden disease (e.g., heart attacks) requiring emergent treatment, those with chronic conditions requiring regular treatment, and childbearing women. Liu Ziwei, a female, aged 26 and 41 weeks pregnant, was rejected by the Hubei Provincial Maternal and Child Care Hospital (湖北省妇幼保健医院) when she went for child delivery on February 4, 2020. Having nobody to turn to, she posted her experience online to call for social attention and help (Liu, 2020). There is a potential risk for everyone to become infected, the relatively high mortality rate caused by the virus,[1] and thanotopower situated citizens in Wuhan within a "limit zone between life and death" (Agamben, 1998, p. 159).

Within this state of exception, death was not directly ordered by any authority. Yet it was not only the virus that killed Chinese locals. During the city lockdown, thanatopower tacitly created structural impasses to facilitate death. For example, in one suicide case that took place on February 10, 2020, in Wuhan, Liang, a male uremia patient in his 70s, committed suicide at home after suffering 8 days without dialysis (the usual frequency would be three times a week). Liang had a fever after the pandemic broke out and was suspected to suffer from COVID. This forced him into a paradox: the hospital where he went for dialysis rejected further treatment because he had fever, while hospitals for fevered patients rejected him because they only accepted confirmed coronavirus cases. Liang turned to the community for help but was told to continue his quarantine at home (Chen, 2020). Such an impasse put many like Liang in a desperate situation. They could either be tortured to death by illness, or commit suicide, as Liang did.

This process can also be understood as social selection by thanatopolitics, screening those in weak health conditions by neglecting or prolonging the time span to get medical assistance. Those who survived the torturous long waiting had access to hospitals. There, they would go through a second round of selection by medical staff. Similar to biopower, thanatopower is no more sovereign-exclusive, meaning the involvement of other power-wielding agents. If most community staff possess this power by deciding who are qualified to receive medical assistance outside the hospital, then inside the hospital, the power completely belongs to medical professionals in deciding whom to save. Yin, a 53-year-old male and a suspected case of COVID, waited more than two weeks to be accepted by one hospital on February 4, 2020. By then he had turned from a mild case to a severe one. Being too weak physically and mentally to beckon for immediate assistance, he was ignored in the hospital. This was made clear by medical staff who told his daughter that doctors would give priority to treating those with a stronger will to survive. In the end, Yin did not receive any hospital treatment and died hours after his arrival in the hospital (Zhang, 2021).

There do appear to be new traits of governance in obligatory death in terms of the relationship between thanatopolitics and biopolitics. Previous studies suggest that thanatopolitics and biopolitics become separate and bounded within the space of exception. In our understanding of obligatory death in China, we find that the two powers coexist and coincide. Policies and regulations implemented in Wuhan included city lockdowns, quarantine and limited freedom of action, which were both therapeutic and thanatological at once. So, in the Chinese context, they are not two powers that function separately on different groups of people as is observed in previous studies (Mbembe, 2003; Esposito, 2008; Alves, 2018); rather, they are like two different sides of one specific power regime that dominated the city. It was up to the agents that possessed this power in Wuhan to decide how to wield it, these agents being primarily community staff and medical professionals.

As the above analysis demonstrates, thanatopolitics helps address how power facilitated death during the citywide lockdowns in Wuhan. However, there are limitations to explaining the rationale as thanatopolitical alone because of the differences between Euro-American and non-Euro-American cultures. In the western context, the social contract is understood to be the basis upon which a sovereign is constituted. This mutual bond requires individuals to delegate the absolute power of life and death over themselves to the sovereign (Foucault, 2003, p. 241), and individuals are granted certain rights in return. As the result, the freedom to live or die is by not legally possessed by the individual, so death, either ordered by power or self-committed, indicates freedom by relieving oneself from the social bond (Foucault, 2003, p. 241). This position corresponds with Murray's argument, which suggests that death is productive in "separating me from myself" (Murray, 2006, p. 211). On the other hand, for Euro-American people, death is established on the assumption of individuality with a clear boundary, and it invokes the image of an ego merging with the surrounding by breaking its boundary when death occurs (Sun, 1991, p. 30). These elements are difficult to locate within the holistic culture in China. In it, the blurred line between self and other makes individual identities inherently enmeshed in a social matrix. Instead of strict individuality, there exists an overriding longing to belong to certain groups (Sun, 1991). The human network is established on the basis of this sense of belongingness and is further confirmed by mutual obligations, which do not come from social contracts. Instead, they are inherent and are rationalized by a sense of indebtedness toward one's family, nation and other groups.

A holistic worldview stresses the existence of something beyond the self (Munro, 1985) in Chinese society: the big me (大我), or overall situation (大局). The pressure of the "big me," internalized and felt on a bodily and psychic level, urges each individual to fulfill her or his social obligations. The big me represents a multitude of different collectives, the two most important being the family and the nation. These two collectives overlap in the Chinese imagination, and a common term for the state is "home country" (家国), a combination of family (家) and country (国). The nation is also referred to as the "motherland" (祖国母亲) – literally, a combination of "homeland" or "ancestral land" (祖国) and "mother" (母亲) – and the emotion of Chinese citizens toward the Chinese nation is commonly one of attachment or love, being permeated by filial piety. This affective link with the nation is established on the already-existing authority of the national state.

Though these traditional ethics and concepts have changed in modern times (Dien, 1983), the modern Chinese state has continued to emphasize citizens' obligations to the nation. When the pandemic hit Wuhan in 2019, administrative bodies at different levels implemented policies and decisions, ranging from city lockdowns to detailed regulations in local communities. These policies defined obligations under the pandemic for everyone living in Wuhan. To fulfill their duties, individuals (including stranded non-locals)[2] exerted self-control to cope with personal inconveniences, including economic hardships and ailments. For them, it was out of awe of state authority on the one hand, but more important, this self-control also reflected an internalized sense of commitment and duty to the state. Expression of negative personal emotions or acting solely for the sake of personal interest (narrowly defined) during that time period would be deemed as selfish (Sun, 1991, p. 30),[3] and most people shared a tendency of not bothering the Chinese nation with individual worries (不给国家添麻烦). For death cases during the Wuhan lockdown, be them from disease or suicide, they were more or less results of following policies and regulations. Death in this case did not relieve oneself from the social contract in the individualistic perspective but it strengthens the already existing bond one has with his community. Death represents a performance of duty for the benefit of the "big me," the nation, and not burdening one's family (不拖累家里人).[4] The dead thereby becomes enmeshed within the webs of social relations that constitute the collective.

"Bad Death" and Its Effects on Grief

In the previous section, we argued that the Wuhan lockdown marked the time span during which both biopolitics and thanatopolitics were wielded by community staff and medical professions to produce death and save life. The two power regimes, overlapping on most occasions, found their most chaotic expression in Wuhan. However, as the state better supplied medical resources, thanatopolitics arguably became absorbed by biopolitics, rendering pandemic-era policies more life-saving than death-producing. This change was ushered in as medical aid teams from around the state arrived in Wuhan and as Huoshenshan and Leishenshan hospitals (specialty emergency hospitals designed to treat people with COVID-19) and 16 mobile cabin hospitals (providing large-scale medical isolation for low-severity cases) were brought into operation in Wuhan after early February. The change was also marked by the implementation of a national strategy to "receive all, treat all, test all, isolate all" (应收尽收，应治尽治，应检尽检，应隔尽隔).

However, during this time, the state and biomedical agents tried hard to hide such (obligatory) deaths from the public. Its existence was either concealed (e.g., through extremely strict criteria in deciding a COVID-related death) or justified by using specific discourses about the virus. For example, because wars are waged for the existence of a whole population (Foucault, 1990), actions against COVID-19 were addressed as a war against the virus, medical workers were addressed as "soldiers in white" (白衣战士), and Wuhan and its people were praised as heroic (CCTV News, 2020). This technique stressed the biopolitical side of power by praising medical professionals for their dedication and strengthening the links subjects have with their nation by taking virus as their common enemy. This logic assisted in obscuring what had occurred. However, the moment when the thanatopolitics revealed itself in producing death was not forgotten. Obligatory death had challenged the public's perception of death, normally constructed under the framework of biopolitics.

In recent years, the concepts of health and well-being have taken on increasingly important roles in Chinese policies, economy and academia. In 2017, Chinese President Xi Jinping put forward a national development strategy called Health China (健康中国战略) in the report of the 19 National Congress of the Communist Party of China (*People's Daily*, 2021). The strategy marks health as an important symbol of national prosperity. This barometer was followed by similar initiatives in other areas including the creation of the Health China Index in economic and the creation of the Health China Research Institute at Qinghua University. These initiatives at both governmental and non-governmental levels confirm a logic of biopolitics. In this context, health is valued as a positive result of the regulation of life, while death, as its negation, is construed as "distant and distanced" (Van der Geest, 2004, p. 902). This is not merely a geographic implication, referring to the relegation of certain death-associated places (including cemeteries, crematorium, and funeral parlors) to the outskirts, but also suggests an estranged position of death in people's minds. As representatives of death itself, dead bodies are removed from the "gaze of the living" (Stepputat, 2014, p. 3). Most city dwellers are able to avoid interaction with or awareness of corpses. Medicalization of death and commercialization of death rituals (Kipnis, 2021) mean that hospitals, medical institutions and crematoriums are relied upon to deal with dead bodies when necessary. In Wuhan, obligatory death shattered this scene. In the chaos of the early outbreak, numerous people witnessed or experienced deaths of loved ones in either hospitals or at home. Death, deprived of all its modern decorations – like decent burial clothes and embalming makeup – was exposed. In one documentary featuring pandemic survivors in Wuhan, a man surnamed Guo broken-heartedly describes his wife passing away in the hospital right under his nose. He even took pictures of the doctor declaring her dead and the medical staff coming in to seal the corpse into a bag and take it away (Figure Video, 2021).

Not only does obligatory death challenge the modern construction of death, but it is also considered as "bad death" in traditional Chinese culture. Connotations of this term have always been changing, but in modern times, professional medical assistance is deemed necessary in constructing good death (Van der Geest, 2004), and this makes numerous cases of obligatory death bad ones. The limited access to medical resources resulting from policies and regulations contributed to power's intervention within a supposedly natural process. In Chinese culture, good death normally refers to death that occurs in a manner that is understood to be natural, not from violence, accidents or malignant disease (Van der Geest, 2004). It also includes a hidden assumption about age: usually a good death involves people who are not younger than about 70 years of age. In this sense, obligatory death is more of a "man-made" or artificial case, with thanatopower interrupting lives that may have otherwise continued. More importantly, it broke with social norms because it denied people their death rituals. Chinese culture holds that death is made complete only when a decent funeral follows – that is, a "joyous funeral" for a good death (喜丧). While during the lockdown in Wuhan, families were not allowed to participate in any rituals due to the risk of contagion. In many cases, they quarantined at home and waited for information about their loved ones: their death, cremation and remains. A simple or symbolic burial of the remains became possible only after the lockdown was lifted months later.

The standards pertaining to death have a therapeutic function, since "goodness" or "peacefulness" of death matters most to the survivors (Van der Geest, 2004). Death rituals play a particularly important role in healing the bereaved. Confucianism advocates using rituals (礼) to humanize people by instilling socially approved moral characters (Jia, 2016). In the case of a death ritual, it allows for a sense of closure and expression of emotions that one has for the deceased. In the case of the death of a parent, a death ritual also functions to refine these raw emotions through a conscious or deliberate commitment to filial piety. By practicing a death ritual, the bereaved fulfill a filial duty, so they can be relieved from a sense of indebtedness. Therefore, through the expression and refinement of grief (over a mourning period that could last years[5]), individuals can obtain psychological comfort. Apart from this, as one of the most important rites of passage, death rituals mark an important transition in life from living to death, bringing peacefulness to the living by suggesting the dead have left the world of the living and properly entered another realm, as suggested in the popular idiomatic phrase "入土为安" (burial brings peace to the deceased). Therefore, a good death followed by a joyous funeral reduces the burden or pain of mourning in Chinese culture. The belief that the deceased will enjoy a good life in the other world is soothing, making death well-accepted by those close contacts of the deceased.

Traditional rituals and associated morals, social obligations and emotions have, however, long been out of date (Jia, 2016). In contemporary China, death rituals have been influenced and reformed by the central government along with the process of urbanization. Traditional death rituals have been simplified to ashes burials and funerals, confining grief into a particular setting that lasts only one day. Regulating grief in this way fits a highly efficient, rationalized modern society, but the importance of burials and funerals is intensified, meaning they now become the most crucial, if not the only, way to process emotions about a loved one's death (Kipnis, 2021). The therapeutic effect of death rituals may now lie primarily in bringing together relatives of the deceased and providing a sphere for a visible expression of grief that enables relatives to achieve a sense of closure and return to their normal lives. In lacking this ritual space and process for mourning, people in Wuhan may have experienced intensified grief without efficacious therapy or healing.

Without an effective channel to release grief over COVID-related loss of life, the intense emotions of survivors led in some cases to self-harm, and even to violence against others. In many cases, conflicts arose between the bereaved and healthcare workers (Gao et al., 2021). In a vlog recording from Wuhan during the first lockdown, a vlogger filmed one girl who had just lost her father to COVID (Zhizhuhoumianbao, 2020). Standing outside the hospital, she told the vlogger that her father was in good condition when he was sent here, but medical workers said the virus was spreading out of control and that he did not make it through. The girl became agitated as she talked, finally bursting out and cursing: "It was all their fault!" She blamed medical professionals for the delayed rescue and for providing vague information about her father's death. The existing tensions between doctors and patients were intensified during the Wuhan lockdown and healthcare workers wielding thanatopower became targets for people's rage.

Apart from the negative emotions caused by obligatory death, there were other factors making the grief from deaths in Wuhan early in the COVID outbreak unique. Some people witnessed the deaths of multiple family members due to COVID being highly contagious (Morris et al., 2020; Tang et al., 2021). Some experienced unexpected deaths of loved ones. Due to the city lockdown and quarantine policies, cases of death were usually handled by the surviving members alone, with very limited social and familial support. These people were also at high risk of possible infection themselves. Therefore, grief related to obligatory death was accompanied by strong emotional distress, including anger, fear, isolation, insecurity, loneliness, denial, self-blame and blame of others (Gao et al., 2021).

These are not experienced so potently in bereavement, rendering grief in Wuhan more like a combined effect of "natural disaster and man-made misfortune" (天灾人祸). It became much more complicated to provide grief counseling in this context, and counter measures at both governmental and non-governmental levels were required when restrictions on traditional cultural practices led to resistance.

Grief Counseling and the "Wailing Wall"

Obligatory deaths as a result of the Wuhan lockdown have resulted in thousands of traumatized survivors, who were under tremendous emotional distress but were denied local, Indigenous or traditional ways of healing and therapy. This made them targets of a new biopolitics of mental well-being. On March 18, 2020, the Joint Prevention and Control Mechanism of the Chinese State Council for COVID-19 (国务院应对新型冠状病毒疫情联防联控机制) issued the "Psychological Counseling Work Plan for the COVID-19 Pandemic" (新冠肺炎疫情心理疏导工作方案), requiring governmental agents at all levels to better understand the psychological condition of different groups of people during the pandemic, so as to maintain the public's mental health. In early February 2020, merely days after the implementation of the city lockdown, the Wuhan Mental Health Center (武汉精神卫生中心) opened a 24-hour hotline providing psychological assistance for citizens (*People's Daily Online*, 2020). Simultaneously, therapists and psychologists nationwide contributed to the healing process by providing online training or counseling services (via phone or the internet). It is estimated that more than 400 psychological hotlines were established in mainland China during this time (Li et al., 2021). Apart from online services, other cities and provinces sent out medical aid teams of therapists to help address mental health issues. Target groups included cured COVID-19 patients, medical workers who had participated directly in COVID treatment, community staff members and bereaved citizens (CCNU Media, 2020).

The Chinese government intervened to deal with grief more or less related to obligatory death, implying a form of therapeutic governance. This refers to psychological or biomedical interventions to heal trauma and distress originating from political or structural causes, or "power . . . exercised through therapeutic activities" (Yang, 2018, p. 597). Apart from biomedical interventions, modern therapeutic governance also emphasizes symbolic justice (Pupavac, 2004; Biehl and Locke, 2010), a therapeutic approach to social justice that encourages people to reconcile with the past instead of addressing the root causes to enable emotional well-being. In the case of the initial COVID outbreak, many official memorial campaigns were launched on the day of the Qingming festival (April 4, 2020), a holiday that traditionally includes commemoration or remembrance of the dead. This was amplified to a national public memorial for those who had died from the pandemic. On this National Mourning Day for COVID, flags were kept at half-mast, all public entertainment was suspended, and a three-minute silent tribute began at 10 am. The Hubei Provincial Government also awarded the honorary title of "Martyr" (烈士) to 14 people who had "sacrificed" themselves in "combating" the virus (Xinhua News, 2020). These 14 martyrs include 12 medical workers, one police officer and one community staff member – 13 of whom had died of COVID-19.

These governmental therapeutic measures to relieve grief were effective to some extent. The first set dealt with individual cases, while the memorial campaigns addressed the whole nation. Yet limitations still existed. The Chinese modes of therapeutic governance adapted the concepts of Euro-American mental health sciences to local problems and needs. Given that Chinese culture is a "less psychologized symbolic medium" (Sun, 1991, p. 6), the adoption of Euro-American psychological concepts to the Chinese context resulted in gaps between theoretical statements and actual practice. This is compounded by the fact that western modes of grief counseling have reached China much later than many other countries, being first introduced to the mainland in 2008 after the Wenchuan Earthquake in Sichuan Province (Cui et al., 2020; Gao et al., 2021). Grief counseling in China is still not included in the national medical curriculum system (Zhou and Zhong, 2021; Gao et al., 2021), and the attitude of Chinese citizens toward it is still not very positive. Most bereaved individuals prefer to process their negative feelings without seeking help from medical professionals (Morris et al., 2020). This is partly attributable to the influence of Confucianism in making death somewhat taboo (Xu, 2007; Yin et al., 2018) and subduing individual emotional responses (Sun, 1991). People would rather bear a personal loss alone or seek help from family and friends (Gao et al., 2021). A saying even spread in the aftermath of the Wenchuan Earthquake in 2008: "be cautious about fire, theft and psychological counsellors" (防火防盗防心理医生).[6] Survivors were reluctant to share their vulnerability with such professionals. Even 11 years later, grief counseling is still not the first choice for the bereaved in China.

The effectiveness of symbolic justice is also limited. These measures including the public mourning campaign and honorary titles were intended to mitigate the past negative effects of thanatopower, including instances of state negligence. But these measures also reminded survivors of the fatal consequences of state authority. Thus, while symbolic justice was emphasized to hide failed attempts at more "substantive social justice" (Biehl and Locke, 2010, p. 329), bereaved individuals and families were still aware of it and deemed themselves to be victimized. This feeling was further intensified by one specific death of Li Wenliang, one of the 14 Martyrs. In the official notice (Xinhua News, 2020) Li Wenlian's profile described him as follows:

[a]n ophthalmologist, he stuck to his position despite the great danger of being infected. He was infected with COVID-19 on January 6, 2020 when receiving

one patient. During hospitalization, he expressed his eagerness to go back to the [COVID]"battlefield" against the virus after recovering. The excellent qualities he bore lived up to his duty as a doctor. He died of COVID-19 on February 7, 2020.

This brief notice omits the important fact that Li was among the first to notify the public about the new virus in a group chat (on WeChat, a Chinese cell phone app) on December 30, 2019. Li was later admonished for spreading "rumors" online by the police. The tragic nature of his case lay in the fact that he was silenced by revealing something that was not supposed to be exposed, which accidentally challenged the implicit political correctness in China.[7] This "rumor" turned out to be true in less than one month's time, but the admonishment he received unveiled sovereign power for the first time during the COVID outbreak. Because Li was a whistle-blower, his infection and death aroused resentment against the state among the public. Li's personal profile on Weibo became itself a platform for public mourning. His last post on January 31, 2020, confirming his illness, has received more than one million comments since, thus forming a virtual Chinese wailing wall.

We have analyzed how governmental apparatuses attempted to deal with grief arising from obligatory death with mixed ramifications. In considering how Chinese citizens, in their response to pandemic-era loss, made up by the deficits and denials of the state, it is helpful to think about the concept of "death system[s]," or sociocultural and symbolic networks by which human beings "meditate and express" their relationships to mortality (Kastenbaum and Aisenberg, 1972, p. 310; Brubaker et al., 2013, p. 153). Because the pandemic prohibited in-person gatherings, the internet became an important channel by which individuals could make contact with the outside world. Weibo, with more than 200 million daily active users in 2021 (The Paper, 2022), became one of the most important spaces for posting individualized eulogies or commenting on the personal accounts of the deceased. Ultimately, this practice served a similar social function to death rituals: it was therapeutic for both those who posted the message and their readers. Online mourning in this sense is not revolutionary; the model of grieving it represents is similar to traditional Chinese patterns of mourning because the deceased are included in the ongoing daily lives of the survivors (Carroll and Landry, 2010, p. 342). This is to say that online platforms create a field (similar to, for example, domestic memorials and altars) upon which the bereaved can express emotions free from the spatial and temporal limitations set by funerals. Among various online platforms, Li Wenliang's final Weibo post acts as a particularly special venue that combines private grieving and collective mourning. In addition, through this post, a more genuine memory of Li persisted after his death, and Li's post served as a powerful symbol allowing Chinese citizens to mourn others that died in the pandemic. The echoing effect of comments like "long live the hero"

(英雄千古) has served to mollify sadness and grief, as it also enshrines the life of Li himself in significance.

Death is given meaning by those left behind (Simpson, 2018), who grieve by establishing a "narrative and identity" for the deceased (Harvey et al., 2001; Brubaker et al., 2013, p. 153). In certain cases, there exist multiple and contradictory narratives of the dead (Brubaker et al., 2013), and state-authorized narratives can contradict or deny personal narratives due to political context (Ngo, 2021). Yet personal narratives and grief practices can challenge or resist such official narratives. A typical example is the Chinese "scar literature" (伤痕文学) of the late 1970s, when writings that were critical of the Cultural Revolution (1966–1976) emerged. These works focused on the trauma and oppression of intellectuals during the 1970s, thereby re-establishing identities for the persecuted and deceased. By directly depicting atrocities and expressing moral outrage, scar literature struck a chord with the public, particularly those who lost loved ones during Cultural Revolution. In Li's case, his unexpected death at the young age of 35 was considered as a bad death, posited against a good death viewed as "natural" and occurring among the elderly. This was worsened because he was believed to have been wronged by state authority. For him, the state-authorized narrative of a fearmonger contradicted with the public opinion and support for him, and the conflict between them reached a climax on the day when he passed away. The strong emotion associated with his death resonated particularly with those who were bereaved. The power behind obligatory death revealed itself when Li was reprimanded for starting "rumors," creating conditions for death in a pandemic-era space of exception. Yet, Li became the epitome for the thousands of deceased, and especially for the victims who were indirectly "killed" as a result of certain state and medical policies. Li was officially admonished till he passed away, and members of the public were trying to establish their own narrative for Li (as well as the victims of obligatory death) by commenting on Li's *Weibo* profile, struggling to give meaning to this event. In March 2020, the government withdrew its admonishment of Li, and granted him the honorary title of a martyr later in April 2020, indicating a rapid change in the state's narrative about him. The online "wailing wall" therefore functioned as a form of spontaneous, grassroots activism allowing personal narratives of Li's death to defy or challenge the state-authorized one, and the wailing wall's success as a means of public mourning and therapy thereby gave meaning and comfort to many survivors.

Conclusion

Almost two years after COVID-19 cases were first reported in Wuhan, we use the notion of "obligatory death" to understand the crippling psychological and physical effects of the continued government-imposed lockdowns. The concept of obligatory death, we posit, reveals the existence of thanatopolitics alongside biopolitics during the lockdowns: the production of death and the regulation of its "afterlives." The ultimate purpose is through selectively letting certain group of people die in order to make other groups live. In this context, it seems that power in China was then focused on preserving a functional social and medical system for a target demographic: "healthy" younger people. More than a linear, and rational selection process, the policy surrounding obligatory death in Wuhan requires consideration of the Chinese cultural background consisting of social obligations and filial indebtedness to one another and between the living and the dead. During city lockdowns, life was reduced to something that needed to be sacrificed for the sake of the overall order and stability, and death became the possible consequence of citizens fulfilling their social and political obligations. And this obligatory death resulted in a tightening of both social and political control and collective benefit.

However, being perceived to be culturally "bad" deaths, obligatory death is complex. It both begets and troubles biopolitical remedies, and it faces defiance and contestation. In response to therapeutic measures at the governmental level, survivors also resorted to online mourning (*yun jisi* in Chinese) when quarantines denied death rituals and in-person gatherings. The significance of such online mourning lies in its ability to construct meaning and bring solace for the living, as well as to situate grief properly into daily life. This everyday practice thus becomes part of the "death system" that helps citizens grasp the cultural force of grief (Rosaldo, 2004).

In this chapter, inspired by the existing discussion of thanatopolitics, we critically engage "obligatory death" as manifested during the COVID-19 pandemic in China. In so doing, we aim to provide new insights as to how biopolitics and thanatopolitics might function, alone or together, in different cultural contexts, and in the culturally and politically specific Chinese context since 2019. We have developed a preliminary understanding of obligatory death from analyzing cases of death in Wuhan. But questions remain for us as the pandemic continues. In other Chinese cities that have implemented more intensified forms of lockdowns after Wuhan (such as Shanghai), the questions that arise include: How do we understand the intersection between thanatopolitics and biopolitics when new agents such as commercial players involved in pandemic response as well as ordinary citizens violate lockdown regulations? How and why might so-called "life-saving" facilities represent sites of "exception"? More importantly, how might thanatopolitical governance incorporate changes brought about by the pandemic in terms of global power relations and structures?

Notes

1 The mortality rate in Wuhan caused by COVID reached 4.9% on February 4, 2020, according to statistics released by National Health Commission of PRC (国家卫健委).
2 Many non-local working or seeking medical help in Wuhan were stranded by the lockdown; when the temporary residence became unavailable due to pandemic, they were homeless, foodless.

3 There were many who fled Wuhan before the city lockdown, especially those who were not local. They were criticized nationwide for selfishly endangering other provinces.
4 In the suicide case of Liang, one hour after his death, his wife was admitted to the hospital. Many assumed that Liang committed suicide to increase the chances of survival for his wife, but his son stated that Liang's suicide was an attempt to un burden his family.
5 As part of death rituals, mourning period of ancient times varied according to the relationship with the dead, the longest last three years on the occasions of parents (father), lord, and husband.
6 This is based on my personal conversation in Shangha with a therapist who volunteered to participate in the psychological counseling of Wenchuan Earthquake.
7 After Li posted the online message, he was immediately called to the district police station. There he filled out the letter of admonishment, admitting he was making false statements and promising would stop such behavior.

References

Agamben, G. (1998). *Homo Sacer: Sovereign Power and Bare Life*. Stanford: Stanford University Press.

Alves, J. (2018). *The Anti-Black City: Police Terror and Black Urban Life in Brazil*. Minneapolis and London: University of Manchester.

Beijing News. (2020, April 10). What did we do before the city lockdown in Wuhan. *Baijiahao*. https://baijiahao.baidu.com/s?id=1663547992002057985&wfr=spider&for=pc.

Biehl, J. & Locke, P. (2010). Deleuze and the anthropology of becoming. *Current Anthropology* 51(3):317–351.

Brubaker, J.R., Hayes, G.R. & Dourish, P. (2013). Beyond the grave: Facebook as a site for the expansion of death and mourning. *The Information Society* 29:152–163.

Carroll, B. & Landry, K. (2010). Logging on and letting out: using online social networks to grieve and to mourn. *Bulletin of Science, Technology & Society* 30(5):341–349.

CCTV News. (2020, February 10). Xi Jinping emphasized that with firmer confidence, more tenacious will and more decisive measures, we will resolutely win the people's war of pandemic prevention and control. *CCTV*. http://tv.cctv.com/2020/02/11/VIDEZoCOTYPB5crt9GwkKIwy200211.shtml.

Chen, Y. (2020, February 12). A 70-year-old suspected COVID patient jumped to his death in Wuhan. *Guancha News*. https://user.guancha.cn/wap/content?id=242378&s=fwckhfbt.

China Central Normal University (CCNU) Media. (2020, April 10). This hotline continues to heal you wholeheartedly. *The Paper*. https://m.thepaper.cn/baijiahao_6917073.

COVID patients seeking help. (2020). *Weibo*. https://weibo.com/p/1008084882401a015244a2ab18ee43f7772d6f/super_index.

Cui, K., Sim, T. & Xu, T. (2020). Psychosocial well-being of school-aged children born to bereaved (*shidu*) families: associations with mothers' quality of life and involvement behaviors. *International Journal of Environmental Research and Public Health* 17(11):4166.

Dien, D.S. (1983). Big me and little me. *Psychiatry: Interpersonal and Biological Processes* 46(3):281–286.

Esposito, R. (2008). *Bíos: Biopolitics and Philosophy*. Minneapolis: University of Minnesota Press.

Figure Video. (2021, April 8). Depressed rooms. *Weibo*. https://m.weibo.cn/status/4623799258974255?wm=3333_2001&from=10BC093010&sourcetype=weixin.

Foucault, M. (1990). *The History of Sexuality: An Introduction*. New York: Vintage Books.

Foucault, M. (2003). *Society Must Be Defended*. New York: Picador.

Gao, X., Wang, Z., Kong, C., Fan, H., Zhang, J., Wang, J., Tan, L. & Wang, J. (2021). Cross-sectional survey to assess health-care workers' grief counseling for bereaved families of COVID-19 victims in Wuhan, China. *Disaster Medicine and Public Health Preparedness* 16(6). Advance Online Publication.

Harvey, J.H., Carlson, H.R., Huff, T.M. & Green, M.A. (2001). Embracing their memory: the construction of accounts of loss and hope. In R.A. Neimeyer (Ed.), *Meaning Reconstruction and the Experience of Loss* (pp. 231–243). Washington, DC: American Psychological Association.

Huntington, R. & Metcalf, P. (1979). *Celebration of Death: The Anthropology of Mortuary Ritual*. Cambridge: Cambridge University Press.

In 2022, does *Weibo* continue to prosper? (2022, March 8). *The Paper*. https://m.thepaper.cn/baijiahao_17010567.

Jia, J. (2016). Li Zehou's reconception of the Confucian ethics of emotion. *Philosophy East and West* 66(3):757–786.

Kastenbaum, R. & Aisenberg, R. (1972). *The Psychology of Death*. New York: Springer.

Kipnis, A. (2021). *The Funeral of Mr. Wang: Life, Death and Ghosts in Urbanizing China*. Oakland: University of California Press.

Li, D., Chang, Y., Liang, H., Ren, Z., An, Q., Lin, X., Wang, Y., Luo, X., Pi, J., Fan, Y., Jia, X., Jiang, G. & Qian, M. (2021). The survey of 427 psychological hotline services during the COVID-19 pandemic in China. *Chinese Journal of Clinical Psychology* 29(3):633–638.

Liu, J., Zhang, L., Yan, Y., Zhou, Y., Yin, P., Qi, J., Wang, L., Pan, J., You, J., Yang, J., Zhao, Z., Wang, W., Liu, Y., Lin, L., Wu, J., Li, X., Chen, Z. & Zhou, M. (2021). Excess mortality in Wuhan City and other parts of China during the three months of the COVID-19 outbreak: findings from nationwide mortality registries. *BMJ* 372:n415. www.bmj.com/content/372/bmj.n415.long.

Liu, L. (2020, February 4). COVID patients in Wuhan seeking help. *Weibo*. https://weibo.com/ttarticle/x/m/show/id/2309404468433877073992?_wb_client_=1.

Liu, Z. (2020, February 4). Woman of 41-week pregnant seeking help in Wuhan. *Weibo*. https://m.weibo.cn/status/4468462095055426.

Mbembe, A. (2003). Necropolitics. *Public Culture* 15(1):11–40.

Morris, S.E., Moment, A. & Thomas, J. (2020). Caring for bereaved family members during the COVID-19 pandemic: before and after the death of a patient. *Journal of Pain and Symptom Management* 60(2):70–74.

Munro, D. (Ed.). (1985). *Individualism and Holism: Studies in Confucian and Taoist Values*. Ann Arbor: Center for Chinese Studies at the University of Michigan.

Murray, S. (2006). Thanatopolitics: on the use of death for mobilizing political life. *Polygraph* 18:191–215.

Ngo, T.T.T. (2021). Bones of contention: situating the dead of the 1979 Sino-Vietnamese border war. *American Ethnologist* 1–14.

People's Daily. (2021, August 7). Laying a solid foundation for the great rejuvenation for the Chinese nation – review of President Xi Jinping's important remarks on health China. *People's Daily*. www.gov.cn/xinwen/2021-08/07/content_5629998.htm.

People's Daily Online. (2020, April 6). Psychological assistance is ready in fighting the pandemic. *Baijiahao*. https://baijiahao.baidu.com/s?id=1663194642105501775&wfr=spider&for=pc.

Pupavac, V. (2004). International therapeutic peace and justice in Bosnia. *Social and Legal Studies* 13:377–401.

Rosaldo, R. (2004). Grief and a headhunter's rage. In A.C.G.M. Robben (Ed.), *Death, Mourning, and Burial: A Cross-Cultural Reader* (pp. 167–178). Malden, MA: Blackwell.

Rose, N. (2007). *The Politics of Life Itself.* Princeton: Princeton University Press.

Shenghuo Newspaper. (2020, February 18). Four members of Hubei director Chang Kai's family died of illness. *Baijiahao.* https://baijiahao.baidu.com/s?id=1658797807011897 479&wfr=spider&for=pc.

Simpson, B. (2018). Death. In *The Cambridge Encyclopedia of Anthropology.* Cambridge: Cambridge University Press.

Stepputat, F. (2014). *Governing the Dead: Sovereignty and the Politics of Dead Bodies.* Manchester and New York: Manchester University Press.

Sun, L. (1991). Contemporary Chinese culture: structure and emotionality. *The Australian Journal of Chinese Affairs* 26:1–41.

Suzhou Release. (2020, February 20). Wife chasing a hearse bidding farewell to her husband. *Weibo.* https://m.weibo.cn/status/4474028515224301?sourceType=weixin&from=10 CB295060&wm=9006_2001&featurecode=newtitle.

Tang, R., Xie, T., Jiao, J., Xu, X., Zou, X., Qian, W. & Wang, J. (2021). Grief reaction and grief counseling among bereaved Chinese individuals during COVID-19 pandemic: study protocol for a randomized controlled trial combined with a longitudinal study. *Environmental Research and Public Health* 18:1–12.

Van der Geest, S. (2004). Dying peacefully: considering good death and bad death in Kwahu – Tafo, Ghana. *Social Science and Medicine* 58:899–911.

Xingshipin. (2020, February 2). Woman in Wuhan bidding farewell to her mother. *Weibo.* https://m.weibo.cn/status/4467580934716599?sourceType=weixin&from=10C3495 060&wm=9006_2001.

Xinhua News. (2020, April 2). 14 people sacrificed on the frontline of pandemic prevention and control in Hubei Province were honored martyrs (X. Zhang, Trans.). *Xinhua News.* www.xinhuanet.com/politics/2020-04/02/c_1125806371.htm.

Xinhua News. (2020, April 16). Notification on the correction of the number of confirmed cases of new coronary pneumonia in Wuhan and the number of deaths of confirmed cases. *Weibo.* https://m.weibo.cn/status/4494653154209693?sourceType=weixin&from=10 CB295060&wm=9006_2001&featurecode=newtitle.

Xu, Y. (2007). Death and dying in the Chinese culture: implications for health care practice. *Home Health Care Management & Practice* 19(5):412–414.

Yang, J. (2018). Officials' heartache: depression, bureaucracy, and therapeutic governance in China. *Current Anthropology* 59(5):596–615.

Yang, J. (2022). Confucius in a self-help group. In N. Bubandt & T.S. Wentzer (Eds.), *Philosophy on Fieldwork: Critical Introductions to Theory and Analysis in Anthropological Practice* (pp. 156–175). London: Routledge.

Yin, Q., Sun, Z. & Liu, W. (2018). Mini review: the mental and physical consequences of Chinese Shidu parents. *Mental Health and Clinical Psychology* 2(3):1–4.

Zhang, Q. (2021, February 19). I guarded my father's memorial tablets for three days. *Living Media.* https://card.weibo.com/article/m/show/id/2309404606656318144863.

Zhizhuhoumianbao. (2020, February 12). Wuhan diary. *Weibo.* https://m.weibo.cn/sta tus/4471524646428699?sourceType=weixin&from=10C4395060&wm=9006_2001.

Zhou, B. & Zhong, Y. (2021). Social media, collective mourning and extended affective space: a computational communication analysis of Li Wenliang's Weibo comments (2020–2021). *Chinese Journal of Journalism & Communication* 3:79–106.

PART 2

Global Surveillance and Trauma

3

AMERICAN EXCEPTIONALISM AND THE CONSTRUCTION OF TRAUMA IN THE GLOBAL WAR ON TERROR

Neil Krishan Aggarwal

In "Old Paradigms in History Die Hard in Political Science: US Foreign Policy and American Exceptionalism," Hilde Eliassen Restad (2012) deconstructs the isolationist/internationalist dichotomy in political science and international relations by interpreting American history through the cultural ideal of "American exceptionalism." Restad (2012) defines American identity as "the widespread and deep belief in American exceptionalism" (p. 54), and American exceptionalism as "the belief in the special and unique role the United States is meant to play in world history, its distinctiveness from the Old World, and its resistance to the laws of history (the rise to power and inevitable fall that has afflicted all previous republics" (pp. 54–55). Restad (2012) argues that American foreign policy can be analyzed by exploring the endurance of American exceptionalism:

When studying US foreign policy, American identity is most usefully defined as American exceptionalism because the belief in American exceptionalism has been a powerful, persistent, and popular myth throughout American history, and furthermore, it has been used in formulating arguments for ever more internationalist and expanding foreign policies.

(p. 55)

This myth is central to America's origins. In Restad's (2012) estimation, American exceptionalism has "always inspired the United States to reform the world in its image" (p. 57), which can be traced to Puritan missionaries who propagated a "millennial narrative view[ing] the Reformation as ushering in a sequence of victories for the forces of good over evil – including the discovery of America

DOI: 10.4324/9781003311843-6

and culminating in the American Revolution" (p. 60). The unlikelihood of the American political experiment succeeding only convinced America's (colonial) pre-independence inhabitants that their futures were blessed:

> The political founding of America acquired its missionary aspect by viewing events as divinely inspired. The success of the Revolution (1776–83) and the subsequent Constitutional Convention in 1787 were seen as so improbable by many founding fathers that they could only explain it in terms of divine intervention.
>
> *(Restad, 2012, p. 60)*

This elevation of ideas over ethnicity is foundational to American identity:

> Since, nevertheless, America's past was British and the Americans themselves were largely Britons (or "Anglo-Scotch"), the new United States had to look to the future, where nothing but ideas existed. American nationality became connected to an instant ideology, forged in revolution as opposed to a secular development of a "community through history."
>
> *(Restad, 2012, p. 61)*

The success of this domestic experiment prompted American leaders to export these ideas:

> What current history of the early republic tells us is that the founding fathers expressed lofty visions for a future "empire for liberty" of the Americas. Expansionism was an integral part of the building of this empire and, as previously mentioned, is intimately connected to the rejection of an isolationist/internationalist dichotomy. The fact that the Americans did not see themselves as invaders, aggressors, or occupiers is testament to the powerful exceptionalist identity that was expressed through its manifest destiny version during the nineteenth century.
>
> *(Restad, 2012, p. 67)*

An exceptionalist identity unites American leaders across the political spectrum:

> This underlies the idea that in every foreigner there is an American waiting to get out. It is an assumption that links the otherwise unlikely grouping of Woodrow Wilson, Ronald Reagan, William Jefferson Clinton, and George W. Bush and their mission to reform the world in the American image.
>
> *(Restad, 2012, p. 70)*

In this chapter, I argue that American exceptionalism characterizes the U.S. government's construction of trauma in its Global War on Terror from 2001 to 2022 for detainees at Guantánamo Bay. Examples of American exceptionalism in the Global War on Terror include the U.S. government's emphasis on military security over international development in formulating policies for the Middle East (Dalby, 2008), President George Bush bypassing the authority of the United Nations Security Council to invade Iraq in 2003 (Foot, 2008; Patman, 2006), and President Barack Obama's claims of a post-racial America that would extinguish terrorism around the world, which has been critiqued as "imperial multiculturalism" (De Genova, 2010) and "American Orientalism" (Nayak and Malone, 2009). Other trends in the United States' Global War on Terror fit key traits of Restad's formulation. For example, in his first prepared remarks after the attacks of September 11, 2001, against the United States, President Bush invoked a narrative of good against evil to inspire American nationalism through an instant ideology, saying, "We're a nation of resolve. We're a nation that can't be cowed by evil-doers. I've got great faith in the American people" (Bush, 2001). In his first State of the Union address after the attacks in 2002, President Bush championed an internationalist foreign policy, declaring: "Hundreds of terrorists have been arrested, yet tens of thousands of trained terrorists are still at large. These enemies view the entire world as a battlefield, and we must pursue them wherever they are" (Bush, 2002). In that speech, he emphasized the unique role of the United States: "America will lead by defending liberty and justice because they are right and true and unchanging for all people everywhere" (Bush, 2002). Hence, American exceptionalism has been fundamental to American foreign policy in the Global War on Terror at the highest levels.

To my knowledge, no one has considered how American exceptionalism has influenced knowledge and practice related to forensic psychiatry in national security settings during the Global War on Terror. Here, I introduce the term *medicolegal exceptionalism* to refer to the American government's modification of psychiatric knowledge and practice to advance belief in the special, unique role that the United States is meant to play in world history. Medical anthropologist Byron Good (1992) suggests that one way to conduct cultural studies of psychiatry is to examine psychopathology as "socially and historically produced," defined as "demonstrating how political and economic structures are embodied in experience every bit as much as early family experience and biology are, and of portraying these issues in our ethnographic and interpretive accounts" (pp. 200–201). This chapter examines the embodiment of political structures in the Global War on Terror through the case of Mohammed al-Qahtani (born 1975), a detainee released from the Guantánamo Bay detention facility in 2022. Through a content analysis of open-source medical and legal documents (Aggarwal, 2015), the chapter follows the theme of medical exceptionalism throughout the evolution of al-Qahtani's case: first, through definitions of torture; second, over competing interpretations of trauma; and finally, in relation to the applicability of international humanitarian law. The next section analyzes the Bush Administration's legal interpretation of "torture" and the choice of Guantánamo as the site to detain suspects, which are explicit policies intended to mark the United States' distinctiveness from "Old World" legal frameworks such as the Geneva Conventions. The chapter concludes by considering the broader potentialities for studying constructions of psychiatric knowledge and practice through the theory of *medicolegal exceptionalism.*

Medico-Legal Exceptionalism in Constructing Knowledge About Torture

After the attacks of September 11, 2001, President Bush declared that international humanitarian law was inapplicable to members of Al Qaeda and the Taliban, and his administration devised a new legal framework. On September 18, 2001, the U.S. Congress passed a bill known as the Authorization for Use of Military Force (A.U.M.F.). The A.U.M.F. asserts the special, unique role of the United States in adopting internationalist, expansionist foreign policies, stating:

> The President is authorized to use all necessary and appropriate force against those nations, organizations, or persons he determines planned, authorized, committed, or aided the terrorist attacks that occurred on September 11, 2001, or harbored such organizations or persons, in order to prevent any future acts of international terrorism against the United States by such nations, organizations or persons.
>
> *(United States Congress, 2001)*

President Bush signed an executive order on November 13, 2001, to establish military commissions for legally trying anyone whom the U.S. government suspected was a member of Al Qaeda or the Taliban who

> has engaged in, aided or abetted, or conspired to commit, acts of international terrorism, or acts in preparation therefore, that have caused, threaten to cause, or have as their aim to cause, injury to or adverse effects on the United States, its citizens, national security, foreign policy, or economy.
>
> *(The White House, 2001)*

In a memo to senior officials on February 7, 2002, President Bush wrote: "Common Article 3 of Geneva does not apply to either al Qaeda or Taliban detainees, because, among other reasons, the relevant conflicts are international in scope and common Article 3 applies only to 'armed conflict not of an international character'" (The White House, 2002). Through such legal acts, the Bush Administration marked its distinctiveness from the Geneva Conventions, which is the prevailing international standard in treating detainees of armed conflicts.

Having decided that international humanitarian law does not apply to suspected Al Qaeda and Taliban detainees, the Department of Justice created new definitions for torture. On August 1, 2002, Deputy Assistant Attorney General John C. Yoo wrote a memo to White House Counsel Alberto R. Gonzales, opining that the definition of torture in the U.N. Convention Against Torture and Other Cruel, Inhuman or Degrading Treatment or Punishment "might be read to require only general intent although we believe that the better argument is that the Convention's use of the phrase 'intentionally inflicted' also created a specific intent-type standard" (Yoo, 2002). That same day, Assistant Attorney General Jay S. Bybee wrote a memo to Gonzales, suggesting that physical torture be defined as "equivalent in intensity to the pain accompanying serious physical injury, such as organ failure, impairment of bodily function or even death" and mental torture as "significant psychological harm of significant duration, e.g. lasting for months or even years" (Bybee, 2002). This new definition of torture contrasted with the prevailing conception of trauma within American psychiatry. At that time, the *Diagnostic and Statistical Manual of Mental Disorders, Fourth Edition, Text Revision* (DSM-IV-TR) established minimal criteria for post-traumatic disorder as:

> The development of characteristic symptoms following exposure to an extreme traumatic stressor involving direct personal experience of an event that involves actual or threatened death or serious injury, or other threat to one's physical integrity; or witnessing an event that involves death, injury, or a threat to the physical integrity of another person; or learning about unexpected or violent death, serious harm, or threat of death or injury experienced by a family member or other close associate (Criterion A1). The person's response to the event must involve intense fear, helplessness, or horror (or in children, the response must involve disorganized or agitated behavior) (Criterion A2).
>
> *(American Psychiatric Association, 2000, p. 463)*

The U.S. Justice Department raised the threshold for injury in redefining torture beyond the definition for trauma that was in medicolegal force for American psychiatrists. In DSM-IV-TR, a stressor only needed to be threatened; for Bybee, torture had to inflict "serious physical injury." In DSM-IV-TR, symptoms could last one month (American Psychiatric Association, 2000) whereas the Bybee memo clarified that the effects of torture must last "for months."

In addition, the U.S. Congress also passed the Military Commissions Act of 2006 which defined "unlawful enemy combatant" as

> a person who has engaged in hostilities or who has purposefully and materially supported hostilities against the United States or its co-belligerents who is not a lawful enemy combatant (including a person who is part of the Taliban, al Qaeda, or associated forces).
>
> *(United States Congress, 2006)*

This Act prevented unlawful enemy combatants from invoking the Geneva Conventions:

> No person may invoke the Geneva Conventions or any protocols thereto in any habeas corpus or other civil action or proceeding to which the United States, or a current or former officer, employee, member of the Armed Forces, or other agent of the United States is a party as a source of rights in any court of the United States or its States or territories.
>
> *(United States Congress, 2006)*

U.S. officials did not anticipate that lawyers for Guantánamo detainees would invoke American law to enforce medical humanitarian protections under the Geneva Conventions, a strategy that al-Qahtani pursued.

Mohammed al-Qahtani and the Embodiment of Torture

The U.S. government has alleged that Mohammed al-Qahtani traveled to Afghanistan, received combat training, and fought with Al Qaeda forces from December 2000 until June 2001 when Osama bin Laden sent him to the United States to be the twentieth airplane hijacker in the September 11, 2001, attacks (United States Department of Defense, 2008). Immigration and Naturalization Service officials denied him entry into the United States after noticing that he did not possess a return ticket and contradicted his account several times (United States Department of Defense, 2008). The U.S. government claims that he returned to Afghanistan until Pakistani forces captured him in December 2001 and transferred him into U.S. military custody (United States Department of Defense, 2008). In January 2002, he was relocated to Guantánamo, and al-Qahtani has consistently denied the U.S. government's charges (Woodward, 2009).

According to classified interrogation logs from Guantánamo that were not authorized for release to the media, health professionals participated in al-Qahtani's interrogations from November 23, 2002, to January 11, 2003, when he was subjected to enhanced interrogation techniques (E.I.T.s) for nearly 20 hours each day (Miles, 2007a). The E.I.T.s consisted of physical strikes, stress positions to induce pain, threats against his family, forced nudity, dogs barking at him, strip searches, sleep deprivation that lasted for several continuous days, prohibiting him from praying, threats to desecrate the Quran, physical restraints, hypothermia, and forced enema and intravenous infusions (O.R.C.O.N., 2006). After a source from the Federal Bureau of Investigation complained about the violent nature of the E.I.T.s, the U.S. Army investigated and concluded in 2005 that the interrogations were "degrading and abusive," but not "torture" or "inhumane" treatment based on the Department of Justice's revised definitions of torture (United States Army, 2005).

Over time, civilian observers and military personnel have drawn different conclusions for why al-Qahtani's treatment at Guantánamo constituted torture. Civilian bioethicists have argued that the government's E.I.T.s met the legal criteria for torture under the Geneva Conventions and the United Nations' Convention Against Torture by subjecting him to interventions from medical professionals that were not in his fiduciary interests (Miles, 2007a, 2007b). Guantánamo's highest administrator, Convening Authority Susan Crawford, agreed that al-Qahtani was tortured, but her reasoning was different. In a 2009 interview, she said,

> The techniques they used were all authorized, but the manner in which they applied them was overly aggressive and too persistent. . . . This was just a combination of things that had a medical impact on him, that hurt his health.
> *(Woodward, 2009)*

In her estimation, the E.I.T.s were each individually legal, but their cumulative impact met the legal standard of "equivalent in intensity to the pain accompanying serious physical injury" for torture. Her statement is an official recognition of how E.I.T.s became embodied for al-Qahtani.

In the same 2009 interview, Susan Crawford announced that she would not refer al-Qahtani's case for legal charges because he was tortured in U.S. custody (Woodward, 2009). Despite her refusal to proceed with a legal case against him, Guantánamo's Periodic Review Board determined in 2016 and 2018 that al-Qahtani could not be released from the detention facility because he posed a "significant threat to the United States"; he could not explain his activities in Afghanistan in 2001 after being refused entry into the United States but before his capture (United States Department of Defense, 2016, 2018). Herein lay the legal dispute: If Guantánamo's Convening Authority refused to press charges, but he could not be released for posing a threat to the United States, then what has been the legal basis to detain him? In 2004, the Supreme Court ruled in *Rasul v. Bush* that the federal habeas statute applies to Guantánamo detainees, whether they are American citizens or foreigners, and al-Qahtani used this precedent to challenge the legality of his detention.

al-Qahtani v. Trump and the Recognition of Trauma

On March 6, 2020, Judge Rosemary M. Collyer of the United States District Court for the District of Columbia ruled in *al-Qahtani v. Trump* that al-Qahtani was entitled to an independent examination by a mixed medical commission to determine if he could be repatriated to Saudi Arabia for treatment. For the first time, foreign medical professionals were granted permission to access the Guantánamo Bay detention facility since it opened in 2002 (Rosenberg, 2020a). The ruling prompted another form of medicolegal exceptionalism at the Guantánamo Bay detention facility, so it is best understood within the context of al-Qahtani's previous legal history and the pivotal role of a forensic psychiatric evaluation in affirming his traumatic experiences.

Judge Collyer's decision referenced the independent psychiatric evaluation of Dr. Emily Keram, a forensic psychiatrist hired by al-Qahtani's defense team. al-Qahtani's attorney submitted Dr. Keram's evaluation to Guantánamo officials before al-Qahtani's case appeared before Guantánamo's Periodic Review Board in 2016. Dr. Keram's sources of information were interviews with al-Qahtani that lasted approximately 39 hours during one week in May 2015, an interview with his older brother in 2016, and a review of clinical records from Saudi Arabia and Guantánamo (Keram, 2016). Dr. Keram asserted several opinions in her evaluation. First, even before reaching Guantánamo, al-Qahtani likely had diagnoses of major depressive disorder, schizophrenia, and a possible neurocognitive disorder from several motor vehicle accidents (Keram, 2016). He was hospitalized in Saudi Arabia in 2000 after attempting to throw himself into moving traffic (Keram, 2016). Second, Dr. Keram (2016) added the diagnosis of post-traumatic stress disorder (PTSD). Her report details the traumas he experienced at Guantánamo, detailing more types of abuses than the account of his interrogation logs that was leaked to the media:

> Included among the conditions of confinement and interrogation to which Mr. al-Qahtani was subjected were periods of solitary confinement, sleep deprivation, extreme temperature and noise exposure, stress positions including short-shackling, forced nudity, body cavity searches, sexual assault and humiliation, beatings, strangling, threats of rendition, and water-boarding. He was not allowed to use the toilet and was forced to urinate on himself repeatedly. Medical and mental health staff members were involved in his interrogations, for example, monitoring his vital signs, administering intravenous fluids, and influencing interrogation approach. This maltreatment took place in various locations, primarily when he was housed in the Brig. Even in the absence of pre-existing psychiatric illness, exposure to severely cruel, degrading, humiliating, and inhumane treatment such as that experienced by Mr. al-Qahtani is known to have profoundly disruptive and long-lasting effects on a person's sense of identity, selfhood. dignity, perception of reality, mood, cognitive functioning, and physiology.
>
> *(Keram, 2016, p. 6)*

In Dr. Keram's (2016) estimation, the traumas impaired his perception of reality: "Mr. al-Qahtani experienced psychotic symptoms during solitary confinement and interrogations. He described auditory and visual hallucinations of ghosts. He also frequently heard a bird talking to him from outside the Brig. reassuring him that he was still alive" (p. 6). Moreover, Dr. Keram (2016) observed that Mr. al-Qahtani developed a psychocutaneous disorder, as trauma literally became embodied:

> Mr. al-Qahtani suffers from a psychocutaneous disorder thought to be either atopic dermatitis or lichen planus. Atopic dermatitis is produced mainly by scratching and flares with stress though psychoneuroimmunomechanisms. Worsening atopic dermatitis can further stress the patient, who then tends to scratch more and further worsen the dermatitis. Lichen planus, an inflammatory pruritic dermatitis, is often triggered or exacerbated by stress. The intense itching and discoloration with hyperpigmentation that typically occur with lichen planus can further fuel the stress.
>
> Mr. al-Qahtani's cutaneous disorder was present throughout my evaluation. Skin lesions worsened in number and severity when discussing extremely traumatic events. These caused Mr. al-Qahtani obvious physical pain and psychological distress.
>
> *(p. 8)*

Third, Dr. Keram (2016) opined that al-Qahtani made statements of questionable veracity to end his interrogations. Her report stated: "He explained that he was unable to successfully suicide and so decided to provide his interrogators with the information he thought they wanted to hear. Thus, Mr. al-Qahtani's statements were coerced and not voluntary, reliable, or credible" (Keram, 2016, p. 7). Finally, she supported his repatriation to Saudi Arabia due to his lack of trust in the mental health staff because medical professionals participated in his interrogations, the lack of culturally informed treatment modalities, and the unavailability of his relatives to participate in his ongoing treatment (Keram, 2016).

With his release denied in 2016, al-Qahtani applied to the Department of Defense in 2017 for medical repatriation and to compel an examination by a mixed medical commission. His defense team noted that detainees in prior cases invoked the Geneva Conventions, which the U.S. government has not recognized at Guantánamo (*Al-Qahtani v. Trump*, 2017). Instead, his attorneys sought to compel examination by a mixed medical commission under a domestic law known as Army Regulation 190–8, which explicitly refers to the Third Geneva Convention for guidance (*Al-Qahtani v. Trump*, 2017). Based on the Third Geneva Convention, Army Regulation 190–8 classifies individuals who commit hostile acts to support enemy armed forces in four ways: (1) enemy prisoner of war; (2) retained personnel who serve in medical, religious, or voluntary capacities attached to enemy forces; (3) civilian internees; and (4) innocent civilians (United States Departments of the Army, the Navy, the Air Force, and the Marine Corps, 1997). According to the Third Geneva Convention, those who are classified as enemy prisoners of war, retained personnel, or are not yet classified but legally designated as "other detainees" are eligible for medical repatriation based on an examination by a mixed medical commission (United States Departments of the Army, the Navy, the Air Force, and the Marine Corps, 1997). The commission must consist of three people: two physicians from a neutral country and one from the U.S. Army (United States Departments of the Army, the Navy, the Air Force, and the Marine Corps, 1997).

al-Qahtani's attorneys argued that he should receive the protections of an "other detainee" since he has not been classified according to one of the four designations in Army Regulation 190–8 (*Al-Qahtani v. Trump*, 2017). Therefore, they requested an independent examination by a mixed medical commission. Prosecution attorneys countered that al-Qahtani was legally designated as an "unlawful enemy combatant," to which al-Qahtani's attorneys responded that "unlawful enemy combatant" is not a recognized designation in Army Regulation 190–8 (*Al-Qahtani v. Trump*, 2020). Prosecution attorneys also contended that al-Qahtani has not availed of the mental health resources at Guantánamo, and al-Qahtani's attorneys referred to Dr. Keram's assertion that the interrogation process caused him to distrust all medical staff there (*Al-Qahtani v. Trump*, 2020). Ironically – given that the U.S. government developed new legal mechanisms to prosecute its Global War on Terror – al-Qahtani's attorneys invoked shared beliefs in the special and unique role of the domestic American legal system to make their arguments for liberating a foreign detainee.

Judge Collyer addressed al-Qahtani's legal designation and medical relief. Acknowledging that the Military Commissions Act of 2006 denies protections under the Geneva Conventions to Guantánamo detainees, she referenced *Al Warafi v. Obama (2013)*, which ruled that domestic laws apply to Guantánamo, and specifically Army Regulation 190–8. Judge Collyer reiterated that Army Regulation 190–8 finds its guidance in the Third Geneva Convention on humanely treating prisoners (*Al-Qahtani v. Trump*, 2020). She affirmed that parts of the Geneva Conventions have been incorporated into domestic law even if Geneva protections as a whole are inapplicable to Guantánamo (*Al-Qahtani v. Trump*, 2020). Hence, al-Qahtani could not receive the legal designation of "other detainee" because he had not been classified through one of four extant designations under Army Regulation 190–8. She ruled that a mixed medical commission must examine him to determine if he qualifies for repatriation.

Army Regulation 190–8 permits medical repatriation based on two medical standards: when detainees are (1) "suffering from disabilities as a result of injury, loss of limb paralysis, or other disabilities, when these disabilities are at least the loss of a hand or foot, or the equivalent," or (2) are ill or injured and "conditions have become chronic to the extent that prognosis appears to preclude recovery in spite of treatment within 1 year from inception of disease or date of injury" (United States Departments of the Army, the Navy, the Air Force, and the Marine Corps, 1997). Judge Collyer did not opine if al-Qahtani's case met either standard and entrusted this determination to the commission. But she included mental health as a reason for medical repatriation, noting,

> Lacking the necessary expertise to evaluate Mr. al Qahtani's physical and psychological condition to determine whether he qualifies for medical repatriation under Army Regulation 190–8, this Court must require Respondent [the U.S. Government] to conduct the necessary evaluation and provide the Court with the record.
>
> *(Al-Qahtani v. Trump, 2020)*

In the waning days of President Donald Trump's administration, however, Secretary of the Army Ryan D. McCarthy attempted another form of American exceptionalism by challenging Judge Collyer's ruling. In a memorandum for the U.S. Southern Command, he wrote,

> Under AR 190–8, JTF-GTMO detainees are not "Enemy Prisoners of War" or "Other Detainees" who are to be treated as Enemy Prisoners of War. A federal district court, nevertheless, has interpreted AR 190–8 to require treating a detainee held at JTF-GTMO as an enemy of prisoner of war for purposes of compelling examination by a Mixed Medical Commission pursuant to Section 3–12 of AR 190–8.
>
> *(McCarthy, 2021)*

The U.S. Congress refused to allow mixed medical commissions with foreign physicians to examine detainees at Guantánamo, but agreed to create the position of a Navy physician who would render an independent medical opinion (Rosenberg and Savage, 2022). The Navy physician concurred with Dr. Keram's findings (Rosenberg and Savage, 2022), and in 2022, Guantánamo's Periodic Review Board announced,

> The PRB recommends the following conditions that relate to the detainee's transfer: Transfer only to Saudi Arabia for participation in the Mohammed bin Naif Counseling and Care Center, or a comparable program, to include provision of mental health care through implementation of a robust treatment plan and implementation of a comprehensive set of security measures including monitoring and travel restrictions.
>
> *(United States Department of Defense, 2022a)*

On March 7, 2022, the U.S. government repatriated al-Qahtani to Saudi Arabia (United States Department of Defense, 2022b).

Conclusion

This chapter has introduced how *medicolegal exceptionalism* refers to the American government's modification of psychiatric knowledge and practice to advance belief in the special, unique role that the United States is meant to play in world history and, specifically, the Global War on Terror. Legal concepts such as passing the A.U.M.F., establishing military commissions to try suspected militants through the Military Commissions Act of 2006, voiding Common Article 3 of the Geneva Conventions, devising new definitions for torture, and creating E.I.T.s reflect just some of the myriad ways that the U.S. government has established its distinctiveness from international laws to advance a narrative of good against evil. Ironically, al-Qahtani's attorneys also invoked American exceptionalism by considering the distinctiveness of Army Regulation 190–8 as a domestic law, only for the Trump and Biden Administrations to void Judge Collyer's legal ruling in a new form of exceptionalism that resisted the introduction of mixed medical commissions at the Guantánamo Bay detention facility. Analyzing interrogation logs and the independent psychiatric evaluation from Dr. Emily Keram demonstrates how psychiatrists continue to grapple with the unintended consequences of American exceptionalism for two decades.

In fact, medicolegal exceptionalism can explain other trends in American psychiatry. For instance, attorneys of Guantánamo detainees have revealed the barriers to care that detainees face when they attempt to describe experiences of trauma that have resulted from their conditions of interrogation and confinement (Aggarwal, 2009), even as the U.S. government has increasingly liberalized the evidentiary standards for American servicemen to receive disability-connected benefits related to war traumas (Aggarwal, 2022). Similarly, American mental health researchers have advocated for an expanded definition of PTSD that accounts for U.S. drone operators who experience trauma after witnessing the killing or maiming of their targets through computer screens without mentioning the thousands of innocent victims of such attacks on Global War on Terror battlefields across West Asia, South Asia or sub-Saharan Africa (Aggarwal, 2018). American military psychiatrists introduced the use of psychoactive compounds in combat zones, even as American antiwar activists were among the first to question the ethics of treating soldiers with the intent of deliberately and repeatedly exposing them to danger (Chua, 2018). American exceptionalism was instrumental to the introduction of PTSD as a psychiatric category after veterans from the Vietnam War lobbied the American Psychiatric Association for its inclusion in DSM-III (1980), and the disorder is now diagnosed worldwide – as well as in civilian contexts – despite its uniquely American conceptions of personhood, memory, trauma, mind–body connections and assumptions regarding treatment (Young, 1995).

Barbara Rylko-Bauer and Merrill Singer (2011) suggest that a central task of medical anthropology is "a critical ethnographic revisualization that discloses and renders visible what often is forgotten or unseen" (p. 221). Their perspective calls us to disclose how political constructions of torture and trauma become embodied in detainees such as Mohammed al-Qahtani, especially as the Global War on Terror wanes from public memory after the United States military withdrew from Afghanistan in August 2021. Researchers of medical complicity in the Global War on Terror have disproportionately focused on the health professionals who have collaborated with the U.S. government in military and national security settings in violation of international laws while forgetting to include the lived experiences of detainees (Aggarwal, 2015). Medicolegal exceptionalism offers a frame to interrogate how belief in the special and unique role that the United States is meant to play in world history motivates the construction of medical knowledge and practices to promote a cultural narrative of good versus evil. Close readings of legal and psychiatric texts reveal how policymakers have debated definitions of exceptionalism, the varying levels of pain that the government considers acceptable in redefining trauma, the cause–effect relationship between redefined trauma and symptoms of Guantánamo detainees, as well as the forms of humanitarian relief that detainees are entitled to under international law.

As of this writing, American military forces currently intervene in Iraq, Libya, Syria and Yemen – among other locations in the Global South – with the justification of protecting national security interests (Kushi and Toft, in press). Future work can offer comparative case studies of how American exceptionalism is invoked across geographical and historical contexts, and the impact of this invocation on forms of medicolegal knowledge and practice. By reconstructing the cases of individuals who are subject to such knowledge and practice, we can disclose the voices of forgotten and unseen victims.

References

Aggarwal, N.K. (2009). Allowing independent forensic evaluations for Guantánamo detainees. *Journal of the American Academy of Psychiatry and the Law* 37(4):533–537.

Aggarwal, N.K. (2015). *Mental Health in the War on Terror: Culture, Science, and Statecraft.* New York: Columbia University Press.

Aggarwal, N.K. (2018). Drone operators, terrorists, and the biopolitics of public health in the war on terror. In R. Parker & J. Garcia (Eds.), *Routledge Handbook on the Politics of Global Health* (pp. 382–391). New York: Routledge.

Aggarwal, N.K. (2022). Psychiatric disorders, military misconduct, and discharge status for U.S. veterans. *Journal of the American Academy of Psychiatry and the Law* 50(1):117–123.

Al-Qahtani v. Trump: Case No. 05-CV-1971 (RMC). (2017, August). *Motion to Compel an Examination by a Mixed Medical Commission.* https://pacerdocuments.s3.amazonaws.com/36/117302/04516171153.pdf.

Al-Qahtani v. Trump, Civil Action No. 2005–1971, D.C. Cir. (2020). https://casetext.com/case/al-qahtani-v-trump.

Al Warafi v. Obama, 716 F.3d 627, D.C. Cir. (2013). https://casetext.com/case/al-warafi-v-obama-3.

American Psychiatric Association. (1980). *Diagnostic and Statistical Manual of Mental Disorders* (Third Edition). Arlington: American Psychiatric Association.

American Psychiatric Association. (2000). *Diagnostic and Statistical Manual of Mental Disorders* (Fourth Edition, Text Revision). Arlington: American Psychiatric Association.

Bush, G.W. (2001, September 16). Remarks by the president upon arrival. *The White House.* https://georgewbush-whitehouse.archives.gov/news/releases/2001/09/20010916-2.html.

Bush, G.W. (2002, January 29). President delivers state of the union address. *The White House.* https://georgewbush-whitehouse.archives.gov/news/releases/2002/01/20020129-11.html.

Bybee, J.S. (2002, August 1). *Memorandum for Alberto R. Gonzalez: Counsel to the President: Re: Standards of Conduct for Interrogation Under 18 U.S.C. §§ 2340–234A.* https://nsarchive2.gwu.edu/torturingdemocracy/documents/20020801-1.pdf.

Chua, J.L. (2018). Fog of war: psychopharmaceutical 'side effects' and the United States military. *Medical Anthropology* 37(1):17–31.

Dalby, S. (2008). Imperialism, domination, culture: the continued relevance of critical geopolitics. *Geopolitics* 13(3):413–436.

De Genova, N. (2010). Antiterrorism, race, and the new frontier: American exceptionalism, imperial multiculturalism, and the global security state. *Identities* 17(6):613–640.

Foot, R. (2008). Exceptionalism again: the Bush administration, the 'global war on terror' and human rights. *Law and History Review* 26(3):707–725.

Good, B.J. (1992). Culture and psychopathology: directions for psychiatric anthropology. In T. Schwartz, G.M. White & C. Lutz (Eds.), *New Directions in Psychological Anthropology* (pp. 181–205). Cambridge: Cambridge University Press.

Keram, E.A. (2016, June 5). *Re: Mohammed al-Qahtani.* www.prs.mil/Portals/60/Documents/ISN063/160606_U_ISN063_DETAINEE_SUBMISSION_PUBLIC2.pdf.

Kushi, S. & Toft, M.D. (in press). Introducing the military intervention project: a new dataset on US military interventions, 1776–2019. *Journal of Conflict Resolution.*

McCarthy, R.D. (2021, January 11). *Memorandum for Commander, US Southern Command: Subject: Army Regulation (AR) 190–8 Clarification, Exception.* https://int.nyt.com/data/documenttools/friday-s-legal-motion-and-army-secretary-ryan-d-mc-carthy-s-guantanamo-memo-dated-jan/e4d98ec9f89d4fc6/full.pdf.

Miles, S. (2007a). Medical ethics and the interrogation of Guantánamo 063. *American Journal of Bioethics* 7(1):5–11.

Miles, S. (2007b). Doctors as pawns? Law and medical ethics at Guantánamo Bay. *Seton Hall Law Review* 37:711–731.

Nayak, M.V. & Malone, C. (2009). American orientalism and American exceptionalism: a critical rethinking of US hegemony. *International Studies Review* 11(2):253–276.

O.R.C.O.N. [Authoring Agency Classified by Originator Control]. (2006). *Interrogation Log Detainee 063.* https://content.time.com/time/2006/log/log.pdf.

Patman, R.G. (2006). Globalisation, the new US exceptionalism and the war on terror. *Third World Quarterly* 27(6):963–986.

Rasul v. Bush, 542 U.S. 466. (2004). https://en.wikipedia.org/wiki/Rasul_v._Bush.

Restad, H.E. (2012). Old paradigms in history die hard in political science: US foreign policy and American exceptionalism. *American Political Thought* 1(1):53–76.

Rosenberg, C. (2020a, March 9). Judge orders medical panel to evaluate tortured Guantánamo prisoner. *New York Times*, p. A16.

Rosenberg, C. & Savage, C. (2022, February 5). Panel backs transfer of mentally ill Guantánamo detainee suspected of 9/11 role. *New York Times*, p. A1.

Rylko-Bauer, B. & Singer, M. (2011). Medical anthropology of political violence and war. In M. Singer, P.I. Erickson & C.E. Abadía-Barrero (Eds.), *A Companion to Medical Anthropology* (Second Edition, pp. 219–249). Hoboken: Wiley-Blackwell.

United States Army. (2005, April 1). *Army Regulation 15–6: Final Report: Investigation Into FBI Allegations of Detainee Abuse at Guantánamo Bay, Cuba Detention Facility*. www.thetorturedatabase.org/files/foia_subsite/pdfs/schmidt_furlow_report.pdf.

United States Congress. (2001). *Public Law 107–40 – September 18, 2001: Authorization for Use of Military Force*. U.S. Congress. www.congress.gov/bill/107th-congress/senate-joint-resolution/23/text.

United States Congress. (2006). Public law 109-366 – October 16, 2006: Military Commissions Act of 2006. *U.S. Congress*. https://www.congress.gov/bill/109th-congress/senate-bill/3930/text.

United States Departments of the Army, the Navy, the Air Force, and the Marine Corps. (1997, October 1). *Enemy Prisoners of War, Retained Personnel, Civilian Internees and Other Detainees*. https://info.publicintelligence.net/USArmy-Detainees.pdf.

United States Department of Defense. (2008). *JTF-GTMO Detainee Assessment*. www.nytimes.com/interactive/projects/guantanamo/detainees/63-mohammed-al-qahtani.

United States Department of Defense. (2016, July 18). *Unclassified Summary of Final Determination: Mohammad Mani Ahmad al-Qahtani*. www.prs.mil/Portals/60/Documents/ISN063/160718_U_ISN063_FINAL_DETERMINATION_PUBLIC.pdf.

United States Department of Defense. (2018, July 24). *Periodic Review Board Determination: Mohammad Mani Ahmad al-Qahtani*. www.prs.mil/Portals/60/Documents/ISN063/SubsequentFullReview1/20180724U_ISN063_FINAL_DETERMINATION_PUBLIC.pdf.

United States Department of Defense. (2022a, February 4). *Periodic Review Board Determination: Mohammad Mani Ahmad al-Qahtani*. www.prs.mil/Portals/60/Documents/ISN063/SubsequentFullReview2/220204_UPR_ISN63_SH2_FINAL_DETERMINATION.pdf.

United States Department of Defense. (2022b, March 7). *Guantanamo Bay Detainee Transfer Announced*. www.defense.gov/News/Releases/Release/Article/2957801/guantanamo-bay-detainee-transfer-announced/.

The White House. (2001, November 13). *President Issues Military Order: Detention, Treatment, and Trial of Certain Non-Citizens in the War Against Terrorism*. https://georgewbush-whitehouse.archives.gov/news/releases/2001/11/20011113-27.html.

The White House. (2002, February 7). *Humane Treatment of al Qaeda and Taliban Detainees*. https://nsarchive2.gwu.edu/torturingdemocracy/documents/20020207-2.pdf.

Woodward, B. (2009, January 14). Guantánamo detainee was tortured, says official overseeing military trials. *Washington Post*.

Yoo, J.C. (2002, August 1). *Memorandum for Alberto R. Gonzalez: Counsel to the President: Re: Standards of Conduct for Interrogation Under 18 U.S.C. §§ 2340–234A*. https://nsarchive2.gwu.edu//NSAEBB/NSAEBB127/020801.pdf.

Young, A. (1995). *The Harmony of Illusions: Inventing Post-Traumatic Stress Disorder*. Princeton: Princeton University Press.

4

MILITARISM, PSYCHIATRY AND SOCIAL IMPUNITY IN KASHMIR

Saiba Varma

Compared to other places of long-term violence, at first blush, Kashmir's public and mental health infrastructure looks remarkably intact. While human rights and humanitarian reports of public health infrastructures in war tend to focus on the most spectacular and egregious violations of medical neutrality, this chapter argues for the need for a more expansive understanding of the effects wrought by militarism and violence on public health systems. In particular, this chapter shifts beyond an accounting of incidents of physical harm – such as destruction of hospitals or attacks on medical professionals – to reveal the phenomenological and affective scars left by violence in psychiatric spaces, as well as in patient and practitioner subjectivities. To do so, I deploy the concept of *social impunity*, a concept that draws on a legal vocabulary to show how Kashmiris themselves theorize dysfunction, disorder and harm in the public health system, and how they see that disorder as directly tied to the politics of Indian state control of Kashmir. Legal and political exceptionalism, they argue, has led to pervasive, ordinary harms that permeate spaces of care. In other words, social impunity refers to how Kashmiris understand how a legal system of exceptionalism affects social relations and the practice of medicine.

This chapter draws on more than 24 months of ethnographic fieldwork conducted between 2009 and 2019, including interviews with clinicians and patients and observations of clinician–patient interactions in public health settings, including a large teaching hospital, a standalone psychiatric hospital, a district hospital and an inpatient substance abuse treatment center.[1] Public healthcare in Kashmir, though protected by international humanitarian legal norms of neutrality, immunity and impartiality, has been subjected to direct attacks as well as more insidious and indirect harms. In ethnographic interviews, both patients and providers

DOI: 10.4324/9781003311843-7

described how militarism had authorized certain social, affective and phenomenological transformations in the practice of medicine and psychiatry. Specifically, they described how forms of legal impunity instituted through more than 30 years of emergency rule in Kashmir had led to widespread corruption and a lack of social accountability. Processes that I gloss here as *social impunity* spread through life like a virus. Medicine, which was supposed to be apart from these dynamics, and ideally an antidote to them, had been corrupted. The practitioners I spoke with described how it was nearly impossible to practice medicine safely or effectively within a colonial milieu, echoing the insights of Frantz Fanon in colonial Algeria (Fanon, 1968; Smith, 2015).

Articles 6 and 7 of the Code of Medical Neutrality in Armed Conflict in the Geneva Conventions and their Additional Protocols, the basis of international humanitarian law, require that "medical facilities, equipment, supplies and transport shall be respected and protected, regardless of whom they serve, and shall not be destroyed." The Code also provides that "medical workers shall have access to those in need of medical care, especially in areas where civilian medical services have been disrupted. Similarly, persons in need of medical care shall have access to such services" (PHR, 1993, p. 18). The organizing distinction between combatants and noncombatants in the framework of medical neutrality is meant to prohibit the targeting of civilian and civilian structures, such as clinics, in war. By documenting violations of medical neutrality, human rights and humanitarian accounts have described how medicine can become an innocent casualty of war. Without denying the seriousness of those violations, I join other anthropologists who have theorized the limits of medical neutrality and posit a more complex relationship between medicine and militarism (Aciksoz, 2016; Hamdy and Bayoumi, 2016; Redfield, 2011).

First, I demonstrate how medicine and public health have been used as tools of statecraft in Kashmir; thus the "neutrality" of medicine and psychiatry have long been compromised by the Indian state for the purposes of furthering its rule in Kashmir. Next, I show how human rights and humanitarian notions of medical neutrality are inadequate to capturing the harms that militarization has produced in everyday clinical practices and relations. I offer the concept of *social impunity* as an alternative to medical neutrality to show how Kashmiris theorize not only how medicine becomes a casualty of violence, but how it is generative of its own, particular forms of harm, produced by a generalized lack of accountability and systemic dysfunction, which are normalized, routinized and become permissible under a regime of military rule.

Indeed, ethnography itself is not immune to these power dynamics. In collecting data on patient and providers' perspectives on state violence, it was necessary for me as an ethnographer to attend to what was sayable and unsayable within institutional settings. Given that there was ongoing state surveillance of hospitals, I was mindful of how, and what kind of data, could be collected in these spaces (e.g., I refrained from taking photographs of patients who were injured by state violence so as to avoid their identification later) (see also Tilley, 2016, p. 107). Through the course of conversations with patients and providers, it also became clear to me that while direct and overt critiques of legal impunity were seen as dangerous, critiquing medicine and public health was still permissible. Indeed, through experiences of anxiety, fear or revulsion in health settings, patients and providers were able to harness these spaces to critique the effects of militarization and violence without coming under the radar of authorities (see also Varley and Varma, 2018).

In the final section, I provide the example of a recovering drug user named Hilal whose dependence to opioids was iatrogenic: that is, it was directly fueled by legitimate encounters with biomedical practitioners. Hilal's first-hand account of clinical iatrogenesis provides a striking example of how Kashmiris theorize social impunity as generative of medicine's corruptibility (see also Varley and Varma, 2019).

Medicine as a Tool of Statecraft

Social scientists have long theorized public health and medicine as tools of nation-building and statecraft in a range of different colonial and postcolonial contexts. In Kashmir, care has thus long been operationalized as a justification for tightening Indian colonial control (Varma, 2020); it helps remake the occupying state from a violent to a palliative apparatus (Aggarwal and Bhan, 2009; Ali, 2010; Bhan, 2013; Varma, 2018, 2020). In Kashmir, public health has been explicitly and implicitly imbricated in projects of colonial rule, even though, until recently, many ordinary Kashmiris did not directly link the biopolitical (public health, run by the Jammu and Kashmir state government) and necropolitical (militaristic, run by the central Indian government) parts of the state together. Until 2019, health budgets and allocations were controlled by the Jammu and Kashmir state government, while military operations were controlled by the central Indian government. While the Indian state's military apparatuses are populated by "outsiders" (non-Kashmiris), its biopolitical apparatuses are run by Kashmiris themselves. Yet, at the state level, healthcare has been used as a tool of biopolitical governance since the former princely state of Jammu and Kashmir was bifurcated, including as part of the state's *Naya Kashmir* (1953–1963) portfolio, an explicitly state-building project that was used to tie the fortunes of the region to the Indian nation-state (Kanjwal, 2017).

In recent years, however, the separation between the biopolitical and necropolitical − state and central − parts of the state have blurred. To contend with the contradictions of an ebbing active conflict corresponding with a rise of a broad-based, youth-led movement for self-determination since the early 2000s, the Indian state has increasingly mobilized humanitarian, biomedical, psychological and therapeutic language and techniques to enact its counterinsurgency operations in the region. It called for a "healing touch" after reports of human rights violations have been publicized and has developed a range of mental health interventions targeting "troubled" youth, such as protestors (Anant, 2011; Varma, 2020). As we have seen in other imperial contexts, public health and medicine can be used to soften or disguise the most egregious effects of militarism. As Jennifer Terry (2017, p. 27) has argued in relation to the US empire, "biomedical logics associate medicine with an ethic of care. As such, when they are mobilized in domestic policing or in imperial military operations, they function to obscure the causes and effects of violence." Or as Jocelyn Chua argues, the medicalization of war-making efforts within the US military also has the effect of "unsettling and reinforcing the boundaries that would distinguish home front from war zone, military from civilian" (2020, p. 43). Building on these insights, I am interested in how legal and military logics of war-making – particularly the guarantee of impunity – spill into and transform medical worlds in Kashmir.

Norms of impunity have become even more central since Kashmir's semi-autonomous status was abrogated in August 2019 and the region was put under an indefinite siege, curfew and seven-month communication blackout, the longest by any democracy in history.[2] The ruling Hindu nationalist BJP party has consistently justified the abrogation of Articles 370 and 35A of the Indian constitution not as eroding the rights of Kashmiri Muslims, but as ensuring "stability, market access, and predictable laws" in the state and facilitating private investment in sectors such as tourism, agriculture, information technology and healthcare (Vaishya, 2019). Social and economic development, care and women's rights were all mobilized to justify increased central government control over Kashmir, even though developmental indicators suggest that Kashmiris are relatively well off compared to the rest of India, with higher life expectancies, lower rates of poverty and better education indicators for women (The Lancet, 2019).

Yet, health development has consistently been used to justify and disguise the norms of impunity that undergird the Indian rule of Kashmir. Following news of the state's reorganization, in a communique, the Health and Family Welfare Minister announced several new health schemes, including improving maternal and child health (ambulance access and networks), reducing tuberculosis incidence, preventing and controlling non-communicable diseases (NCDs), such as hypertension, diabetes and three common cancers of breast, cervix and oral cavity, for local residents. In addition to these new budgetary allocations, two premier medical teaching institutes (modeled after the All India Institutes of Medical Sciences, AIIMS) are scheduled to be established in Vijaynagar (in Jammu) and Awantipura (south Kashmir). While done in the name of development, many of the proposed reforms transfer wealth from the public to the private sector and, in the case of healthcare workers, change secure, public-sector employment to short-term, contractual labor. The transformation of Kashmir's legal status from a state to a union territory means that the central Indian government will now exert greater control over state budgets. While many in Kashmir welcome the promise of new investment and development, they are far more ambivalent about the changes to domicile and land ownership laws that these promises depend upon.

In the aftermath of the autonomy decision, many Indian medical professionals supported the government's moves, eschewing the apolitical, neutral and professional stance that is exemplary of the profession. For example, a senior Indian doctor writing in the *Times of India* defended the government's position by noting that Kashmir's autonomous status had prevented private corporate investment in public hospitals. The doctor concludes his op-ed on an optimistic note, "The people of Jammu and Kashmir may have to face some difficulties, but I am confident that the decision to bifurcate J&K would certainty benefit the people of Jammu and Kashmir in the near future" (Vaishya, 2019). Meanwhile, *The Lancet*, one of the world's premier medical journals, published a short article titled "Fear and Uncertainty around Kashmir's Future" that raised concerns about the effects of the lockdown, suspended communication and curfew on the "health, safety and freedoms of the Kashmiri people" (The Lancet, 2019). The journal has often commented on the effects of political conflict on civilian life and health throughout its history, but the retort from the Indian medical fraternity was swift. In a sharply worded letter, the Indian Medical Association as well as the American Association of Physicians of Indian Origin condemned the editorial and hundreds of people posted negative comments in response to the Lancet editorial on Twitter (Timsit, 2019). The Indian Medical Association noted that the editorial had forced "the medical fraternity of India" to "withdraw the esteem we have for The Lancet," given that the journal "has committed breach of propriety in commenting on this political issue" (Kaur, 2019). By opposing the Lancet editorial so vociferously, however, Indian and Indian-origin medical professionals themselves were tacitly supporting the revocation of Jammu and Kashmir's autonomy, thereby also taking a political position.

In my work, I have shown how Kashmiris are increasingly experiencing and theorizing connections between the public health system and the militaristic aims of Indian state occupation at different scales: at the level of the body and subjective experience, intersubjective experience (such as clinical encounters), and systemic failures (Varma, 2016, 2020, p. 14). At the level of subjective experience, patients commonly recognize their illnesses as "outcomes of social and political failures" (Smith, 2015, p. 274). In both Indian- and Pakistan-controlled Kashmir, hospitals are sites of intimate contact between citizens and states (Das and Poole, 2004; Linke, 2006; Varley, 2016; Varley and Varma, 2018), with both patients and providers agitating against problems of access, the inadequacy of healthcare delivery, and deliberate efforts to erode medical neutrality. The enduring effects of histories of military and police interference in public health institutions are palpable. Kashmiri patients and medical professionals alike theorized militarism as having much broader and wide-ranging effects than what could be captured by the concept of medical neutrality. They pointed to the indirect, less visible, but insidious effects of militarism as directly related to the legal impunity and emergency laws that had been instituted since Indian military occupation began in 1990. Over time, this legal impunity has transmuted into a social impunity, which has taken hold of Kashmiri society and is responsible for the proliferation of corruption and a lack of accountability in the medical system.

Kashmir studies scholars have done important work on impunity as a legal and constitutional project (Duschinski, 2010; Duschinski and Ghosh, 2017). As Duschinski notes, in human rights discourse, "impunity refers to a condition in which perpetrators are immune to or exempt from punishment for their crimes committed." In Kashmir, a network of emergency laws enacted since the beginning of the armed insurgency have granted the Indian military extraordinary powers and have protected Indian security forces and state officials from prosecution. Despite well-documented cases of human rights violations committed by Indian security forces in Kashmir, including extrajudicial killings, enforced disappearances, illegal detentions and torture, not a single member of the Indian security forces has been prosecuted or punished for any crime. Soldiers, paramilitaries and police are routinely shielded by both uniformed and civilian superiors who make such prosecutions next to impossible (Human Rights Watch, 2006).

In addition to this legal form of impunity, extralegal impunity proliferates in Kashmir. Because the Indian state has invested large, unknown quantities of money into Kashmir in the form of economic and humanitarian aid, as well as through more secretive arrangements to buy Kashmiris' loyalty over decades, there was also a sense that systems of "patronage democracy" has made Kashmiri elites addicted to easy money (Staniland, 2013). Many people argued that this corruption – rarely prosecuted, although widely known – had bred immoral and unethical practices. According to Kashmiris, impunity has spilled out from military and legal institutions and become an everyday and commonplace practice that was necessary for survival. In this sense, Kashmiris understand impunity as having much wider and deeper effects than merely legal or military action; rather, it has permeated every aspect of social life as corruption, bureaucratic mismanagement, treachery and neglect. While Duschinski (2010) defines impunity as "a strategy for demarcating a *certain kind of political, economic and social 'order'* that benefits the state while creating conditions of misery for ordinary people who find their social worlds transformed through social violence, economic hardship and political terror" (emphasis added, p. 115), I build on this definition to think about impunity not as a "certain kind of order," but rather, as *disorder*. Kashmiris understood *social impunity* as a general lack of accountability, mistrust, unruliness, disorder and unpredictability in existing systems. While many of these features will be familiar and recognizable to readers working in other settings, Kashmiris argued that they existed at a different scale and intensity here than elsewhere. For them, this disorder was tied to the state's machinations and shadowy dealings to further colonial control.

Social impunity had led to medicine and psychiatry bending toward a harmful rather than caring or curative practice. While some medical providers felt the weight of social impunity constantly impinge on their work and lives, for others, social impunity emerged most clearly when the health system was hit by crisis. In the following section, I explore the range of violations that health professionals in Kashmir have had to endure in three decades of Indian military occupation (1990–2020). These range from direct physical attacks that register in human rights and humanitarian accounts of medical neutrality, but also militarism's harms that are unaccounted for. Social impunity was used to explain both medical crises, illustrating medicine's potential for harm.

More and Less Visible Harms

Recent scholarship from anthropology and other disciplines has shown how medical neutrality has been systematically eroded and how civilians and medical institutions have been deliberately targeted in war contexts (Aciksoz, 2016; Benton and Atshan, 2016; Dewachi, 2015; Smith, 2015; Varley, 2016). In one of the most egregious examples of the violation of medical neutrality, in 2015, US military airstrikes destroyed a trauma hospital run by Médécins sans Frontières (MSF) in Kunduz, Afghanistan, killing 42 people, including humanitarian aid workers and patients. While the US military eventually described the incident as a "mistake," MSF aid workers described how they had desperately called US military authorities while the airstrikes were ongoing and had tried to plead with them to stop. In a statement after the incident, MSF's general director stated that "the view from inside the hospital is that this attack was conducted with a purpose to kill and destroy. But we don't know why" (MSF, 2015). For many medical humanitarian professionals, the Kunduz attack demonstrated the inadequacy of a juridical and humanitarian language of "violation" to describe how the battlefield might extend to protected spaces such as clinics and the inability to account for intentionality and culpability within dominant legal framings.

Medical neutrality has been eroded by using medicine not just as a *target*, but a *tactic* of war (Dewachi, 2015; Dewachi et al., 2014; Kherallah et al., 2012; Pfingst and Rosengarten, 2012). For example, in 2011, Bahrain's Salmaniya Hospital was occupied by the police and military after unrest and became the site of a stand-off between the state and opposition, with doctors arrested for treating Shi'a demonstrators. In Gilgit-Baltistan, hospitals have served as sites of what Emma Varley (2015) calls "exclusionary infrastructures," in that they operate as sites that mirror and perpetuate the social and structural inequalities associated with Shi'a-Sunni hostilities in the region. Similarly, the US Central Intelligence Agency and Pakistan state security agencies' uses of a polio vaccination campaign to locate and kill Osama bin Laden reveals another example in which medicine was deliberately used as a cover for military and intelligence operations. Pfingst and Rosengarten (2012, p. 118) trace how occupying Israeli forces have obstructed access to medical care, exacerbating health problems, delaying and refusing passage through checkpoints for patients, and actively destroying hospitals and ambulances. By its proximity to the precariousness of life, medicine becomes "a technique of combat" (Pfingst and Rosengarten, 2012, p. 100). As scholars have pointed out, the concept of medical neutrality only makes sense in a conflict in which both sides are relatively equally positioned. In incidents of domestic protest or revolt, however, where the nature of conflict is highly asymmetrical, medical neutrality's limits – as well as the cost of its violation – become evident. In Turkey and Egypt, for example, when doctors and other medical providers interceded on behalf of unarmed civilians or protestors, they suffered personal harm and injury (Aciksoz, 2016; Hamdy and Bayoumi, 2016). In occupied Palestine, paramedics and medical personnel have been deliberately targeted by Israeli snipers. Since the Great March of Return began, more than 238 health personnel and 38 ambulances have been targeted (Gadzo, 2018).

A framework of medical neutrality helps us understand how public health infrastructures and medical professionals in Kashmir have experienced, and continue to experience, violations in the form of direct violence, such as physical assaults, bombings and kidnappings. These violations were at their peak in the 1990s, when fighting between Kashmiri pro-independence forces and the Indian state was most intense. In 1993, Physicians for Human Rights (PHR) and Asia Watch published a report on detainee torture and assaults on the medical community in Kashmir, for which they interviewed 45 health professionals, including doctors, residents, medical students, ambulance drivers and other medical staff and inspected six health facilities. In the report, the authors described how Kashmiri health professionals had frequently been detained, assaulted and harassed while attempting to perform their duties. Indian security forces prevented ambulance drivers from transporting injured persons to hospitals for emergency care, and had beaten, shot or strafed ambulance drivers attempting to provide care to the wounded. In the early 1990s, one ambulance driver was shot while he was on duty. The PHR and Asia Watch report also documented how security forces detained injured persons for prolonged periods before allowing them to seek medical care and rarely provided medical assistance to the wounded. The 1993 report described how

> Security forces [had] repeatedly raided hospitals and other medical facilities, even pediatric and obstetric hospitals, [forcing] doctors at gunpoint to identify recent trauma patients. . . . Injured patients had been arrested from hospitals,

in some cases after being disconnected from intravenous medications or other treatments. . . . Doctors and other medical staff frequently were threatened, beaten and detained. Several have been shot dead while on duty; others have been tortured.

(PHR and Asia Watch, 1993, pp. 2–3)

However, what does not receive much coverage in these reports are the ways in which doctors themselves eschewed claims to neutrality and supported the movement for self-determination. As pro-independence fighters initially gained the upper hand in the conflict in the early 1990s, doctors "eschewed their commitments of neutrality and many became staunch supporters of the armed movement" (Varma, 2020, p. 76). In some cases, hospitals were used as hiding places for militants and some well-known physicians actively spoke out against Indian rule. Medical neutrality was thus multiply disrupted – by doctors, who became more vocal and open about their support for the movement (*tehreek*), armed groups, who used the neutrality of medicine to hide, seek refuge, and receive emergency care, and security forces, who attacked public health infrastructures and doctors, whether or not they were aligned with pro-independence forces. During counter-insurgency and military operations, clinics were often repurposed into interrogation and torture chambers, forever marking them with a carceral taint (Ahmad, 2012; Varley and Varma, 2018). As Ahmad describes, these incidents left lasting traces on hospital and health infrastructures, including in how clinics were spoken about in everyday life. These examples show how, in the Kashmir Valley in the 1990s, medicine and public health were not protected. Neither were they outside of the forces of militarism and violence sweeping the rest of Kashmiri society; rather, they were contiguous with them.

Yet, the concept of medical neutrality appears myopic when we try to apply it to conditions in Kashmir in the last two decades. By the mid-2000s, as levels of active combat decreased, and the movement shifted from violent to nonviolent tactics, overt and direct attacks on hospitals and medical professionals declined, but never completely disappeared. Direct attacks on hospitals and medical professionals still occur during periods of crisis or emergency. For example, although medical professionals are all given "curfew passes" and technically allowed to move freely during curfews, these passes are often not respected at checkpoints. Many providers fear that their person or property will be attacked, that the red "+" sign taped on their cars and their curfew passes will be ignored and they may be physically harmed. I had met many a doctor who had had the windshields of their cars smashed by either pro-independence protestors (stone pelters) or Indian soldiers and knew several who had been physically assaulted on their way either to or from the hospital during curfews.

These incidents had traumatized many medical professionals, yet they remained under the radar of human rights accounts of medical neutrality because they did not rise to the level of "violation." For example, in August 2019, a few days into the communication blackout, I spoke to Dr. Jamshed, a psychiatrist who works in a public hospital in Srinagar. I asked him how he felt about coming to the hospital in the midst of a siege. He replied:

> Now, coming to the hospital every day, I feel on edge. It's not like I can just come here. I have to think about *how* I will get here. Do I take my personal car or the hospital bus? Which route do I take? Which will be the safest? [As doctors] We hope no one misbehaves with us, we feel scared, *pathar lag jaye mat* [hoping that we won't get hit by a rock or stone] on our way. Then, on a normal day, the clinic is full of people and we can't get proper supplies. We have to compromise on the medicines we give. The medicines we want to pre-scribe are not available. When you have crises like this, then it adds even more to everyone's overall stress. Now for the last 10 days, since this siege began, doctors, ambulances, buses are being stopped [at checkpoints]. Everyone is extremely stressed.

Dr. Jamshed described a high level of insecurity that he regularly experiences as a medical professional, insecurity that never totally disappeared during "normal" times – because, those, too, had their own stresses, such as shortages of essential medicines and supplies, which forced him to compromise on the kind of care he was able to give. Despite being a highly qualified professional, with multiple advanced degrees, he felt unprotected from what he saw as the unruly forces of violence. Some of these contingencies were located outside the clinic, on the streets, but others had found their way into the clinic. In the following section, I describe one crisis that hit Kashmir's public health system and which people explained and theorized as evidence of social impunity.

Poisonous Medicine

In the spring of 2013, media outlets reported that counterfeit versions of the anti-biotic amoxicillin trihydrate had flooded Kashmir's public health system. Labora-tory tests showed that generic drugs marketed under the names Maximizen 625 and Curesef, which were supposed to contain 500 milligrams of amoxicillin each, contained no trace of the antibiotic. To make matters worse, the test results had been kept secret for over a year, while more than 100,000 fake antibiotics were prescribed and dispensed in public health settings across the region. Some health professionals estimated that the fake drugs had contributed to the early deaths of up to 300 patients, including children (Harris, 2014). Tests of other medi-cines that had been dispensed in public hospitals found dozens more that were substandard, including an intravenous antibiotic used for sick infants, as well as antibiotic prophylaxis given to women after C-sections.

As the amoxicillin story unfolded, systemic corruption and governmental neglect crystallized as the crisis' etiology. Despite the fact that Kashmiris have had extensive experience with corruption in the public sector, the amoxicillin crisis caught the public imagination. Some Kashmiris interpreted the amoxicillin scandal as a direct and purposeful strategy of the Indian state's necropolitics. Syed Ali Shah Geelani, one of Kashmir's most famous politicians, described the supply of spurious drugs as a "conspiracy [by the Indian government] to carry out genocide" against Kashmiri civilians. Not everyone shared Geelani's impassioned and hyperbolic statement that fake drugs were *deliberately* being given to Kashmiris. Instead, they attributed the scandal to a more nefarious process in which forms of impunity, a lack of accountability, and the proliferation of shadowy practices had been sanctioned or encouraged. Doctors and the public alike held Kashmiri public health officials ultimately responsible for the amoxicillin crisis, but their corruptibility was blamed on social impunity that had originated from the state's breach of the social compact.

On May 3, 2013, a few days after the scandal broke, several Kashmiri medical organizations and political parties called for a statewide shutdown (*bandh*) of all commercial activity to protest what they saw as endemic corruption in the public health system. Angry protestors called for the resignation of senior government bureaucrats and health officials. Many patients I spoke to were not surprised at the revelation of corruption in medicine, but what appeared to be particularly disturbing about this scandal was the wanton risking of life, including the lives of children.

While the media hype around the scandal faded in a few weeks, the scandal left long-lasting effects on the affects and subjectivities of patients. For example, one news report described how the scandal had made patients skeptical of the medications and treatments they were receiving in public health settings. One patient, Raja Begum, regarded the prophylaxis she was being given with suspicion. "How can I be sure it will relieve my suffering?" the 49-year-old asked. "Everyone says we are being fed fake drugs in Kashmir" (Parvaiz, 2013). The amoxicillin scandal thus did not register as a surprise as much as it confirmed what patients already feared: that medicine was not immune from the disorder and harms that militarism had unleashed. Though most did not go so far as viewing the supply of fake drugs as "genocide," they nonetheless worried about a generalized climate of corruptibility. Confirming Dr. Jamshed's confession about the compromises doctors have to make, patients similarly questioned the quality of (subsidized) drugs they were being prescribed in public health settings. For example, although "patented" and "generic" drugs have the same chemical makeup, patients preferred patented (which they colloquially called "branded") drugs, which were generally from European or American pharmaceutical manufacturers and were several times more expensive than generic brands, which were made by Indian pharmaceutical companies (India is the largest producer of generic drugs in the world). "How can one drug cost 15 rupees and the other drug cost 150 rupees, and they be the same thing?" one of my interlocutors asked me rhetorically.

Social impunity had led to a mistrust of pharmaceuticals as well as of clinicians. Patients told me that the quality of medicines was directly related to the integrity of the doctor. They wondered about the deeper, more subterranean motivations that might underlie certain actions or behaviors on the part of medical professionals. There was a sense that doctors could prescribe whatever they wanted – and no one could hold them accountable. This was a form of "paranoid thinking" justified by decades of counterinsurgency operations, networks of informers and collaborators, the illicit flow of money, and widespread impunity (Fassin, 2008), but in this context, it was perfectly rational. As one middle-aged patient named Bashir memorably said to me, "how do I know if the doctor is going to prescribe me a medicine or a poison?" referring to the amoxicillin scandal. Patients frequently expressed how they could no longer trust the assessments of medical professionals who were motivated by profit and had been corrupted by decades of systemic dysfunction and disorder.

While many of these concerns are shared by patients in capitalist health systems beyond Kashmir, patients in Kashmir specified that *their* public health system was *particularly* corrupt due to the social impunity unleashed by the occupation. When I asked them to compare hospitals in Kashmir with other parts of India, for example, they insisted that hospitals in major Indian cities were significantly more professional and provided better care than hospitals in Kashmir. "Why do you see all the well-off Kashmiris run off to get their medical tests and procedures done in big cities in India?" Bashir asked me. "Don't we have hospitals here? It's because you cannot get good care here. It's impossible." Bashir's statement exemplified how Kashmir was cast as an exceptional space – of not just legal exceptionalism, but social and moral exceptionalism – that made it impossible for ordinary Kashmiris to receive proper care uncorrupted by other interests. While patients recognized the good intentions of individual providers, they told me that the "habit" (*aadat*) and milieu of corruption and impunity overdetermined individual agency.

The amoxicillin scandal was thus woven into a broader narrative of generalized mistrust, impunity and disorder that were directly tied to the politics of Indian state occupation. Social impunity meant that unintentional and intentional harms were difficult to distinguish, and medicine could become the source rather than the solution to pain and suffering. In the next example, I further show how a former drug user used the notion of social impunity to explain his own spiral into drug use, which was iatrogenic in nature. Iatrogenesis refers to the "health-denying or disease-making effects of specific medical interventions" (Illich, 1975, p. 79; see also Varley and Varma, 2021; Chary and Flood, 2021). While clinical iatrogenesis is again not particular to Kashmir, the narrative I offer shows how forms of social impunity were seen to have corrupted medicine and to have produced real, long-lasting harm in the lives of patients.

Circuits of Harm

While Ivan Illich's classic work (1975) on iatrogenesis focused on how technology and liability-based models of care enhance the possibility of clinical iatrogenesis, here, I show how medicine's iatrogenic potentials are heightened in places where impunity has been legally and socially authorized. I provide an example from a patient named Hilal Ahmed, who was seeking substance abuse treatment at an inpatient mental health facility. Through his iatrogenic experience, Hilal had intimately felt and lived the effects of social impunity *as well as* militarism's co-imbrication with medicine in the form of coercive treatment.

During his admission at the substance abuse clinic, Hilal had repeatedly come to the attention of the clinic's staff because of his "non-adherence": he had repeatedly refused to consume medications that he had been prescribed as part of his detoxification regimen. In his medical file, which I read with his permission, Hilal had refused to take his medication for two successive days (in June 2010). For doctors at the clinic, Hilal's refusal constituted a medical crisis. When I asked Dr. Wani, the clinic's practicing psychiatrist, about Hilal's non-adherence, he said: "Yesterday, he refused medicine. I discussed it with him for a long time, but he bluntly refused. Medicine cannot be forced, but this is where the skill of the practitioner comes in . . . he will have to be motivated again."

Rather than explore why Hilal was refusing to comply, clinicians saw his resistance as a sign of his continued dependency on opioids. According to Dr. Wani, Hilal's refusal to take his medications was a problem of "motivation" that could be overcome. Yet while clinicians verbally distinguished between "motivation" and "coercion," and claimed that "medicine cannot be forced," the next day, as Hilal refused to take his medication again, I heard Dr. Mir, the clinic's psychologist, threatening Hilal that he would have to leave the treatment center if he did not comply with clinicians' orders. I asked Dr. Wani if such threats were necessary: "Yes, it was a sort of threat," he confessed, "but a necessary one because otherwise his case amounts to custodial care, and we're not here for that." Ironically, in order for the clinic to "motivate" Hilal, they had to use custodial logics, such as threats and coercion. These forms of violence were always already present in clinical setting, given that the substance abuse treatment center was run by the Jammu and Kashmir police and located in its highly militarized police headquarters (Varma, 2016).

I interviewed Hilal to try to better understand his non-adherence. I learned about his checkered medical history, one in which his history of substance abuse was linked to clinical iatrogenesis (as with many other cases of opioid addiction):

I went to a doctor, Ghulam Rasool Sheikh, with complaints of *tension* [lit. feelings of anxiety], mainly because my father was abusive [Hilal's father also suffered from mental health issues]. He gave me Ativan [a sleeping pill] and Diazepam [a benzodiazepine used to treat anxiety]. After taking these, I would feel my mouth forcibly close. I wouldn't be able to speak or form words [possible symptoms of benzodiazepine-induced central nervous system toxicity].[3] . . . To treat this, I went to another doctor and he told me to drink 2–4 capfuls of Corex [Codeine] every day. I got into the habit of consuming Corex. Slowly, I started using more and more because it would make me feel peaceful [sakoon] and I felt like I couldn't do without it. . . . I took Codeine because, unlike other drugs, Codeine is medicine [davai]. I felt that other drugs were dirty. I knew that Codeine was not sharab [alcohol], it was nasha [an intoxicant], but it was also a medicine [davai].

Hilal's history of addiction was, like many other opioid users, woven together with encounters with 'official' medical systems and 'qualified' medical profession-als. Yet, when Hilal sought treatment for anxiety, he was overmedicated, result-ing in him possibly developing nervous system toxicity. For this, again, he was prescribed Codeine (a narcotic analgesic), which gave him temporary relief at the cost of his becoming entirely dependent on the drug. Hilal was infuriated by the fact that this drug use had been produced by *licit* channels, by medical profession-als who had prescribed him highly addictive substances and yet who would never be held accountable. Hilal was deeply affected and angry by this experience of clinical iatrogenesis and sense of impunity in medicine.

Not only had Hilal's spiral into addiction been caused by a genuine pur-suit of care, but he had also experienced corruption in the laboratory testing industry, which had further eroded his faith in medicine and convinced him of the pervasiveness of social impunity. He described how he had gotten the same laboratory test done at two different labs – Qadri labs and Lal Path labs – but while the former had charged him 750 rupees, the latter had charged him 1,750 rupees for the same test. "Who do I trust?" he asked me, rhetorically. "How can the same test cost such a different amount?"[4] He eventually ended up getting tested by both labs but came back with different results. "How is anyone supposed to get well? These people are intent on keeping us sick," Hilal stated. These experiences had led Hilal to be highly skeptical of and to refuse the medications he was being given at the substance abuse clinic. "It is not these doctors that will cure us," he told me, "we will have to do it for ourselves." Ironically, this message of self-motivation was often what doctors themselves told patients, but in reality, patient success depended to a great extent on their willingness to follow strict rules and guidelines that verged on the coercive. Hilal's story showed how even official channels of medicine and care were shot through with contradictions and unaccounted harm. These contradictions and harms were directly attributed to the larger context of disorder and impunity that the Indian state had unleashed in Kashmir. Now, impunity had also infil-trated the practice of psychiatry.

Conclusion

In this chapter, I have tried to show how medicine does not simply absorb or register the effects of violence or militarism, but rather, as we see in the case of the amoxicillin crisis and the example of iatrogenesis, it produces its own, unique forms of harm. Occupied medicine has acquired its own strange flavor of impunity. Ethnographic research on health systems in Kashmir shows how the manifold, negative effects of occupation include egregious gaps and acts of malintent in public health services (Varley, 2016). The emergencies experienced by Kashmiris in medical facilities produce similar feelings of acute precariousness and erode faith in medical systems. Gaps in care are linked to a general state of social impunity, which is directly tied to the state's necropolitical acts.

These examples offer a way to rethink the place and function of public healthcare in systems of colonial governance. For ordinary Kashmiris, public health has not only been severely compromised by histories of violence and militarization, but medicine and public health have actually become sites of harm themselves. This is not to say that this is all they are. Both providers and patients reflect on, critique, and at times mourn how violence impinges on care. This piece is by no means an indictment against individual practitioners, who are themselves highly vulnerable and precarious in this system, and as I showed in the case of Dr. Jamshed, susceptible to social impunity themselves. Many doctors I met thought conscientiously about how to mitigate these harms and reflected on their own, constrained ability to act ethically. Meanwhile, patients like Hilal and Bashir drew on an existing social language of impunity to try to find meaning in clinical encounters gone deeply awry. Medicine and public health are fecund sites to imagine, reimagine and interrogate how techniques of state power seep into bodies and lives.

Notes

1 Research was approved by Cornell University's Institutional Review Board, as well as the University of California, San Diego's Institutional Review Board. Research for this article was generously funded by the Institute of Practical Ethics at UC San Diego and the Wenner-Gren Foundation for Anthropological Research. I use pseudonyms for all my participants and public health settings. I have previously elaborated in detail my research ethics and methods in detail (please see https://escholarship.org/uc/item/217248s8).

2 On August 5, 2019, the Home Minister of India announced the abrogation of Article 370 and Article 35-A of the Indian Constitution which granted "special status" to the state of Jammu and Kashmir, including the capacity of the Jammu and Kashmir state legislature to define state permanent residents and limited land ownership to those permanent residents, along with a number of other rights and privileges. The state was also demoted to a "union territory" status, bringing it under direct control of the central Indian government. The revocation was accompanied by the imposition of curfew-like conditions across the Kashmir Valley and the invocation of Section 144 of the Criminal

Procedure Code, which prevents the assembly of more than four persons in public. To accompany the news of "decades long privileges being undemocratically and unceremoniously ended" was a total communication blackout, with mobile phones, landlines, internet and other messaging facilities blocked. The region also suffered more than US$1 billion US in economic losses during the blackout (Rather et al., 2020, p. 510).

3 Common side effects among benzodiazepines (BZDs) include drowsiness, lethargy and fatigue. At higher dosages, impaired motor coordination, dizziness, vertigo, slurred speech, blurry vision, mood swings and euphoria can occur, as well as hostile or erratic behavior in some instances. BZDs are eliminated slowly from the body, so repeated doses over a prolonged period can result in significant accumulation in fatty tissues. Thus, some symptoms of overmedication (impaired thinking, disorientation, confusion, slurred speech) can appear over time. Tolerance, dependence and withdrawal are adverse effects associated with long-term use (Griffin et al., 2013).

4 While Hilal's fears were treated as irrational by the clinic staff, there have been several alarming reports about the lack of regulations around private medical laboratories and the lack of qualified staff in testing facilities in Kashmir (www.risingkashmir.com/news/jk-lacks-testing-labs-technical-staff-drug-controller-to-shrc-333936.html).

References

Aciksoz, S.C. (2016). Medical humanitarianism under atmospheric violence: health professionals in the 2013 Gezi protests in Turkey. *Culture, Medicine, and Psychiatry* 40(2):198–222.

Aggarwal, R. & Bhan, M. (2009). 'Disarming violence': development, democracy, and security on the borders of India. *The Journal of Asian Studies* 68(2):519–542.

Ahmad, W. (2012, June 6). Appointment with terror. *Fountain Ink*. Retrieved November 1, 2022, from http://fountainink.in/essay/appointment-with-terror.

Ali, N. (2010). Books vs bombs? Humanitarian development and the narrative of terror in Northern Pakistan. *Third World Quarterly* 31(4): 541–559.

Anant, A. (2011). *Counterinsurgency and 'Op Sadhbhavana' in Jammu and Kashmir*. ISDA Occasional Paper 19. Retrieved November 2, 2020, from https://idsa.in/occasionalpapers/CounterinsurgencyandOpSadhbhavanainJammuandKashmir.

Benton, A. & Atshan, S.E. (2016). 'Even war has rules': on medical neutrality and legitimate non-violence. *Culture, Medicine, and Psychiatry* 40(2):151–158.

Bhan, M. (2013). *Counterinsurgency, Democracy and the Politics of Identity in India: From Warfare to Welfare?* London: Routledge.

Chary, A. & Flood, D. (2021). Iatrogenic trainwrecks and moral injury. *Anthropology and Medicine* 28(2):223–238.

Chua, J.L. (2020). Pharmaceutical creep: US military power and the global and transnational mobility of psychopharmaceuticals. *Medical Anthropology Quarterly* 34(1):41–58.

Das, V. & Poole, D. (2004). *Anthropology in the Margins of the State*. Santa Fe: School of American Research Press.

Dewachi, O. (2015). Blurred lines: warfare and health care. *Medical Anthropology Theory* 2(2):95–101.

Dewachi, O., Skelton, M., Nguyen, V.K., Fouad, F.M., Sitta, G.A., Maasri, Z. & Giacaman, R. (2014). Changing therapeutic geographies of the Iraqi and Syrian wars. *The Lancet* 383(9915):449–457.

Duschinski, H. (2010). Reproducing regimes of impunity: fake encounters and the informalization of everyday violence in Kashmir valley. *Cultural Studies* 24(1):110–132.

Duschinski, H. & Ghosh, S.N. (2017). Constituting the occupation: preventive detention and permanent emergency in Kashmir. *The Journal of Legal Pluralism and Unofficial Law* 49(3):314–337.

Fanon, F. (1968). *Black Skin, White Masks*. New York: Grove Press.

Fassin, D. (2008). The embodied past: from paranoid style to politics of memory in South Africa. *Social Anthropology* 16(3):312–328.

Gadzo, M. (2018, May 28). Palestinian medics struggle to provide healthcare amid attacks. *Al Jazeera*. Retrieved November 1, 2022, from www.aljazeera.com/news/2018/5/28/palestinian-medics-struggle-to-provide-healthcare-amid-attacks.

Griffin, C.E., Kaye, A.M., Bueno, F.R. & Kaye, A.D. (2013). Benzodiazepine pharmacology and central nervous system–mediated effects. *Ochsner Journal* 13(2):214–223.

Hamdy, S.F. & Bayoumi, S. (2016). Egypt's popular uprising and the stakes of medical neutrality. *Culture, Medicine, and Psychiatry* 40(2):223–241.

Harris, G. (2014, February 14). Medicines made in India set off safety worries. *The New York Times*. Retrieved November 1, 2022, from www.nytimes.com/2014/02/15/world/asia/medicines-made-in-india-set-off-safety-worries.html.

Human Rights Watch. (2006, September 11). *Everyone Lives in Fear: Patterns of Impunity in Jammu and Kashmir*. Retrieved November 1, 2022, from www.hrw.org/report/2006/09/11/everyone-lives-fear/patterns-impunity-jammu-and-kashmir.

Illich, I. (1975). Iatrogenic tort. *Journal of Medical Ethics* 1(2):78–80.

Kanjwal, H. (2017). *Building a New Kashmir: Bakshi Ghulam Muhammad and the Politics of State-Formation in a Disputed Territory (1953–1963)*. PhD Dissertation. Ann Arbor: University of Michigan.

Kaur, B. (2019, August 19). IMA slams the Lancet on Kashmir editorial. *DownToEarth*. Retrieved November 1, 2022, from www.downtoearth.org.in/news/health/ima-slams-the-lancet-on-kashmir-editorial-66226.

Kherallah, M., Alahfez, T., Sahloul, Z., Eddin, K.D. & Jamil, G. (2012). Health care in Syria before and during the crisis. *Avicenna Journal of Medicine* 2(3):51–53.

The Lancet. (2019, August 17). Fear and uncertainty around Kashmir's future. *The Lancet* 394(10198):542.

Linke, U. (2006). Contact zones: rethinking the sensual life of the state. *Anthropological Theory* 6(2):205–225.

Médécins sans Frontières. (2015). *On 3 October 2015, US Airstrikes Destroyed Our Trauma Hospital in Kunduz, Afghanistan, Killing 42 People*. Retrieved August 31, 2020, from www.msf.org/kunduz-hospital-attack-depth.

Parvaiz, A. (2013, June 5). When the health system is ill. *Inter Press Service*. Retrieved September 1, 2022, from www.ipsnews.net/2013/06/when-the-health-system-is-taken-ill/.

Pfingst, A. & Rosengarten, M. (2012). Medicine as a tactic of war: Palestinian precarity. *Body & Society* 18(3–4):99–125.

Physicians for Human Rights and Asia Watch. (1993, March). *The Crackdown in Kashmir: Torture of Detainees and Assaults on the Medical Community*. Retrieved July 1, 2022, from https://phr.org/wp-content/uploads/1993/03/crackdown-in-kashmir-1993.pdf.

Rather, T.A., Wani, G.M. & Suhrawardy, B.M. (2020). Abrogation of article 370 of the constitution of India: socio-economic and political implications on Jammu and Kashmir. *International Journal of Research and Analytical Reviews* 7(3):501–517.

Redfield, P. (2011). The impossible problem of neutrality. In P. Redfield & E. Borstein (Eds.), *Forces of Compassion: Humanitarianism Between Ethics and Politics* (pp. 53–70). Santa Fe: School for Advanced Research Press.

Smith, C. (2015). Doctors that harm, doctors that heal: reimagining medicine in post-conflict Aceh, Indonesia. *Ethnos* 80(2):272–291.

Staniland, P. (2013). Kashmir since 2003: counterinsurgency and the paradox of 'normalcy'. *Asian Survey* 53(5):931–957.

Terry, J. (2017). *Attachments to War*. Durham: Duke University Press.

Tilley, S.A. (2016). *Doing Respectful Research: Power, Privilege, and Passion*. Halifax: Fernwood Publishing.

Timsit, A. (2019, August 19). Why India shouldn't be angry at a British medical journal's comments on Kashmir. *Quartz*. Retrieved November 10, 2020, from https://qz.com/india/1690677/why-indians-are-upset-about-the-lancets-editorial-on-kashmir/.

Vaishya, R. (2019, August 30). Will scrapping article 370 ensure better healthcare environment in Jammu and Kashmir. *The Times of India*. Retrieved January 1, 2022, from https://timesofindia.indiatimes.com/readersblog/arthritis-care-foundation/will-scrapping-article-370-ensure-better-healthcare-environment-in-jammu-and-kashmir-5378/.

Varley, E. (2015). Exclusionary infrastructures: crisis and the rise of sectarian hospitals in Northern Pakistan. In M. Sökefeld (Ed.), *Spaces of Conflict: Perspectives Across Asia* (pp. 187–220). Bielefeld: Transcript.

Varley, E. (2016). Abandonments, solidarities, and logics of care: hospitals as sites of sectarian conflict in Gilgit-Baltistan. *Culture, Medicine and Psychiatry* 40(2):159–180.

Varley, E. & Varma, S. (2018). Spectral lines: haunted hospitals across the line of control. *Medical Anthropology* 37(6):1–15.

Varley, E. & Varma, S. (2019, April 17). Attending to the dark side of medicine. *Anthropology News*.

Varley, E. & Varma, S. (2021). Medicine's shadowside: revisiting clinical iatrogenesis. *Anthropology and Medicine* 28(2):141–155.

Varma, S. (2016). Love in the time of occupation: reveries, longing and intoxication in Kashmir. *American Ethnologist* 43(1):50–62.

Varma, S. (2018). From 'terrorist' to 'terrorized': how trauma became the language of suffering in Kashmir. In H. Duschinski, M. Bahn, A. Zia & C. Mahmood (Eds.), *Resisting Occupation in Kashmir* (pp. 129–152). Philadelphia: University of Pennsylvania Press.

Varma, S. (2020). *The Occupied Clinic: Militarism and Care in Kashmir*. Durham and London: Duke University Press.

PART 3

Culture, Displacement and Healing

5

HEALING THE SICKNESS OF FIGHTING

Medicalization and Warriordom in Postcolonial North America

Christopher M. Webb

After the Vietnam War, the conspicuous suffering of U.S. veterans of the conflict was recognized by both U.S. society and the American Psychiatric Association. In 1980, the Post-traumatic Stress Disorder (PTSD) diagnosis was codified in the Diagnostic and Statistical Manual of Mental Disorders (DSM) (American Psychiatric Association, 1980). Since this time, the object of "combat trauma" has grown to occupy significant space in popular culture. In the contemporary world, PTSD is now the primary lens for translating a wide range of military (and military-adjacent) experiences to both the public and veterans themselves.

However, the diagnosis and all of its clinical appurtenances fall short of contextualizing the full range of traumas associated with military service and its treatments often fail to relieve sufferers of their symptoms. An early example of this was observed in American Indian veterans of the Vietnam War, who demonstrated marked "treatment resistance" to novel PTSD therapies that were developed in the 1980s (Kulka et al., 1990; Holm, 1995; Friedman et al., 1997). In response to this, a Veterans Affairs (VA) hospital in southern Puget Sound responded to requests by local tribal leaders to make Indigenous healing and purification rituals available for American Indian veterans. Noting the efficacy of these rituals, a ritual community of Indigenous veterans became established there who continue to practice their ceremonies today on a piece of sacred land adjacent to the VA Hospital. The Indigenous peoples of North America experience a unique combination of circumstances that shape the ceremonial practices of this community. The majority of Native Americans belong to a diaspora that is composed of multiple tribal groups, within the borders of the nation-state of which they are citizens, but removed from their various respective ancestral lands. Within the United States, their lived historical realities are flattened by public narratives that

DOI: 10.4324/9781003311843-9

conflate diverse cultures and the perpetuation of stereotypes that can be traced to the colonial era.[1]

Working as a medical anthropologist, I conducted ethnographic fieldwork with this healing community. Over a period of 36 months, I made several trips to the site, including seven months of continuous fieldwork in 2019. As a combat veteran with a PTSD diagnosis, my fieldwork centered on extended participation in the ceremonial life of this ritual community. I became close with the Elder Council, the team of experienced Native chaplains who officiate ceremonies in the ritual community. Drawing from several tribal traditions, particularly from Lakota/Plains traditions, these elders conduct sweat lodges, "talking circles," and other ceremonies. These rituals serve a dedicated cohort of regular attendees, a segment of patients from the hospital's inpatient PTSD program, and periodic visitors who are seeking healing after the failure of clinical therapy. My findings detail two developments: first, the ritual community exposes the limits of the 20th-century process of medicalizing trauma associated with war/military service. For instance, ritual participants draw on the Lakota concept of iwáyazaŋ azúyeya, "the sickness one acquires from fighting others and the self" as the therapeutic object at stake, in contrast to "PTSD." Ceremonies directly address this sickness by highlighting Native experiences of colonization, the unique ways that trauma was experienced by Native veterans (particularly from the Vietnam War era), and the connections between violence and masculinity. Second, the site shifts the ways "warriordom" connects concepts of violence to concepts of culture. The notion that the warrior is a unique kind of person who both suffers and heals differently from civilians may account for the increasing appeal of ritual therapy among non-Native veterans (Telonidis, 2012; Lifson, 2015; Lodono, 2020). However, the ceremonies compel veterans to confront warrior identity as a feature of white settler violence and effectively turn healing into a process of social critique.

Indigenous Roots

The ceremonies at American Lake trace their roots into the Indigenous faiths of the Northern Great Plains, particularly from the Lakota Tribe. After a set of sociopolitical phenomena in the mid-20th century, the traditions of the Northern Great Plains spread across North America and were adopted by Indians across the continent, especially the diaspora who had been relocated to urban areas during the Indian Termination Policy era (the 1940s–1960s). The product is a postcolonial healing religion that is practiced by thousands of Native Americans today, often referred to as the "Red Road" in vernacular. The ceremonial community at American Lake follows this tradition and the rituals and traditions in action on the site are extensive. However, the ceremonial anchor of the community, including the bulk of ceremonial work that first-time attendees encounter revolves around the inípi sweat lodge ceremony, the čhaŋnúŋpa pipe ceremony, and work with five sacred plant medicines: sage, sweetgrass, cedar, bear root and lavender. In addition, biweekly talking circle ceremonies alternate between "sweat" weeks. Sweat lodges and sweat lodge ceremonies exist in various forms all over the world, notably in the Americas. However, the particular sweat lodge ceremony that is practiced in the American Lake thiyóšpaye has a genealogy that can be traced, through various routes, to the North American northern Plains. Describing this ceremony comes with some implicit complications, which I will do my best to address both thoroughly and sensitively. Some of these complications are:

1. The most common ceremony practiced at American Lake is the Inipi sweat lodge ceremony. This ceremony comes from the Lakota people, though it is practiced at American Lake on Salish land, managed somewhat by a government organization, by many people who are non-Lakota. There is a complex history through which things came to be this way (these are described in greater depth in another chapter). This is, not surprisingly, controversial to some people.
2. This is not a public ceremony. There is a confidentiality agreement that governs a lot of what is said and done on the ceremonial grounds and, especially, in the lodge. While the community is magnificently inclusive in their treatment of people, there is an exclusivity to the experience and Indigenous people have, understandably, long made clear that they oppose people capitalizing on these ceremonies or representing them out of context. There are a lot of things said and done that I simply cannot, and would not want to, repeat.
3. The sacred nature of the space, and the requirements of navigating it in a good way, dictated that I could not use some common anthropological research methods while on-site. I never carried a camera, phone, recording device or notebook onto the sacred grounds. This means that I was sometimes unable to write about things until hours or, in some cases, days after they occurred.
4. Though it was well established that I am an anthropologist conducting research, the community at American Lake embraced me primarily as a human being on the healing path. I remember academic peers/mentors talking about things like the accessibility of counseling and mental health resources "in the field" when I was leaving to conduct my field research. I had the thought: "my counseling and mental health support network in the field is actually my community of interlocutors." This is a manifestation of the fact that my "fieldwork" was something other than sterile, empirical data collection by an unbiased observer. A substantial part of my research is my sincere attempt to experience growth and healing in the aftermath of the violence of my own life. Though the community and elders were always dismissive of this concern (and sometimes overtly hostile toward it), I am aware that there is a justified tradition in anthropology of suspicion toward anthropologists who can be seen as inappropriately "using" their interlocutors. I admit

that over the several years I have spent with this community, I have at times leaned very hard on them, asking them to help me live a better life, be a better person, and process heavy emotions like grief, guilt and self-hatred. The archetypal image of the anthropologist sitting at the edge of the ceremony, observing and writing field notes, does not really apply to my experience, which involved a much more visceral embodiment of participant observation. I am deeply grateful to my thiyóšpaye and everything they have given to me. Perhaps some might feel that they have given me too much, which is what I am trying to communicate here.

With these complications in mind, I have to be strategic in recreating the ceremony. Some parts of the Inipi ceremony have been published in other sources, with the blessing of the Lakota people. Raymond Bucko's The Lakota Ritual of the Sweat Lodge is exemplary (Bucko, 1998). Of course, the rituals at American Lake are, as is the case with all respective thiyóšpayes, distinct in some ways. My descriptions of the rituals will draw from my own experiences at American Lake, emphasizing the things that are not intended to be kept secret. Some things vary a bit from ceremony to ceremony but others are inflexible.

Genealogy

The genealogy of the ceremonies performed at American Lake traces ultimately to the American northern Plains and they are often described on site as "Lakota ceremonies." However, there are other Indigenous influences as well and many of these roots have passed through the Pan-Indian tradition. A common manifestation of the Pan-Indian tradition is a spiritual system and way of life that is often referred to in vernacular as the "Red Road" (sometimes the "Good Red Road"). This is due to the massive, national spread of Great Plains spirituality across reservations and Urban Indian populations during the 20th century. While practitioners earnestly endeavor to follow established Lakota parameters and consider sacred all things called sacred by the Lakota, this relationship is not universally seen as reciprocal from the Lakota side. For their part, Lakota people are divided over whether or not the Red Road counts as a legitimate expression of Great Plains spirituality. The debate over this has been public and profoundly emotional, with members of the Lakota people who passionately argue both sides of this. On the Red Road side (which is populated primarily with Urban Indians of multi-tribal ancestry), opinions are just as diverse, with some people feeling very hurt by their sense of being "rejected" by the Lakota, others who embrace the acceptance they receive from other Lakota, and others still who are personally committed to the practice of their faith and do not care what other people think. By my observation, there is no question that the Red Road is just as "real" as any other faith/

way of life practiced by anyone in the world and it is foundational in the lives of thousands of people. As was noted by Lakota scholar Vine Deloria Jr., the Red Road has indisputably brought a lot of good into the lives of a lot of people and has the potential to do more. The real and legitimate anger that Lakota people feel is ultimately against white New Age practitioners who have appropriated the system and made a mockery of it, through using it to gain status for themselves and trying to make money "selling" their religious services/items to paying clients (Deloria, 1972/2003). This kind of behavior is very far from what I observed at American Lake, where there is no exchange of money and humility is embraced as a great virtue (a goal is to become ikčé wičháša, "just a common man").[2] With this in mind, I will generally refer to the faith/way of life at American Lake as the Red Road or Pan-Indian faith, for the purpose of acknowledging that some practices there are not Lakota in origin and there is a Lakota way of life that does not feature them. However, the influence of the cosmology of the Great Plains is enormous, and understanding them requires some knowledge of their origins, which are disproportionately Lakota.

In this vein, it is also important to note that "Lakota faith" is itself a diverse set of things that vary through time and across different assemblages of people. The Lakota language and its usage is a major part of this. Though I've never seen it described as such, within Pan-Indian/Red Road spirituality, the Lakota language functions as a liturgical language (I have heard it referred to, broadly, as "Indian language" by a number of practitioners). The majority of regular attendees at American Lake, as well as adherents to the Red Road in general, are not fluent in Lakota. However, most know enough prayers and songs to participate actively in the ceremonies. When people attend for a long time and begin to attain greater responsibility in the community, they have to learn more of the language to take on more active roles. It is conventionally accepted that one cannot lead an Inipi ceremony or carry a Čhaŋnúŋpa (sacred pipe) without being able to competently pray/sing in the language. Lakota spiritual leader Arvol Looking Horse has declared formally that an Inipi or Čhaŋnúŋpa ceremony is only legitimate if the person leading it can do so in "Plains tongue" (Looking Horse, 2003).[3] The language also serves an important role in structuring spiritual development in the faith as people follow the Red Road. Its unique grammatical structure (in contrast to English) serves as a metaphor for the ways that a person can live in a good way. Ideas and concepts that are presented in the Lakota language are taught in a way that allows the unique grammatical structure of the language to frame the ideas themselves as inherently different from European/colonial ways of thinking. This helps people imagine future possibilities that were previously difficult to conceive of. As Lakota linguist and activist Albert White Hat said: "when you learn Lakota, you gain a new heart" (White Hat, 1999).

The Healing Community

The very existence of the healing community that exists at the American Lake VA is the product of numerous intersecting histories, many of which came together in the 1980s. One of these is the volume of American Indian veterans, the majority of whom live in the western United States. The Seattle area, in particular, has a significant population of urban Indians, including many veterans among them. Urban Indians, moved to Seattle by relocation programs in the early-mid 20th century, comprise the largest population of American Indians in the United States. American Indians, across tribes and the urban/rural divide, serve in the military at a rate higher than any other demographic and also utilize VA medical care at the highest rate of all veteran groups (Schilling, 2018; Simkins and Barrett, 2019). After PTSD was recognized in the DSM in 1980, VA medical centers began working to address the PTSD "epidemic" that had been identified, very publicly, in Vietnam War veterans. This included the establishment of the unique PTSD inpatient clinic at the American Lake VA. This inpatient clinic subsequently became the site where a significant amount of early research on PTSD was conducted, particularly with regard to the responses of veterans to various forms of therapy. The uniqueness of this clinic resulted in "severe" cases of PTSD from several western states being sent to American Lake. This included many veterans who were reservation Indians, as well as several veterans from the Seattle urban Indian population (Scurfield, 1995). Shortly afterward, clinicians, social workers and tribal leaders collectively observed that for unknown reasons, the response of American Indian veterans to PTSD therapy was markedly poor in comparison to other groups (some clinicians were documented as saying that they no longer wanted to work with American Indian patients, whom they considered difficult). Tribal leaders and VA officials consulted with each other to address this issue and identified several disjunctures between clinical therapy and Indigenous culture. The combination of hundreds of years of colonial violence and "top-down" power structures intrinsic in western clinical practice doomed "doctor/patient relations" from the beginning. Furthermore, it was determined that American Indians belonged to a "warrior culture" context that was ontologically distinct from the culture that modern biomedical practices were designed to operate within (Scurfield, 1995).

During a series of meetings with American Indians, where hospital staff traveled to reservations and Indigenous cultural centers to discuss these issues, clinicians and other hospital staff observed profound differences between their own "presentation" style and the way that American Indian groups facilitated public events and meetings. For example, meetings hosted by American Indians ordinarily involved ritualized exchange of objects, gifts and food, while speakers utilized a more conversational approach with audiences (in contrast to the lecturing style used in "western" meetings, where a single speaker is given privileged space to dictate information to quiet listeners). These staff recognized this as a mechanism to establish a more egalitarian social structure prior to accomplishing any sort of "business." In reflection, these clinicians realized not only that their presentation style had made Indians feel like they were being "talked down to" but also that their claims to exclusive medical expertise were being coded as "over-promising," which was received badly after centuries of being deceived by the US government.[4]

Ultimately, American Indian veterans wanted to use their own purification and healing rituals, as a VA service. VA officials were at first opposed, fearing that embracing Indigenous ritual would set a precedent that would necessitate individualized therapy for all ethnic groups serviced by the VA. But ultimately, the VA granted this request, after determining that American Indians were a special category, apart from the majority of other, non-Indigenous veterans. Unlike other veterans, American Indians were labeled "warriors," which was seen as something distinct from "veterans." As "warriors," it was believed that American Indians would heal best in a "warrior culture" context, in contrast to the clinical therapy that was seen as most efficacious for non-Indigenous veterans (Scurfield, 1995).

The other histories that contribute to the existence of this healing site and its unique contemporary dynamics transcend its local contexts. The Vietnam War itself, the Civil Rights Movement, intense late 20th-century medicalization, the spread of healing religion among North American Indigenous peoples, and different forms of "warrior" identity (including a nascent 21st-century phenomenon that repackages warriordom in the context of contemporary wars) all necessarily contribute to how "healing" dynamics occur at American Lake.

In 1923, 377 acres of Fort Lewis were set aside for the construction of a hospital campus to provide care for WWI veterans. The buildings of the VA medical center were built in a beautiful Spanish terracotta style; many of them are now on the National Register of Historic Buildings. In 1924, the hospital was dedicated and was immediately designated as a psychiatry-focused institution. While the American Lake VAMC later became a multi-care hospital, its mental-health focus remains a core part of its identity. In the 1980s, after the PTSD diagnosis was recognized in the DSM, the American Lake VAMC began its PTSD inpatient program for severe PTSD. American Indian-specific programming at the American Lake VAMC, which is now much more of a "stand-alone" entity on that campus, originally grew out of the inpatient PTSD clinic.

In its earliest iteration, this option was explored through the admission of an all-American Indian cohort in the inpatient PTSD clinic. Though "cultural activities" were incorporated, this cohort was held to a therapeutic regimen that was built around the same three-month PTSD program that was already established within the clinic. Originally as an addendum to the established clinically oriented PTSD program, sacred ceremonial grounds on the property were designated for the construction of a sweat lodge. The sweat lodge was built to support the cohort by making purification rituals available on an as-needed basis.

Though the program was being developed to serve a multi-tribal group of veterans from nine states, elders agreed that the ceremonies would be neither legitimate nor appropriate without the blessing of the people who were Indigenous to the land being used. For this reason, the local Nisqually people were asked to conduct the ceremonies that established the grounds as sacred for these ceremonial purposes. They did so and the Nisqually continue to maintain formal ceremonial authority over this property. However, the ceremonies conducted on the property often derive from non-Salish traditions and the medicine men who conduct the ceremonies have diverse tribal backgrounds.

The separateness of the sweat lodge from the first cohort's official therapeutic regimen derived from concerns held by VA officials about seeming to endorse a particular religious practice.[5] Cohort members had to request the use of the sweat lodge and it saw the majority of its use during this period before and after "official" therapy hours.

Significant tensions developed during the cohort's journey through the 3-month inpatient program. These included tensions between American Indian patients and hospital staff (who were all either white or African American) and between different groups of Indians in the program. Hospital staff were frightened by the American Indian cohort and there was significant turnover among these staff during the cycle. Unexpected conflicts also developed between urban Indians and the reservation Indians who were brought in from other regions, often over matters regarding ancestry and "real" Indianness (urban Indians were accused by reservation Indians of being "assimilated" and being culturally too "white").[6] After experimenting with an all-Indian cohort, the program experimented with having it only half Indian, with the same structure as before. While hospital staff reported feeling much more comfortable with this arrangement, the greatest benefit seemed to go to the non-Indigenous veterans who participated with that group. Non-Indigenous veterans reported a significant reduction in PTSD symptoms and responded very affirmatively to participation in American Indian community events.[7] However, witnessing the volume of investment that the surrounding Native American community had in the success of this cohort, through ceremonies and performances given at their graduation, struck a bittersweet chord in the non-Indigenous veterans who participated in that cohort (as well as staff members). As one participating clinician said:

> The bittersweet aspect was the recognition by non-native veterans that we never have had or would have this depth of mutual affinity with, let alone such support and recognition from, the communities in which we had been raised.

Perhaps as much anything that can be gleaned from the ceremony itself, the above statement signals to something that is too often left out of conversations about health and wellness: the role of community support during healing (as well as beforehand). Amidst the structural violence and public health barriers experienced by American Indigenous people, the presence of a strong community context stands out as one variable to their advantage. One feels tempted to speculate about the possibility that the distinct, robust response that *non-Natives* showed to the program could have been associated with exposure to a form of community support previously unexperienced.

Though relegated to the sidelines early on, it is the sweat lodge that is now the center of American Indian programming at the American Lake VA. During the initial two cohorts that were observed in their movement through the inpatient PTSD program, the usage of the sweat lodge stood out as the most efficacious and useful intervention. During the all-American Indian cohort, the sweat lodge was available on an as-needed basis. This was physically taxing for the individuals conducting the ceremonies, which led to the decision to hold one structured sweat lodge ceremony every other week.[8] Though there has been slight variation over the years, this continues to be the general pattern for sweat lodge ceremonies at American Lake. In alternating weeks, the community meets for "talking circle" ceremonies, which are held indoors in the American Lake VAMC's campus chapel.

During and after the 1980s, the concept of warriordom would transform. While originally thought of as something "primitive" and projected onto ancient or non-European peoples, multiple factors led to its adaptation by contemporary peoples of European descent (Gibson, 1994). Over time, the dynamics (including racial/ethnic dynamics) of the ceremonies at American Lake would also have to adapt, as new wars brought new cohorts of traumatized veterans to the sacred grounds seeking healing.

Warriordom

The clinical PTSD diagnosis has evolved in accordance with medicalizing trends in the four decades since its recognition in the DSM (Young, 1997; Stein et al., 2007; Moghimi, 2012; Clarke, 2014). However, the social construct of combat trauma that is often known discursively as "PTSD" has grown and become increasingly entangled with various sociopolitical projects associated with war, gender, and racial/ethnic identity. In the 21st century, veterans increasingly prefer the signifier "warrior" over the civil term "veteran." The warrior signifier conjures a more mythical notion of timeless, transcultural castes located in martial societies. At the same time, this warrior identity is being embraced by many outside of the military, including police and civilian defense contractors. Warriors are seen as a distinct kind of person who experiences war, suffering and healing differently than civilians. Within this context and among soldiers/veterans, the combat trauma construct that is often generalized as "PTSD" becomes the fundamental marker of legitimate warrior experience.

When the VA approved of making space for Indigenous ceremony in the 1980s, it was because Indigenous veterans were seen as denizens of "warrior cultures," and understood to be ontologically distinct from non-Indigenous veterans who were expected to heal best in a clinical environment. Until relatively recently, the ritual healing community was almost exclusive to the Indigenous veterans it was created for. However, the ceremonies increasingly appeal to non-Indigenous veterans and are now being seen as a therapeutic option for treatment-resistant veterans of all ethnicities. This situation creates the conditions for the complex intersection of several socioepistemological projects, including medicalization, race, indigeneity, militarism and "warrior" identity among many other things. While non-Indigenous veterans may see their admiration of Indigenous warriors as respectful (along with their own claim to warrior identity), this concept of warriordom remains an artifact of colonial violence.

Indigenous scholar Tom Holm has noted that colonizers endow their enemies with superhuman qualities, often for the purpose of increasing the prestige of their own ability to conquer them. As long as the United States has existed, Holm argues, American Indians have been imagined as a martial race, with the belief that superhuman individual combat competence is inherited. This inheritance has been ascribed to genetics, as the study of genes developed in science. Prior to and through the Vietnam War, American Indian soldiers were commonly forced into dangerous "scout" positions, due to what some soldiers have referred to as "Indian Scout Syndrome." Indian Scout Syndrome refers to the tendency for white commanders and soldiers to assume that American Indian soldiers have an inherited proclivity and skill with respect to certain combat-related tasks. Woodcraft, acute senses of sight/smell, as well as fearless ferocity in combat are parts of this construct. This fetishizing form of "veneration," combined with the overt racism experienced by Indigenous peoples at home in the United States, has been attributed as a source of the disproportionate suffering (represented by a high PTSD diagnosis rate) experienced by Indigenous veterans (LaDuke, 2013, pp. 13–18).[9]

The relationship between Native Americans and the US Military is both deep and complex; while the United States Army was often the deliverer of the Government's campaign of genocidal violence against the continent's Indigenous peoples, Native Americans serve in the military at a rate higher than any other ethnic group in the United States (Schilling, 2018; Vergun, 2021). Much like the VA in its justification for making ceremonial therapy available for Indigenous veterans, the public often attributes this high rate of service to the "warrior tradition" of Native Americans (Ault, 2020). This colonial sense of warriordom is sometimes expressed by Indigenous veterans themselves (Viola, 2008). Native

Hawaiian anthropologist Ty P. Kāwika Tengan has observed in his research with Indigenous Hawaiian men that his interlocutors often see themselves as having genetically inherited warriorhood, as the progeny of a warrior culture (Tengan, 2008). In an interview with two Native Hawaiian veterans, Tengan recorded their expressed belief that warriorhood was in their DNA and that their Native American peers in the military similarly demonstrated particular prowess under the conditions of war (Tengan et al., 2015, pp. 229–235). It is important to note here that, regarding statements like this, Kim TallBear (2013) argues that Indigenous peoples do not necessarily mean to reference actual genetics in statements like this. In communication with Ty P. Kāwika Tengan over these particular interviews, TallBear states that most Indigenous people understand that who they are as people is comprised of cultural and political factors, and they understand physical bodies to be directly descended from the bodies of their ancestors. TallBear cautioned that linking Indigenous peoples and their DNA with soldiering and warriordom potentially ignores the political economic conditions that shape their high enlistment and denies how profoundly US colonization disrupted their ancestors' life ways and the degree to which it continues to oppressively structure their lives (TallBear, 2015, p. 240).

Lumbee scholar Robert Williams Jr. identifies the colonial concept of Indigenous warriordom in the writings of Thomas Jefferson, though Jefferson attributed warrior prowess to social factors rather than DNA. However, though Jefferson praised Native Americans for their skill in battle and woodcraft, he saw these as indicative of the limited and primitive culture of Indigenous peoples, "which call for a display of particular talents only" (Pearce, 1965; Sheehan, 1973). Even today, the usage of Native American names and nations is abundant in the military, particularly in the naming of units and equipment. I recall being told by a high-ranking officer during my time in the military (every Company in my Battalion was named after a Native American tribe) that we used the names of tribes that we (the Army) had conquered, so that we could mobilize the power of those peoples.

The Vietnam War itself, particularly its aftermath, began the process of reconfiguring veteran subjectivity in North America. As the United States' invasion of Southeast Asia was met with unexpected domestic unpopularity, even among soldiers and veterans, the Nixon administration responded with a massive propaganda campaign. The propaganda argued both that: A. countless veterans were being held in communist prisoner of war camps and B. veterans experienced mass abuse upon homecoming at the behest of leftist anti-war protesters (Franklin, 1992; Lembcke, 1998). The goal of this propaganda campaign was to frame domestic anti-war leftists as the veterans', and thus the state's real enemies. Film and popular culture representations of Vietnam War veterans reified this image in the public imagination. In the aftermath of the war, an effluence of popular fiction in the form of movies and novels exalted Vietnam War veterans who struggled at home against a corrupt, abusive society.[10] The core, shared plot device in these works utilized the abused veterans' struggle as an allegory for a massive conflict that pitted masculinity, traditional values, patriotism, strength and order against femininity, queerness, amorality and naïve weakness. In this context, the promise of a connection to the "ancient" is, theoretically, fundamental to the emergence of this warrior identity.[11]

Warrior identity did not develop on an island, isolated from greater cultural processes. Rather than an archetype universal to humanity, it could be argued that the concept of warriordom as understood here may be a direct expression of, and exclusive to, western ontological schemas. Sociocultural anthropology observed long ago that the ontological categories of nature and culture powerfully structure western cognition. Anthropologist Philippe Descola termed this schema naturalism, further exploring how this shapes the ways in which people understand and relate to other people and beings around them (Descola, 2013). Understanding the warrior turn in contemporary society is facilitated by engagement with this schema. According to Descola, naturalism can be viewed as a category of nature within the realm of a kind of "natural law." In contrast, the realm of culture is contingent upon human thought and action. Historically, non-European "warriors" would have been seen as closer to nature than the colonial war machines of modern Europe. Within a world (predominantly the west) that still relies on this schema, identification with warrior identity entrenches behaviors that are ostensibly those of warriors within the realm of nature. Thus, the contemporary warrior's violence and alienation from society can be understood as nature in action, rather than a pathology of culture. Emergent warrior identities are not only translatable through ontologies of nature/culture dualisms, but these also reflect contemporary society's deep historical and nascent struggles with these categories. Climate change, globalization, civil rights campaigns, Indigenous/anti-colonial movements, and debates over land and resource management have powerfully challenged classic western assumptions about nature and culture. The warrior turn may be seen as an expression of western culture's attempt to muster a riposte to these challenges. Rather than an evil set out to conquer and oppress nature, the colonial violence of western society can be understood to *be* nature.

Today the rituals at American Lake are no longer seen as specific to Native American veterans and, likewise, Euro-American veterans no longer see "warriors" as something different from them. Though uncommon prior to the 21st century, the term has been widely embraced by contemporary veterans and others, such as domestic police (an approach and mindset that has recently come under well-deserved scrutiny), defense contractors, and even civilians who arm themselves to defend their families from threats. Veterans see themselves as warriors and less so as "citizens who served." Veterans who embrace the term warrior use it to mean a distinct kind of person, often imagined as a privileged caste in "warrior cultures" throughout human history. In contrast to World War II veterans who returned to the United States from war with the intent of strengthening their nation as civilians, contemporary veterans who embrace a warrior identity often feel an "otherness" in relation to civilians. This sense of otherness has been documented in scholarly works (MacLeish, 2013; Wool, 2015). However, instead of seeing veteran otherness as a public health concern in need of correction, the contemporary turn toward warriordom frames this otherness as normative and good for human social order. They come home with the intent of continuing to be warriors, strengthening their society through maintaining their inherent martial values.

This worldview has been reinforced by contemporary literature and media. One analogy for this, already popular from retired Lt. Col. David Grossman's 2004 book *On Combat*, achieved ubiquity after it appeared in the 2014 film *American Sniper*. This analogy posits that there are three kinds of people in the world. The vast majority of people are "sheep," who are virtually helpless and naïve about the dangers of the world. The remaining people are either "wolves," who prey on the sheep, or "sheepdogs," who protect the sheep from the wolves.

In applications to US society, the sheep represent the majority of citizens. Wolves are the criminals, terrorists and gangsters who are seen as constantly trying to penetrate our borders. The sheepdogs are the "warriors" of our society, a category that includes not only military personnel but increasingly domestic police as well. In his book, Grossman explains that the sheepdogs should expect to be disliked by the sheep for their brutality and disagreeable nature. But, he argues, the sheep do not realize how helpless they are and that it is only through the violence of the sheepdogs that they do not become the immediate prey of wolves. According to Grossman:

> We know that the sheep live in denial, that is what makes them sheep. They do not want to believe that there is evil in the world. They can accept the fact that fires can happen, which is why they want fire extinguishers, fire sprinklers, fire alarms and fire exits throughout their kids' schools. But many of them are outraged at the idea of putting an armed police officer in their kid's school. Our children are thousands of times more likely to be killed or seriously injured by school violence than fire, but the sheep's only response to the possibility of violence is denial. The idea of someone coming to kill or harm their child is just too hard, and so they chose the path of denial. The sheep generally do not like the sheepdog. He looks a lot like the wolf. He has fangs and the capacity for violence. The difference, though, is that the sheepdog must not, can not and will not ever harm the sheep. Any sheep dog who intentionally harms the lowliest little lamb will be punished and removed. The world cannot work any other way, at least not in a representative democracy or a republic such as ours. Still, the sheepdog disturbs the sheep. He is a constant reminder that there are wolves in the land. They would prefer that he didn't tell them where to go, or give them traffic tickets, or stand at the ready in our airports in camouflage

fatigues holding an M-16. The sheep would much rather have the sheepdog cash in his fangs, spray paint himself white, and go, "Baa." Until the wolf shows up. Then the entire flock tries desperately to hide behind one lonely sheepdog.

(Grossman, 2004)

Grossman has been training police for two decades to think of themselves as warriors. Recently, he has come under heavy criticism for his "bulletproof mind" training program that teaches cops to kill with less hesitation. When I first went to American Lake, I wondered if such notions of "warriordom" might inspire non-Native veterans to pursue healing in the sweat lodge community, seeing it as a form of warrior-specific therapy. The struggles of Vietnam War veterans were one of the primary motivations for the construction of the PTSD diagnosis and came to be seen as the signature wound of that war. However, PTSD is commonly diagnosed in the survivors of many kinds of trauma, including violent but morally neutral events like natural disasters and accidental car crashes.[12] As warriors who distinguish themselves from civilians, they can imagine postwar suffering to be unique and transcendent of PTSD, which can be experienced by civilians due to ostensibly less "profound" forms of trauma that can be treated by biomedicine in a clinical setting.[13] From my conversations with first-time attendees, I have learned that some veterans are attracted to the ceremonies for this very reason; first-time attendees often express that they anticipate that the ceremony is going to be "bad ass." However, the ceremony itself challenges these preconceived notions. Rather than a macho-warrior event where men demonstrate their strength and capacity to endure pain, the ceremony escorts veterans through a deeper and potentially more challenging journey that decidedly unravels the social contexts that buttress warriordom.

Mike Lee, the elder who leads ceremonies at American Lake, grew up on the Blackfeet Reservation in Montana and is a veteran of the Vietnam War. Many times, I have heard him share his wisdom with new attendees before they go into the lodge for the first time. In addressing the notion of "warriordom," Lee explains that the English word "warrior" is an artifact of European worldviews and Hollywood. It fails to adequately describe many of the Indigenous people, including his own ancestors, to whom it is applied. Even within contemporary North American society, Lee cautions that "a 'warrior' and a 'soldier' or 'veteran' are not exactly the same thing." The overwhelming brutality of western war, where people travel far from home and lay waste to foreign people and lands, would be incomprehensible to his ancestors. Lee explains, "Often, the goal was not even to kill but rather to take the enemy's spirit – challenge their bravery."

Though aspiring to primitive non-modernity, the warrior turn is in fact a medicalization of culture, folding masculinity and race in with science. Warriordom is evoked as a radical departure from modernity, but constructed to conform to modern biomedical logics.

As noted earlier, one of the primary justifications for creating a separate, decid-edly Indian space for healing was the argument that Native American veterans required special non-biomedical healing interventions due to their warrior cul-ture provenance. Biomedical PTSD therapy treats a neuro-physical disorder that manifests in response to chemical/hormonal changes that occur during moments of extreme fear. However, warrior cultures ostensibly relate to war violence in deeper, more categorically fundamental ways than do the modern soldiers who are meant to relate to war in a more professional, transactional manner. It warrants repeating here that this reflects the amorality of framings of war trauma that are intrinsic to the classic PTSD diagnosis. The marked treatment resistance of Native Americans diagnosed with PTSD was attributed to this fundamental difference in how these Indigenous veterans were understood to relate to war.

Conclusion

According to Eduardo Viveiros de Castro, warriordom as a concept is fundamen-tally a descriptor of relationships between "self" and "other" (Viveiros de Castro, 2004). A warrior can only exist in binary opposition to something else; as a sub-ject it exists in binary opposition to an enemy other, and as an object, it exists in binary opposition to a modern soldier self. From its inception after the Vietnam War, the healing community at American Lake has been a site of negotiation of these categories. Simultaneously, the United States (and the rest of the world as well) has also been negotiating the meaning and method of combat trauma. The ceremonial community at American Lake, though seen by many on the outside as a form of "alternative therapy" for military PTSD, is a remarkable focal point for healing the unique trauma of the Indigenous people who pursue it there. Its appeal and efficacy for the non-Indigenous people who experience healing there signals the depth and reach of the trauma that devastated Indigenous communities worldwide subsequent to the colonial project.

Notes

1 During the Colonial era, it was common for colonizing societies to portray colonized Indigenous people as ferocious. This continues today in environments such as the military, where Indigenous soldiers are often expected to be particularly fierce in battle (Holm, 1986).
2 During ceremonies and in other places, I often heard people use this term to refer broadly to values of simplicity and "ikčé" is translated as "common" and "wičháša" is translated as "man." However, it is noteworthy that the word "ikčé" can also be inter-preted to mean something more like "unmarked" or "regular" or "standard." For this reason, Lakota people have historically used the phrase "ikčé wičháša" (regular people) to refer to Native American people as opposed to other ethnicities of people they encountered after colonization.
3 Arvol Looking Horse is the 19th keeper of the pipe given by the White Buffalo Calf Woman. Though some people describe him as the "Chief of the Sioux," his role is as

spiritual leader for the three Western Sioux bands (Lakota, Dakota and Nakota) and bears closer resemblance to the role of the Dalai Lama in Tibet (with whom Looking Horse collaborates) than to the western concept of a "chief." As the keeper of the White Buffalo Calf pipe, Looking Horse's opinion on matters of Lakota spirituality is deeply influential. In 2003, he made a declaration sharing his position on the role of non-Lakota practice of Lakota faith. In spite of the high esteem that is held for Looking Horse by Lakota and non-Lakota people alike, his complex declaration remains controversial among people in and out of the Lakota nation.

4 This references the long practice of the United States government signing treaties that promised to respect Indigenous land rights and then stealing the land anyway.

5 VA officials worried that if their programming began to look too "religious," they would ultimately be bombarded by requests from every religious group represented among VA clientele to provide services specific to their respective religions (Scurfield, 1995).

6 This tension was identified by Raymond Scurfield (1995) during a review of Native American programming at the American Lake VA in the early 1990s. I also observed this tension, rarely, between participants during my time with the community.

7 This observation was also made during Scurfield's study (1995).

8 The sweat lodge ceremony itself is physically difficult and requires endurance of extreme heat in a dark, cramped enclosure, sometimes for a period of hours. Participants have to recover from it. Even regular participants rarely participate in more than two sweat ceremonies per month.

9 It isn't my intention to suggest that PTSD isn't "real" or to dismiss the array of traumatic experiences that are accounted for by the diagnosis. Rather, I hope to show that as a sociopolitical object, the PTSD diagnosis can be used to flatten the understanding of multiple complex social factors that contribute to human suffering after trauma.

10 In film, the *First Blood* series of films starring the fictional character John Rambo are exemplary of this. The *Missing in Action* franchise starring Chuck Norris exalts the (unsupported) hypothesis that the United States abandoned and covered up the existence of perhaps thousands of prisoners of war, who were purported to still be held in POW camps in Southeast Asia. This theme also appeared in films including *Uncommon Valor, Good Guys Wear Black,* and *P.O.W. The Escape.*

11 First applied through the stigmatization of Indigenous warriors as "primitive," this connection to the ancient is now pursued by non-Indigenous people who identify as warriors.

12 In the aftermath of the Vietnam War, the biomedical neutrality of the PTSD diagnosis's construction was beneficial to sufferers who understood themselves to be blamed for the war's violence and who were also framed as suffering due to their own weakness.

13 This recalls Ken MacLeish's argument that the nascent "moral injury" quasi-diagnosis is being normalized in part for the purpose of creating a category more profound than PTSD.

References

American Psychiatric Association. (1980). *Diagnostic and Statistical Manual of Mental Disorders* (Third Edition). Washington, DC: American Psychiatric Association.

Ault, A. (2020, November 11). The remarkable and complex legacy of Native American military service. *Smithsonian.* www.smithsonianmag.com/smithsonian-institution/remarkable-and-complex-legacy-native-american-military-service-180976264/.

Bucko, R. (1998). *The Lakota Ritual of the Sweat Lodge: History and Contemporary Practice.* Lincoln: University of Nebraska Press.

Clarke, A. (2014). Biomedicalization. In W.C. Cockerham, R. Dingwall & S. Quah (Eds.), *The Wiley Blackwell Encyclopedia of Health, Illness, Behavior, and Society*. Hoboken: Wiley-Blackwell.

Deloria, V. (2003). *God Is Red: A Native View of Religion*. Golden: Fulcrum. (Original work published 1972).

Descola, P. (2013). *Beyond Nature and Culture*. Chicago: University of Chicago Press.

Franklin, B. (1992). *M.I.A., or Mythmaking in America: How and Why Belief in Live POWs Has Possessed a Nation*. New York: Lawrence Hill Books.

Friedman, M.J., Ashcraft, M.L., Beals., J.L., Keane, T.M., Manson, S.M. & Marsella, A.J. (1997). *Matsunaga Vietnam Veterans Project* (Volume 1–2). West Haven: National Center for Posttraumatic Stress Disorder and National Center for American Indian and Alaska Native Mental Health Research.

Gibson, J.W. (1994). *Warrior Dreams: Violence and Manhood in Post-Vietnam America*. New York: Hill and Wang.

Grossman, D. (2004). *On Combat: The Psychology and Physiology of Deadly Conflict in War and Peace*. Paris: Hachette.

Holm, T. (1986). Culture, ceremonialism, and stress: American Indian veterans and the Vietnam War. *Armed Forces and Society* 12(2):237–251.

Holm, T. (1995). PTSD in native American Vietnam war veterans: a reassessment. *Wicazo Sa Review* 11(2):83–86.

Kulka, R.A., Schlenger, W.A., Fairbanks, J.A., Hough, R.L., Jordan, B.K., Marmar, C.R. & Cranston, A.S. (1990). *Trauma and the Vietnam War Generation: Report of Findings From the National Vietnam Veterans Readjustment Study*. New York: Brunner, Mazel.

LaDuke, W. (2013). *The Militarization of Indian Country*. Lansing: Makwa Enewed Press.

Lembcke, J. (1998). *The Spitting Image: Myth, Memory, and the Legacy of Vietnam*. New York: New York University Press.

Lifson, A. (2015). Veterans tackle PTSD with traditional Indian healing. *Humanities* 36(1). www.neh.gov/humanities/2015/januaryfebruary/statement/healing-spaces.

Lodono, E. (2020, August 30). 'A Hail Mary': psychedelic therapy draws veterans to jungle retreats. *The New York Times*.

Looking Horse, A. (2003, April 25). Looking horse proclamation on the protection of ceremonies. *Indian Country Today*. https://newsmaven.io/indiancountrytoday/archive/looking-horse-proclamation-on-the-protection-of-ceremonies-2IW86M5KiUm71NiBOX0PlA.

MacLeish, K. (2013). *Making War at Fort Hood: Life and Uncertainty in a Military Community*. Princeton: Princeton University Press.

Moghimi, Y. (2012). Anthropological discourses on the globalization of posttraumatic stress disorder (PTSD) in post-conflict societies. *Journal of Psychiatric Practice* 18(1):29–37.

Pearce, R. (1965). *The Savages of America: A Study of the Indian and the Idea of Civilization*. Baltimore: The Johns Hopkins University Press.

Schilling, V. (2018, September 13). By the numbers: a look at Native enlistment during the major wars. *Indian Country Today*.

Scurfield, R. (1995). Healing the warrior: admission of two American Indian war veteran cohort groups to a specialized PTSD inpatient unit. *American Indian and Alaska Native Mental Health Research* 6(3):1–22.

Sheehan, B. (1973). *Seeds of Extinction: Jeffersonian Philanthropy and the American Indian*. Chapel Hill: University of North Carolina Press.

Simkins, J. & Barrett, C. (2019, November 15). A warrior tradition: why Native Americans continue fighting for the same government that tried to wipe them out. *Military Times*.

Stein, D., Seedat, S., Iverson, A. & Wesseley, S. (2007). Post-traumatic stress disorder: medicine and politics. *The Lancet* 369(9556):139–144.

TallBear, K. (2013). *Native American DNA: Tribal Belonging and the False Promise of Genetic Science*. Minneapolis: University of Minnesota Press.

TallBear, K. (2015). Quoted in T.P.K. Tengan, T.K. Kaulukukui, Jr. & W.K. Richards, Jr. The face of Ku: a dialogue on Hawaiian warriorhood. In R.A. Innes & K. Anderson (Eds.), *Indigenous Masculinities: Legacies, Identities, Regeneration*. Winnipeg: University of Manitoba Press.

Telonidis, T. (2012, May 28). In sweat lodge, veterans find healing down to the core. *NPR*.

Tengan, T.P.K. (2008). *Native Men Remade: Gender and Nation in Contemporary Hawai'i*. Durham: Duke University Press.

Tengan, T.P.K., Kaulukukui, Jr., T.K. & Richards, Jr., W.K. (2015). The face of Ku: a dialogue on Hawaiian warriorhood. In R.A. Innes & K. Anderson (Eds.), *Indigenous Masculinities: Legacies, Identities, Regeneration*. Winnipeg: University of Manitoba Press.

Vergun, D. (2021, November 1). *DOD Honors Native Americans and Their Many Contributions to the Nation*. U.S. Department of Defense. www.defense.gov/News/Feature-Stories/Story/Article/2825658/dod-honors-native-americans-and-their-many-contributions-to-the-nation/.

Viola, H. (2008). *Warriors in Uniform: The Legacy of American Indian Heroism*. Washington, DC: National Geographic.

Viveiros de Castro, E. (2004). Exchanging perspectives: the transformation of objects into subjects in Amerindian cosmologies. *Common Knowledge* 10(3):463–484.

White Hat, A. (1999). *Reading and Writing the Lakota Language*. Salt Lake City: University of Utah Press.

Wool, Z. (2015). *After War: The Weight of Life at Walter Reed*. Durham: Duke University Press.

Young, A. (1997). *The Harmony of Illusions: Inventing Post-Traumatic Stress Disorder*. Princeton: Princeton University Press.

6

JINNS AND TRAUMA

Unbounded Spirits and the Ontology of Mental Illness in Pakistan

Sanaullah Khan

Introduction

After 9/11, the Pakistani state joined hands with America in the global war on terror. The Pakistani State began its own operations against homegrown militants, because of accusations from the United States about not doing "enough" (US Government Publishing Office, 2016). The war led to the deaths of 70,000 Pakistani citizens through terror attacks and counter-offensives by the Pakistan Army (Crawford, 2018). Meanwhile, many thousands continued to be displaced due to the US drone strikes in areas known since colonial times as Federally Administered Tribal Areas (FATA), until their merger with the neighboring province of Khyber Pakhtoonkhwa in 2018 (Maqsood, 2019). Multiple factors such as suspicion toward the state, a dearth of psychiatrists to provide treatment to those experiencing mental illness, and, I argue, a denial of patients' ontological realities made them much more likely to visit local healers than state-run psychiatric institutes.

Populations which had been displaced due to conflict experienced a range of mental health problems such as post-traumatic stress disorder (PTSD), depression and anxiety. This was accompanied by the strict surveillance of everyday life. Many continued to refer to their experiences of dissociative states as forms of jinn affliction in which they experienced periodic unconsciousness accompanied by the experience of "multiple personalities," attributed to self and non-human agents (referred to in Islamic contexts as jinns) (World Health Organization, 2022; Verweijen, 2015). The kind of dissociated states expressed in scenes of healing may be interpreted from a biomedical lens as the loss of bodily, emotional and subjective "integration" as defined by the DSM-5, but the question I am interested in asking is how such states are interpreted by healers and families as they

DOI: 10.4324/9781003311843-10

borrow spiritual ideas about health and disease in the context of displacement, Islamic revivalism and war in contemporary Pakistan.

Local healers, some of whom served in the army, or those who had been displaced, provided treatment for jinn afflictions by taming memories and spirits representing "multiple selves" and attempting to make them cohabitate with their human counterparts. The resort to traditional healing has to be understood in the context of the lack of recognition of people's social experiences of illness and the coloniality of state-run psychiatric institutions, as I will describe below, which results in many illnesses to be normalized and thus under-diagnosed (Philbin, 2014; Yu, 2013; Estroff et al., 1991; Foucault, 2006). I have discussed elsewhere the suspicions around mental illness and accusations of malingering by the state, especially toward soldiers, under conditions of colonialism in India (Khan, 2022), and a similar concern is raised by Roberto Beneduce in his chapter in this present volume, when he suggests the need to consider simultaneously the genealogy of suspicion and of trauma.

In this chapter, I first consider how in the context of Islamic revivalism and the increasing burden of mental illness, people understand recovery in terms of moral transformation and the need to become pietistic subjects. Then I show how conversations between jinns and Sufi healers involve domesticating spirits and making them live peacefully with their human counterparts through their conversion to Islam (*shahadat*). Finally, I ask how religious obedience is considered essential to keep symptoms of affliction at bay. In so doing, I also ask how the lines between jinns, *nafs* (souls) and the unconscious become blurry, which helps us consider how dualisms based on mind and body, and splits between the self and other, underpinning western biomedicine and psychiatric discourse, are put under pressure. Methodologically, the data used in the chapter were collected through household surveys in Pakistan, participant observations with two healers in Rawalpindi and Lahore, and interviews and participant observation in a state-run psychiatric hospital in Lahore during 2021. In the sections below, I refer to the voices of entities other than the patient during healing sessions as those of the jinns'. The reason for doing this is to take people's understanding of the etiologies of illness seriously without imposing any external ideas of selfhood.

The Coloniality of Mental Health

During colonial rule in Pakistan, with the passing of the Lunacy Act of 1912, the role of the magistrate became central in referring people to psychiatric hospitals (Mills, 2000). This power was often exercised to remove vagrants from the streets (Ibid.). The magistrate's help would also be sought strategically by families in order to admit relatives in psychiatric hospitals. These powers were instituted in the figure of the magistrate in 1912, and have existed to this day, even with the passing of the Punjab mental health ordinance of 2001, which has sought to de-criminalize mental health. Existing histories of colonial asylums in South Asia have thrown light on the way asylums classified populations based on social class and ethnicity (Arnold, 1993). In the postcolonial context, the power of the magistrate remained central in the admission of the prisoner in a mental hospital. Even with the government's attempt to de-criminalize mental health, family members still seek to admit patients to exclude them from households or to extract revenge.

Historians and anthropologists have commented on how diagnoses in South Asia could be used strategically by families to reinstate patriarchal authority when it was challenged by the sick (Waxlar, 1977; Mills, 2000). To this day, institutionalization implies families trying to get rid of troublesome members, which plays a significant role in stigmatizing mental health services. This perception continues to plague psychiatric hospitals. Occasionally on my way to meet psychiatrists in one of the oldest psychiatric hospitals in the country, whose offices were next to inpatient wards, I would hear voices of patients begging me to get them a phone so they could call their relatives. Some patients, roaming around with friends, or mowing lawns and helping in the preparation of meals, shared that they had been left by their loved ones many decades ago and no longer maintained any connection with them. It took over a week for the family to finally be able to admit the member, but this too was possible only by bribing or using connections with relatives already in the hospital bureaucracy (*taluqaat*) to facilitate the institutionalization of the sick.

Using mental health discourses to admit patients also means that minorities such as Christian groups continue to be targeted. During the ongoing war on terror and the increase in political and sectarian violence since the early 2000s, policing of neighborhoods and targeting or minorities based on blasphemy accusations and sedition charges has been on a rise. While initially the state considered psychological causes as mitigating factors in acts of blasphemy, there were new forms of state-led violence experienced by these individuals in prisons. As I learned in my fieldwork, prisoners were construed indefinitely as mentally unfit to stand their trials, which exposed them to new forms of bureaucratic violence.

During the 1920s, after the assassination of a publisher of a book named *Rangila Rasul*, published in Lahore, Punjab and under pressure from the Muslim community, the administration of the British Raj enacted Hate Speech Law Section 295(A), a part of the Criminal Law Amendment Act XXV. This made it a criminal offence to insult the founders or leaders of any religious community. After the creation of Pakistan in 1947, anti-blasphemy laws and clauses were introduced in Pakistan's Penal Code. From 1967 to 2014, over 1,300 people were accused of blasphemy, with Muslims constituting most of those accused. More than 75 people were murdered for blasphemy between 1987 and 2017. The punishment for blasphemy is life in prison or death sentence. In a curious combination, blasphemy laws and the remnants of the Lunacy Act have been used to screen any signs of disrespect toward Islam and the Prophet Muhammad in the ongoing war on terror.

In the Imdad Ali and Safia Bano murder cases, the court relied upon precedents from *Khizer Hayat vs. the State* which had used *The State vs. Balahari Das Sutradhar* to reject the plea of the convict and "observed that not every person who is mentally disturbed or is suffering from some mental illness (es) is ipso facto, exempted from criminal liability" (C.R.P. 420, 2016, p. 20). However, when reviewed in the Supreme Court, it was decided that

> in the view of the medical opinion placed on record regarding the mental health conditions of convicts Imdad Ali and Kaneezan Bibi, we [the Supreme Court] direct the Government of Punjab to immediately shift them from prison to Punjab Institute of Mental Health, Lahore for treatment and rehabilitation. . . . They shall be released from the hospital as and when the said Medical Board opines that they are fit for themselves and for society.
>
> *(Ibid., p. 47)*

Prisoners interpreted their delusions, such as having seen the Prophet Muhammad, as signs of divine inspiration whereas the state viewed such experiences and expressions as acts of blasphemy. In contrast to the scientific rationality of psychiatric care, prisoners defended their "blasphemy" by recourse to a more spiritual logic. During my research in the Out-Patient Department in Lahore, I also observed patient-prisoners brought for their regular treatment to the hospital. Prisoners tied to each other through chains and handcuffed would be accompanied by policemen (in almost all cases men), who sat right next to them waiting for the patient-prisoners to have their turns for check-ups. The officers and patient-prisoners could be seen chatting with each other. In the gray zones of bureaucracy, I saw police officers variously sympathizing with prisoners, and also defending the scientific-rationality invoked by the courts. The intimate conversations between the police officers and the mentally ill showed how mental illness was treated with ambivalence – in some cases officers sat and listened intently to the spiritual experiences of the patients, and in other cases, the officers' respect for spirituality was overridden by a punitive attitude toward prisoners. In this chapter, though, my concern is not so much with psychiatric institutions, but the healers to whom patients turn under conditions of political violence and poor psychiatric care.

Recovery and Moral Transformations

During my household surveys in Pakistan, a mother-in-law referred to the daughter-in-law's depression as a product of her daughter-in-law's *hasad* (jealousy). She referred to her condition by saying, "She is dying in the fire of her own jealousy (*hasad*)." Often families viewed family conflicts and jealousies as a cause of mental illness but the only solution to them was to engage oneself in the remembrance of God. It was not enough to simply bear markers of piety, but one was also expected to embody patience and love for others. In many cultures, the locus of psychopathology may in fact be the family instead of individuals, where possession by spirits gives expression to the deep impacts of broader socio-economic changes and modernization upon families (Ong, 2010). Afflictions, especially those by supernatural entities, may also be considered to be transmissible from one person to another (Skultans, 1987). This means that just as illness is shaped by pressures in kinship, affliction may implicate multiple individuals. Thus healing, as I observed, entailed providing relief not only to the patient but the relation causing an illness. Illness evokes not only the question of *how* but *why*, as Evans-Prichard showed among the Azande, and gives voice to structural inequalities and family jealousies (Evans-Prichard, 1976).

Anthropologists have considered the ways in which illness allows patients and their families to craft narratives around moral struggles (Mattingly, 2014). Anthropologists have also considered moral striving as present even in conditions of psychosis which represent breakdowns through which patients try to arduously regain a semblance of normality (Zigon, 2007). Healing of mental illness is effective because it helps to pacify tense relations among family members, which are understood to be caused by jinns. Healing entails, I argue, turning the patient into a pietistic subject who is spiritually cleansed. Another aspect of treatment in this context includes getting the jinns to accept *shahadat* to enter the fold of Islam in order that they may learn to live peaceably with the patient.

In Rawalpindi, at the Islamic healer's *astana* (gateway), I observed large crowds in which people had come from all around Pakistan to seek treatment for what most described as *jadoo* or magic. Some had even come from as far as Afghanistan for their treatment. The healer, Ahmed, belonged to the Qadria Silsila, a major order in South Asian Sufi Islam. His son mentioned,

He felt spiritual energy within himself over 25 years ago during his employment in the Pakistan Army. . . . During those days, Pir Ahmed sought the guidance of his mentors and other spiritual scholars who informed Pir Ahmed sahib about Allah's blessing on him as well as his capability of spiritual power. He was advised to leave the army and concentrate on his spiritual learning and relation with Allah through prayers.

Often jinns professed identities that pre-existed national divisions. Many of these jinns claimed to be Hindus. Ahmed used verses of the Quran to invite jinns to appear through the bodies of the patients without touching the patient physically (Csordas, 1994). Other healers, with whom I worked, used force and were involved in showcasing their strength to the jinn by physically holding or restraining patients under possession. One patient had been brought by his aunt's son to Ahmed. The Afghan patient said after his treatment, "I had stomach problems (*mayday ka masla*) and I went to many doctors but received treatment only when I came here." The jinn had supposedly left the body after Ahmed had converted the jinn and asked him to repeat the *shahadat* to convert him to Islam.[1] The crowd rejoiced the moment as Ahmed used a range of performances, anger, persuasion and empathy as "semiotic ideologies," that served as privileged channels for divine apprehension (Engelke, 2007; Keane, 2018).

While 19th-century psychiatrists like Jean-Martin Charcot would have considered the emergence of different voices among patients as "hysteria," I ask what implications such a type of treatment has for the cultivation of ethical selves. I use this observation to ask how traditional healing involves the creation of a pious self, but more importantly, the continual regulation of pious selves by warding off the effects of sinning which make a patient vulnerable to afflictions by jinns (Mahmood, 2011). My questions are informed by the work of Ahmed Ragab (2018), who shows how healing in medieval Islamic hospitals involved creating pious subjects. Without having to resort to psychoanalytic notions such as the "unconscious," which arguably retain core dualisms of western psychological thought, I consider *nafs* as a central category, understood in the medieval Islamic context as the Islamic counterpart of Greek pneuma or breath, to open an ontological space for considering a site that bears the residual impacts of hostilities in kinship and wider political traumas.

The word *nafs* also forms the root of the Urdu world *nafsiyat* (used for psychology) showing close connections between spiritual and psychological recovery, at least etymologically. Sufi Islam posits a complex relationship between soul expressed in a spiritual dualism between the *nafs*, the vital self or the eternal soul, the *ruh*. The move toward self-purification is considered as the transformation of the self, the *nafs*, through a transcendence of bodily needs. *Nafs* in some contexts may even be referred to as the *shaytan's* sister (Pandolfo, 2018, p. 315). By totally denying the self, however, the *nafs* is purified and may in the context of saints, even return to instruct the living (Werbner, 2003). In dying, the *nafs* is therefore eternalized. Conversely when one is alive, *nafs* has to be morally cultivated for the pious self to emerge through remembrance of God. Scholars have also differentiated between *nafs* in its different states, such as *nafs al-ammarah* where the *nafs* incites evil (Schimmel, 1975), *nafs-luwwamah* where the *nafs* aspires for perfection, and *nafs al-mutaminnah*, when the *nafs* is at peace, which is the perfect state for any believer.

An ontological space of engagement with non-human agents is opened by treating bodies as porous to spiritual affliction and treatable through divine redemption. Untrammeled desires have been seen, among Islamic thinkers, as causing disorders of the soul since medieval times. These questions acquire a new salience in the context of political conflict and modernization in contemporary Pakistan. Translated works of medieval Islamic thinkers show the intersections between desire and the disturbances of the soul. Ibn Sina (2005) suggested in the *Metaphysics of Healing* that only a virtuous soul could be prepared to suffer the agony of detachment from the body upon death, and it was this separation toward which the believer needed to devote his or her energies. Al-Razi (1950), wrote about how excessive appetite of the soul led to melancholia. He wrote in *Spiritual Physic,*

> Excess in the rational soul is proved when a man is so swayed and overmastered by the consideration of such things as these that the appetitive soul cannot obtain the food and sleep and so forth to keep the body fit, or in sufficient quantity to maintain the temperament of the brain in a healthy state. Such a man is forever seeking and probing and striving to the utmost of his powers, supposing that he will attain and realize these matters in a shorter time than that which is absolutely necessary for their achievement. The result is that the temperament of the whole body is upset, so that he falls prey to depression and melancholia and he misses his entire quest through supposing that he could quickly master it.
>
> (*p. 32*)

How are magical practices as causes of jinn affliction detected through frameworks of piety in the engagement between the patient's family, the healer and the jinn? To answer this question, it would be necessary to explore how affliction is seen as caused by the *nafs*. One father had come to Ahmed and complained that he saw *beysharmi* (shamelessness) in the eyes of his son. Ahmed the healer asked the jinn to become present (*haziri*) by reciting a few verses. The child's voice, now visibly different, became furious and responded to Ahmed's question, "I used to annoy him, did not let him study, used to disturb his mother and used to steal." Ahmed asked the jinn, "Does the child have *mirghi* [epilepsy] or not?" The child's father added that he had once taken the child to neurosurgeon, but it did not help. The jinn added, "I didn't let him eat." When asked about how the jinn had impacted the child's health, he said, "I used to give him pain in his legs and head." Then Ahmed asked if the jinn had come through a *taweez* (amulet). The jinn replied, "There is a woman, a bad woman, she is their relative. Afzal's mother." The father interjected, "She is a very pious woman [*woh tou bohat naik aurat hai*]." Ahmed said, "Don't believe him, this is the *shaytan*." Thus, piety or its lack thereof resulted in accusations and counter-accusations about the identity of the bewitcher, which was something strategically concealed by the healer to avoid causing any further conflict in the family.

Later, the jinn continued about how he had been responsible in destroying the father's business. The session ends with Ahmed asking the healer to remove all the afflictions. The father used the occasion to inquire about what the jinn had done to the younger sister, if it was mirghi [epilepsy] or *jinnat* (plural of jinn). Thus, the jinn could also provide an insight into the health of other family members who had been afflicted as mentioned earlier. The slippage between infractions by *shaytan* (satan) and afflictions by jinn, in other words, the moral weakness of a self, showed the workings of the *nafs*, which represents base and uncultivated human instincts that need to be ethically cultivated and restrained for the pious self to emerge. Jinns afflict where *nafs* has not been tamed or brought control. Piety interestingly also provided a lens to determine whether the identity of the one behind the magic, revealed in conversation with the jinn, was true or not.

Piety also allowed jinns to peaceably cohabit with the jinn. Bilqees, a 50-year-old jinn, who had supposedly afflicted the patient Sammaiya, said, "We also have a world. We also live in this world." She continued, "Some jinns are dangerous. I was captured. The magician was behind it. The girl (patient) was pious. I got attached to her. I was harassed by some healers. They touched me at the wrong places. They did not have much power. As soon as I heard the *kalima*, I began to feel better."[2] The jinn then said, "Please read the Quran for spiritual benefits (*Iman kay lyay Quran ko khola karein*)." The jinn then left the body and the patient's voice reemerged. Summaiya, the patient, said that while the jinn destroyed her home, she had become subservient to her. She said, "My sisters could not get married. Brothers left home. It is all because of the *faiz* (benefit) from Pir Sahab that I feel better." Thus, conversion to Islam and reaffirming faith in the unity of God were seen as prerequisites to the integration of the jinn with the human self.

Taming Jinns

The heterotrophic character of jinn rites blurs distinctions between the distant past and the present, and while the rites transcend time-space dimensions, they also provide a moment to experience political history as personal memory (Taneja, 2017; Kwon, 2008). It is important to note that some jinns, even in a country where the majority is Muslim, claim to be Hindus. As Crapanzano has suggested, foreign names of jinns invoke the globally circulating images and technologies that jinn rites now incorporate (Crapanzano, 1980). Jinns do not follow the temporalities of the nation-state, but healers tried to make them co-habit with their human counterparts through *shahadat* or conversion to Islam. Some jinns were hundreds of years old. For instance, in one case, a Hindu jinn emerged aggressively when Ahmed, the healer, asked him to swear by the name of Kali (Hindu goddess) that he was going to tell the truth. When asked about the damage to the patient's health, the jinn said, "I gave him diabetes; I destroyed his kidneys and was behind his divorce." Ahmed asked Raju if he could leave after the amulet was taken out. Ahmed asked a *muakkal* to do *parwaaz* (flight), and to get all the *putlay* out.[3] Ahmed asks the *muakkal* who engages with the jinn to hold the jinn and to beat him if necessary. Later Raju, the jinn, is asked to remove all the nails from the kidneys and the neck. The patient's sibling adds, "All his tests are fine, and the doctor says everything is alright. But we still don't know what's wrong with the patient."

One Hindu jinn admitted that he worshipped Kali Mata, a Hindu goddess. He admits that the magician had asked him to make sure that the patient's mind did not work anymore. His brother adds during the engagement between Ahmed and the jinn: "We had a shop in Dubai. Everything has been devastated. The situation at home is also really bad. His [the patient's] eyes turn red, and he hits people. Everyone in the house is worried because of him." After the patient regains consciousness, his brother continues, "As long as he takes his medicine, he is fine. His mind just shuts off." The patient himself adds, "When I feel unwell, I feel very dizzy (*cheezein ghoomti hein*)." His brother added, "He fights a lot with his brother. We give him a sleeping pill to make him sleep because he just becomes uncontrollable." Upon regaining consciousness, he mentions notable differences in how he felt.

In other cases, jinns have claimed to have caused pancreatic dysfunction (*lablaba kamzoor kiya*) or loss of memory (*hafiza kamzoor*). Another Hindu jinn said that he made the patient kill his child. He said, "I swear by Bhagwan, I was the one who got him [the patient] to kill his child. I destroyed his mind." The jinn was also responsible for creating indebtedness. The affliction was caused by brother-in-law's wife (*bhabi*). He also admitted to making the patient lose his mind (*dimag kharab kar diya hai*). The patient was from Naushera, when asked if the jinn actually made him kill the child (after regaining consciousness) he agreed. He said, "At 12 one night, he was lying in another room. I made him drank acid [*tehzaab*]." The patient shared that he had been to Peshawar, Mardan and Swabi but with little success. The jinn refused to convert but promised not to return again. Thus, there was a range of negotiations that need to be undertaken to keep the influences of the jinn at bay. Jinn afflictions also allowed people to invoke a more "displaced" or a "distributed" form of agency than is conventionally permitted by the singular subject of western psychiatric discourses.

The healer exerted considerable force over the jinn, fluctuating between letting the jinn converse, but also demonstrating his power to audiences, by causing the jinn, as well as the human agent (whose body had been occupied as a medium) to suffer. The healer's attempt to create a relationship of dominance over the jinn also meant making the jinn become subordinate to the patient's will. The immense spiritual power and the paternal touch of the healer was necessary to get the jinn to leave the human subject or to come to live with it peaceably.

Existing studies in Pakistan have shown that there are at least three categories of supernatural beings who can help in such operations – a dead person's spirit who had emerged from the graveyard, a jinn, or a *pari* (Csáji, 2011). However, there are also instances when the jinn is asked to be burnt, especially when the jinn is insistent in not leaving the patient. Another jinn told Ahmed that he was from the Hindu Jati, and continued to resist Ahmed's demands.[4] He said,

> Rohani (spiritual) operation does not work on me. The patient had a dream about you. Initially I thought it was the Prophet, but then I realized that it was someone else. I have taught *bhashan* (Hindi word for speech) to him. I am a Brahmin and have married him. He used to always be with his wife, and I did not like them, so I got them to fight with each other. Now I cannot leave him, nor live without him.

The jinn says, "If I stay with him, he will remain unconscious." Ahmed replies, "You can stay with him as long as you become Muslim." After reciting the *kalima* behind Ahmed, the jinn says, "I have become a Muslim, please call me Hussein from now." Thus, in a lot of cases, the goal was not to completely destroy the jinn or to detach him from the agent, but to make it live with its human counterpart. Having discussed the treatment provided by Ahmed, an army veteran and healer in viewing *nafs* as the site of afflictions and attempts to improve patients' symptoms by integrating the jinn and the patient, I now consider spiritual power as a tool to combat the afflictions caused jinns.

Piety, Obedience and Recovery

There is also a push to recognize that some maladies are simply untreatable, except through spiritual guidance. In one case, a jinn claimed to have been from the British Army, speaking in broken English but in a British accent. This is followed by another voice, a person who appears to serve as a mediator between the British jinn and the healer. The latter spirit admits to the spiritual power of the healer by saying,

> There is a lot of spiritual power, your *buzurg auliya* (religious elders), and it starts from Sheikh Amir Qadir Jilani, and you are provided with *shifa* (cure).

What is important to consider here is how the ability to heal is understood to be inherited in a master–discipline relation within the Sufi order, where the healer in a way comes to imbibe curative powers via his link to a Sufi saint. The patient's son, who is in the police, says that he had grown up witnessing his father having frequent *dauras* (seizures) when jinns became present (*hazir*). He also had to be taken to the hospital periodically, until he was brought to Ahmed.

In other cases, some physicians and psychiatrists even deferred to the authority of spiritual leaders for the treatment of soldiers, when they felt that they were not able to fully understand the patients' causes of illness. One officer had been deployed to Kohat. One night he went to an empty hill. He found an empty cooking pot. He was curious to open it to see what was inside. As soon as he opened it, he experienced a strange smell. He found the smell unbearable and began running back toward his unit. When he was running, he heard a voice, "I am leaving you because you are a Sayyid. If you were not a Sayyid, I would have killed you" (O'Brien, 2001, p. 224; Spadola, 2013).[5] With this voice resounding in his head, he reached his unit, out of breath and full of sweat. He said that he was taken to the hospital where doctors could not come up with a cure. He said that the military doctors "accepted their shortcoming" and advised him to consult a pir (Sufi leader). When he went to the pir, he told him that to prevent the effect of the spirit, he could not afford to miss even a single prayer. He said,

> My pir has told me to always remain in a state of *wuzu* and to never miss my prayers if I wanted to maintain my sanity.[6]

I interpret this episode as suggesting both the limitation of medical expertise and the role of piety in safeguarding the person's mental well-being, which was thought to be affected by jinns and magic. Thus, obedience to a religious elder, which could result in new spiritual challenges due to greater intensity of satanic inclinations (*waswasay*) was another pre-condition of successful healing.

During my fieldwork with Muhammad, a healer who had been displaced from Waziristan after war, one patient said that he was constantly being bothered by the jinn. He said, "As soon as I leave here, I begin to be bothered. I am really tired." Muhammad had earlier suggested *bayt*, but now he said that he was going to send a *muakkal* with him.[7] *Muakkal*, a word derivative of *wakil*, was an invisible entity, used to negotiate with the jinn, bearing qualities of jinns (fire) as well as angels (light). The invocation of the *muakkal* showed the blurry lines between spiritual and malevolent uses of spirits for affliction and treatment (Khan, 2006). Affliction could be caused when the patient was impious, and the causes of witchcraft were similarly attributed to those who lacked signs of piety. Yet greater piety also exposed individuals to a greater exposure to the mischief of the *shaytan* to divert the patient from faith.

One soldier had been traumatized during operations in Waziristan. He mentioned that he was from Chakwal and only knew Punjabi, hence proving that the jinn and the patient were separate entities, as the latter conversed in Pushto. After convincing the jinn to convert to Islam by getting a Pushto-speaking patient from the audience to converse with the jinn, Ahmed prays with the crowd, "Allah please give him strength to safeguard the frontiers of the country." Ahmed now says, "The doctors thought that he had been completely finished mentally (*Dimaagi taur pay bilkul khatam hogya hai*). He could not speak, talk or move. He had a *rohani* (spiritual) problem, *not a medical problem*." Ahmed proudly declares that the problem was not so much with the brain as much as related to affliction by the jinn.

Conclusion

The undetachability of the jinn in a lot of cases means that healers play an important role to keep patients' afflictions at bay through various kinds of negotiations. Moreover, the chapter has considered how jinns reveal temporalities that exceed imaginaries of the nation-state, where healers are involved in taming the unbounded nature of jinns to make them peacefully co-habit with their human counterparts. The healer takes the jinn's conversion to Islam (*shahadat*) as the only way to make it habitable with its human counterpart. The coloniality of mental health and the poor conditions of psychiatric hospitals in the country have meant that the Islamic healer is often the first person to visit in the patient's hierarchy of resort (Schwartz, 1969). The costs of warfare in Pakistan have been great, and given the poor conditions of psychiatric hospitals and a wide-ranging distrust in them, both civilians and servicemembers visit local healers for their psychiatric problems. Instead of relying on patient–physician encounters within a strictly biomedical setting, this chapter explores what it means to think about jinn affliction as giving expression to the maddening effects of political violence and domestic conflicts during the ongoing war on terror. Jinn afflictions further raise ontological questions about what it means to be sick, as they also reveal how unconscious experiences can be shaped by both individual and collective memories, especially as collective memories permeate the intimate relations between self and other. In this context, the work of the healer entails re-integrating the jinn with the patient. This is possible only through ethical cultivation as well as through reliance on the spiritual power of Sufi lineages.

Notes

1 *Shahadat* refers to the belief in the oneness of God and the finality of Prophet Muhammad. It is also used for the act of testifying (being a witness) or for martyrdom.
2 Kalima is the formal content of *shahadat* which is "There is no God but Allah, and Muhammad is the messenger of Allah."
3 *Putlay* are miniature objects used for sympathetic magic.
4 Jati is used for one's caste but can also be used for tribe or one's kin belonging.
5 Families who can trace their lineage to the prophet refer to themselves as Sayyid. Healing also involves a class element, as Susan O'Brien has put it succinctly in the case of Kano, "Forms of involvement with the spirit world index distinctions of class, education and gender" (O'Brien, 2001, p. 224).
6 Ablution required before praying.
7 *Bayt* refers to taking allegiance on the hands of a religion figure. After taking *bayt* on the hands of Sufi pirs, they are typically consulted for everyday affairs, as they are considered to have a privileged connection with the divine. Bayt also brings the follower or a disciple (*mureed*) directly in the lineage of religious figures that often go all the way back to the Prophet or his companions.

References

Al-Razi, I.Z. (1950). *The Spiritual Physick of Rhazes*. London: Butler and Tanner.

Arnold, D. (1993). *Colonizing the Body: State, Medicine and Epidemic Disease in 19th Century India*. Berkeley: University of California Press.

Crapanzano, V. (1980). *Tuhami: Portrait of a Moroccan*. Chicago: University of Chicago Press.

Crawford, N. (2018). Human cost of the post 9/11 wars: lethality and the need for transparency. In *Costs of War*. Providence, RI: Watson Institute for International and Public Affairs, Brown University.

C.R.P. 420. (2016). *The Supreme Court of Pakistan*. https://www.supremecourt.gov.pk/downloads_judgements/c.r.p._420_2016.pdf.

Csáji, L.K. (2011). Flying with the vanishing fairies: typology of the shamanistic traditions of the Hunza. *Anthropology of Consciousness* 22(2):159–187.

Csordas, T. (1994). *The Sacred Self: A Cultural Phenomenology of Charismatic Healing*. Berkeley: University of California Press.

Engelke, M. (2007). *A Problem of Presence: Beyond Scripture in an African Church*. Berkeley: University of California Press.

Estroff, S.E., Lachicotte, W.S., Illingworth, L.C. & Johnston, A. (1991). Everybody's got a little mental illness: accounts of illness and self among people with severe, persistent mental illnesses. *Medical Anthropology Quarterly* 5(4):331–369.

Evans-Prichard, E.E. (1976). *Witchcraft, Oracles and Magic Among the Azande*. Oxford: Oxford University Press.

Foucault, M. (2006). *Michel Foucault: Psychiatric Power: Lectures at the Collège de France, 1973–1974*. London: Palgrave Macmillan.

Ibn Sina. (2005). *The Metaphysics of Healing*. Provo: Brigham Young University Press.

Keane, W. (2018). On semiotic ideology. *Signs and Society* 6(1):64–87.

Khan, N. (2006). Of children and jinn: an inquiry into an unexpected friendship during uncertain times. *Cultural Anthropology* 21(2):234–264.

Khan, S. (2022). Medicine and the critique of war: military psychiatry, social classification and the malingering patient in colonial India. *Medical History* 66(1):47–63.

Kwon, H. (2008). *Ghosts of War in Vietnam*. Cambridge: Cambridge University Press.

Mahmood, S. (2011). *Politics of Piety: The Islamic Revival and the Feminist Subject*. Princeton: Princeton University Press.

Maqsood, A. (2019). The social life of rumors: uncertainty in everyday encounters between the military, Taliban and Tribal Pushtun in Pakistan. *Comparative Journal of South Asia, Africa and Middle East* 39(3):462–474.

Mattingly, C. (2014). *Moral Laboratories: Family Peril and the Struggle for a Good Life*. Berkeley: University of California Press.

Mills, J. (2000). *Madness, Cannabis and Colonialism: The 'Native Only' Lunatic Asylums of British India 1857–1900*. Basingstoke: Palgrave Macmillan.

O'Brien, S. (2001). Spirit discipline: gender, Islam, and hierarchies of treatment in post-colonial Northern Nigeria. *Interventions: International Journal of Postcolonial Studies* 3(2):222–241.

Ong, A. (2010). *Spirits of Resistance and Capitalism Discipline: Factory Women in Malaysia*. Albany: State University of New York Press.

Pandolfo, S. (2018). *Knot of the Soul: Madness, Psychoanalysis, Islam*. Chicago: University of Chicago Press.

Philbin, M.M. (2014). 'What I got to go through': normalization and HIV-positive adolescents. *Medical Anthropology* 33(4):288–302.

Ragab, A. (2018). *Piety and Patienthood in Medieval Islam*. Abingdon: Routledge.

Schimmel, A. (1975). *Mystical Dimensions of Islam*. Chapel Hill: University of North Carolina Press.

Schwartz, L.R. (1969). The hierarchy of resort in curative practices: the Admiralty Islands, Melanesia. *Journal of Health and Social Behavior* 10(3):201–209.

Skultans, V. (1987). The management of mental illness among Maharastrian families: a case study of a Mahanubhav healing temple. *Man* 22(4):661–679.

Spadola, E. (2013). *The Calls of Islam: Sufis, Islamists, and Mass Mediation in Urban Morocco*. Bloomington: Indiana University Press.

Taneja, A.V. (2017). *Jinneaology: Time, Islam and Ecological Thought in the Medieval Ruins of Delhi*. Redwood City: Stanford University Press.

U.S. Government Publishing Office. (2016). *Pakistan: Friend or Foe in the Fight Against Terrorism? Joint Hearing Before the Subcommittee on Terrorism, Non-Proliferation and Trade*. Serial No. 114–173. www.govinfo.gov/content/pkg/CHRG-114hhrg20742/html/CHRG-114hhrg20742.htm.

Verweijen, J. (2015). *The Ambiguity of Militarization*. Doctoral Dissertation. Utrecht: Utrecht University.

Waxlar, N.E. (1977). Is mental illness cured in traditional societies? A theoretical analysis. *Culture, Medicine, and Psychiatry: An International Journal of Cross-Cultural Health Research* 1(3):233–253.

Werbner, P. (2003). *Pilgrims of Love: The Anthropology of a Global Sufi Cult*. New York: Hurst & Co.

World Health Organization. (2022). *ICD-11 for Mortality and Morbidity Statistics*. https://icd.who.int/browse11/l-m/en#/http://id.who.int/icd/entity/1829103493.

Yu, Y.J. (2013). Subjectivity, hygiene, and STI prevention: a normalization paradox in the cleanliness practices of female sex workers in post-socialist China. *Medical Anthropology Quarterly* 27(3):360.

Zigon, J. (2007). Moral breakdown and the ethical demand: a theoretical framework for anthropology of moralities. *Anthropology Theory* 7(2):131–150.

PART 4

Global Bodies, Logics and Clinics

7

FEMINIZED TRAUMA, RESPONSIVE DESIRE, AND SOCIAL/GLOBAL LOGICS OF CONTROL

A Dialogue

Alyson K. Spurgas and Elliott Schwebach

Introduction (Elliott)

How do psychology and psychiatry persist in maintaining gender-based oppression? What are the ways in which, and the reasons for which, sexuality is constructed and conscripted? And what relation do feminized trauma and gender-based resistance bear to global logics of control?

Alyson and I were compelled to explore these questions together via dialogue. Our discussion ended up lasting hours, notwithstanding pandemic-era Zoom fatigue, air conditioning troubles for Alyson and a large spider wandering across the ceiling of my Albuquerque apartment.

Beyond my interest in Alyson's work on the sexual politics of medical and therapeutic interventions for low desire in women, I am inspired by the intensely critical, avowedly liberatory, deeply caring and psychoanalytic ambitions of their research. It is uncommon, I find, to come across a scholar whose work is all at once.

At one point, given that Alyson's book *Diagnosing Desire: Biopolitics and Femininity into the Twenty-First Century* exposes oppressive assumptions that are endemic to contemporary sex therapy (Spurgas, 2020), I asked Alyson if they would consult for the opening of a sexual health clinic were they asked to do so, and how they might aim to contribute to the therapeutic vision. Acknowledging the "historical process by which intimacy *as an idea* [has become] reduced to sex" (Blatterer, 2016, p. 72), the hegemony of compulsory sexuality today (Gupta, 2015), and how dominant sexual treatment modalities, by their recourse to evolutionary psychological assumptions, tend to essentialize and universalize particular

DOI: 10.4324/9781003311843-12

(white, bourgeois, cis-heterosexual and nondisabled) constructions of femininity, Alyson responded:

> If people want help having better sex and they see that as part of sexual health, whatever that means, then that would be great. I would hope that it could be friendly and feminist and intersectional and not ableist and that it could make space for the idea that you don't have to have a lot of sex to be a healthy person.

Altogether, this is critical, liberatory, and healing; this is my kind of research.

The basis of our encounter also included a shared interest in the analysis of unconscious mental functioning and a shared investment in interdisciplinarity. My research has thus far centered upon the psychopolitical legacy and implications of the work of Frantz Fanon, and Alyson's upon the embodied constructions of gender through medical and psychological research.

Together, we discover that despite these disparate areas of study, our similarities in approach allow us to draw connections and theorize possibilities that speak directly to the questions posed earlier. What follows is our conversation – lightly edited, of course – as it unfolded over video chat, and a short conclusion by Alyson.

Our Dialogue

I want to begin with a somewhat straightforward question. In your book Diagnosing Desire: Biopolitics and Femininity into the Twenty-First Century, you chart how recent trends in sexology, psychology, psychiatric medicine and therapeutic intervention – many of which claim the title "feminist" – reproduce a conception of female sexuality that continues, in different guises, a long tradition of oppression and control.

Given that the understanding of female sexuality in question is one that supposes (and naturalizes) that female sexual desire must be activated by men, that is, that it is innately receptive and thus characteristically different than male sexuality, you call this the "feminized responsive desire framework." I am interested in your choice of the word "feminized" (rather than "female," "feminine," etc.) here. Would you be willing to unpack this word a little bit?

I should start by saying that the language that I used around gender throughout the book was really difficult to form. I had to think a lot about it, and I had a lot of feedback from reviewers and conversations where I was kind of pressed and pushed on it. And I really appreciated that. I began conducting these interviews and doing this research as early as 2010. Most of it was ultimately conducted probably between 2012 and 2014 with the monograph-writing coming later than that. So, when I began this study, it was a different moment and I don't think

I was thinking as critically about gender as I do now. I should start by just being honest about that.

This isn't about the word "feminized," specifically, but I ultimately did decide to use the term "women" throughout the text and I used she and her pronouns for the participants because at the time, most – no, *all* of the participants that I spoke with did use those pronouns and identified as women. But I think that kind of strangely, at the time, I didn't realize how much my study was actually about gender. I know that sounds odd.

I thought of it as being more about sexuality, more about medical sociology, kind of a sociology of diagnosis. And it wasn't until years later that I realized, "oh, this is really kind of about gender itself." So I think that the word "feminized" here is meant to indicate that it's a process: that the treatment of people as women and the *becoming woman* that occurs under modern psychology and psychiatry and sex therapy is a process. It's the simple idea that discourses and diagnoses push different norms and expectations upon people and in so doing they *produce gender as such*. And they in some sense produce or at least deeply impact people's experiences of gender, including via sex itself – meaning sexual activity.

I should say, I did know that *Diagnosing Desire* was about gender by the time I wrote the book. But when I started to initially ruminate on these ideas as a graduate student and I initially started to make contacts and begin the interview process, I didn't know how much about gender it actually was. On the one hand, I'm looking at this female sexual interest/arousal disorder (FSIAD) diagnosis in the *DSM-5*, that's about gender. And then I'm doing these interviews. And I kind of . . . I'm just being really honest here that I assumed that the people I was talking to were women.

It wasn't until I had really processed the interview data and thought about it next to, and in conjunction with, the diagnosis and all these discourses that I realized, "oh wow." I don't think that as many people identified as non-binary or at least not as openly – and to be clear, now I am someone who identifies on a kind of gender-fluid non-binary spectrum, and I use they and she pronouns – but I think that wasn't quite in the air in the exact same way between 2010 and 2014, or at least it wasn't in my world. It was starting to percolate, but my point is that even though I knew that the diagnoses were absolutely about gender and in this kind of Foucauldian feminist way that they were *productive* of gender, I didn't realize how much was at stake with the actual identities and phenomenological experiences of my participants as feminized people until the interviews were conducted. And until I had analyzed that data and really sat with it.

What I also came to know is that some of the folks in my study were now in different places, gender-wise. So I think that the argument that I make about the regulatory nature of these diagnoses and discourses is absolutely correct, because I think that the people I interviewed did feel pressed or pressured into a kind of femininity that wasn't working for them.

I'm wondering how you approach the relationship of this feminized responsive desire framework to contemporary trends in gender theory. What does feminized responsive desire imply about the politics of sexual difference and the contours of feminism, or of different feminisms, as you understand them?

What I don't want to see is just a "liberalizing" of sex.

There is some contemporary work being done that pushes back on the medical and psychological discourses that push people into the two boxes of male or female, masculine and feminine. But a lot of that is firmly in the realm of . . . I don't know how to say it. Maybe normative psychology? It is where lots of people are given a survey or put into an experiment and it's about how they feel if they are non-binary, for example. How do they experience sex? I think that it is important to gather that data.

But I don't want to see. . . . What I don't want the takeaway to be is basically just that we have more "boxes" for sex, gender, and sexuality.

So the fear is maybe losing the power element?

Yes, exactly. There's a proliferation of categories, you know, and now I think there are genuinely more psychologists, including the ones I critique in the book, who would be more likely to make spaces for folks who identify as non-binary or trans within their work. But I don't know how much that challenges the system of sex, sexuality and gender as an apparatus of control. There are still hierarchies. There will still be power.

The other thing I wanted to briefly say. . . . You asked about the contours of feminism as I understand them? I would say that I see my work in this book and elsewhere as Foucauldian feminist, as well as queer feminist, and I'm hoping to make it as intersectional as possible. But I also think that what I'm really trying to do is recuperate the best parts of radical and Marxist or materialist feminisms.

Radical feminism can be trans-exclusionary and also kind of weirdly cis-hetero-normative, especially cultural feminism. But I believe that there are useful aspects of radical feminism that have been lost. We now associate it so strongly with trans-exclusionary feminism but there are pieces of radical feminism that I think are important. Someone like Gayle Rubin and her pieces "The Traffic in Women" (1975) which is then followed later by "Thinking Sex" (1984), for example, are part of a lineage that thinks about how gender is structural and how it can be oppressive in many ways.

So, how should I say this? Thinking about feminization as a process, one that can be oppressive and dominating and painful or hurtful, is in line with certain tenets of radical feminism. And I think that may need to be reclaimed, and that it can be fully aligned with trans feminisms. I think this is actually in line with a lot of contemporary trans feminisms, because trans women are incredibly oppressed as a group. We know that feminization can be something really wonderful, femininity can be a great thing that can be celebrated, but feminization, when it is unwanted or when it only manifests in certain restrictive, mechanistic ways, can feel *not* great. It can feel bad.

It can be accompanied by harm and violence and it can feel bad, *and* it can still be wanted. Andrea Long Chu (2018, 2019) writes about this, that there can be a kind of melancholic femininity, wherein it can still be desired, even as it is injurious.

When I think of radical feminism, I also think of approaches that interrogate and confront the idea of a public space, or the public/private distinction, which is so central to the foundation and maintenance of the modern state. As opposed to liberal feminism, where sexual politics – and this might be a little bit of a caricature, but I don't think it fully is – where sexual politics remains limited to a kind of private realm. Where the idea is that we can just create a structure whereby people can live safely and happily in their own little bubbles and not bother anyone else. (Laughs)

Exactly, exactly. And I think that liberal feminism too often valorizes the idea that gender is just a totally happy thing. I guess I'm really trying here to balance taking seriously the idea that gender is fluid, which I believe for myself – part of the process of doing these interviews and writing this book was also my own kind of coming into a non-binary experience – I want to take seriously that while on the one hand there is something really great and pleasurable about coming into gender fluidity or in some cases living out the gender norms that you were assigned at birth and feeling great about that, on the other hand it doesn't always feel great. We have to take seriously that misogyny is real. Feminization is often accompanied by violence.

And I guess that's what I'm saying is in line with a certain radical feminist tendency in my work. I think it's in keeping with trans feminist writers like Andrea Long Chu, I think it's in keeping with some Black feminist writers today who talk about misogynoir, like Moya Bailey (2010). I think it's in keeping with other people whose work I really love, like Sophie Lewis's (2019) work, critiques of the family, abolition of the family . . . I think here, you can also see my kind of anarchist tendencies coming out, as well. (Laughs)

But before we move on from this point, it is also important to recognize that liberal feminism also claims to put women on the same plane as men. But we know that this is not a politically serious or efficacious approach because they are not asking "*which* men?" They're obviously not talking about trans men, they're not talking about queer men, they're not talking about men of color. They're talking about a certain kind of white cis male figure. So liberal feminism – including as it manifests in psychology, psychiatry, sexology and sex therapy – can both accept a kind of proliferation of sex/gender/sexuality categories or "boxes" to check on a survey while also failing to take seriously the overarching apparatus of domination. And it thereby remains complicit with that apparatus of domination.

I want to flag these anarchist commitments because I think they are relevant to the volume, and because I share them. But at some point, I would also like to ask you about allyship and what that looks like in relation to your work. Maybe especially in relation to your more recent work on fracturing and falling apart. I want to pick your brain about fracturing as a liberatory method.

And I am curious about fracturing and falling apart as it is relevant to this conversation about different "categories" of women. Is fracturing and falling apart to any extent an affirmation of the ways that female subjectivity is already so fractured (e.g., into white woman, woman of color, etc.) by an overarching apparatus of domination and control?

The idea of fracturing as it appears in the last chapter of *Diagnosing Desire*, and then also in my *Lateral* piece, "Solidarity in Falling Apart" (Spurgas, 2021), absolutely can harken to different groups of women and different kinds of experiences of oppression. You're right. It is partly about being honest about the fact that feminization, as I'm describing it, which can be violent or at least associated with violence and harm, is not experienced by all feminized individuals in the same way.

I think more about accompliceship than allyship. I think about coalitions because, again, because of my anarchist commitments, I want to think about the violence that's done by the state, too, by the capitalist state, and ways to resist that. And by the way, thank you so much for noticing that and for really homing in on that. I think that's a part that people sometimes miss in the book, but there have been a few people that I've talked to that really like the falling-apart thing, which I really appreciate. (Laughs)

So yeah, on the one hand, it's about a kind of accompliceship and coalitional resistance of different groups who are a fractured group. There's no perfect cohesion there. And I think this is anarchist, or anarcho-communist, for sure. It's not assuming that there's any kind of perfect cohesion or similarity among feminized people, and it does not believe we have to have similarity to have solidarity.

But then the other piece of fracturing and falling apart for me is also that it's about internal processes, as well. So it's also about the idea. . . . This is a little complicated and I need to flesh it out a bit more. . . . And maybe if I had psychoanalytic training I could think more deeply about it. . . . But it's partly about questioning the idea that dissociation is so necessarily attached to trauma. There's an idea that with trauma, you *will* dissociate.

In the "Solidarity in Falling Apart" piece, I critique the psychologist and therapist Judith Herman. As much as she did for feminized populations with the addition of complex post-traumatic stress disorder or C-PTSD, and going beyond just PTSD, to show that trauma is enduring, it doesn't just "go away" after a brief treatment, it can't always be cured . . . as much as this contribution is huge and super important, I want to argue that we can question the normative implications of dissociation and the politics that are bound up within our discussions and interpretations of it. I propose that not all trauma survivors experience dissociation in the same way and that an uncritical emphasis on dissociation risks causing medical providers or therapists to question the credibility of feminized trauma when it appears without dissociation, or at least without dissociation in a certain image or form.

But instead of just fully eschewing dissociation, I suggest that there's something potentially akin to dissociation, something that I call dissociation-adjacent states, that may be operative for feminized trauma. The bottom line is that there is a world that is often experienced by feminized folks that *breaks you open*. This is worth embracing because medical discourses and sex therapy are normatively committed to kind of helping people "keep it together." And they are generally complicit in a kind of compulsory sexuality, compulsory heterosexuality and in compulsory ideas about gender.

In these discourses, it's about getting by to get by. Keeping it together. And I mean, obviously we sometimes have to keep it together under the capitalist state, which tells us that we have to be productive. So I think that there is this radical possibility of saying, "no, we're just going to fucking fall apart."

Sorry . . . you can scratch the f-word. (Laughs)

I'd kind of love to keep it! (Laughs)

You mentioned psychoanalysis. You and I share a lament about the contemporary abandonment of psychiatry's Freudian roots, given that trauma is more fundamental to (and might be rendered more visible from within) a psychodynamic approach. Yet, you also document the role that Freud and psychoanalysis played in constructing the feminized responsive desire framework by reinforcing essentialistic binaries of sexual difference.

In my work, I appreciate the extent to which Freud's early work on libidinal energy (which he defines as "objectless") allows him to normalize sexual experiences and identities such as those classified as homosexual, particularly in contrast to the evolutionarily/biologically reductionist and moralistic hostilities toward homosexuality that loomed large during his time. Yet Freud also classifies homosexuality as a perversion, implying at least some degree of pathology. I struggle with what we are to do (conceptually, therapeutically, politically) with frameworks such as these that seem to straddle precariously between continued oppression on the one hand and liberatory validation and care on the other.

Both of us also share a commitment to interdisciplinary engagement with psychiatrists, psychoanalytic thinkers, educators and practitioners, and other psychotherapists. In your work with these professionals, how do you aim to inspire dialogue across wide theoretical rifts? And how do you work to retain a commitment to radical justice and care when, between the pitfalls of both Classical Freudianism and contemporary psychiatry, the entire terrain remains so slippery and fraught?

I guess I would say . . . I think it's important, first of all, to honor people's change and growth, and people's contradictions. I feel that I can hold the fact that Freud posited some really messed up stuff. The same sort of stuff that liberal feminist psychologists and clinicians get up in arms about. But that is all they see. Education in psychology and psychiatry today, at least the last time I checked, tends to denounce Freud completely.

I asked a student of mine once, a Psychology major, how much she learned about Freud in her classes. She told me that her freshman Psychology teacher told the class that Freud is discredited, and that was it. That was the extent of Freud.

Yeah, exactly. And if or when anything comes up about Freud, it's like "penis envy, oh my god!" Or "the Oedipal complex – what a joke!" That's how it is framed. So obviously, you [Psychology teacher] and I don't agree about Freud. He provided a framework for thinking about psychic life that is imperative for understanding desire. There is a place to rethink things like penis envy but we don't have to – to use a poor idiom – throw the baby out with the bathwater. And to discredit him completely is bizarre and honestly such nonsense. Psychology and psychiatry owe *so much* to Freud. So anyway, I just think that it is possible to hold the contradictions and acknowledge that occasionally he said some bad stuff.

The same is true for me, as well. I wrote an article about body image that was published in 2005. I think when I started it, I was like 22 years old. A lot of the language that I used, a lot of the way that I describe women, I would do a lot differently now. Maybe it was fine at the time; I won an award for it, and it is my most cited piece, but it is a far cry from where I ended up, intellectually and theoretically. We are always learning and growing. Even the book that I wrote, the dissertation that I wrote – I will be completely honest that I was not thinking about gender in the same way that I am now.

I would also say that that is true for other people that I critique. I have critiqued some contemporary sexologists and clinical psychologists, who probably now kind of hate me (laughs), but who I think have also changed a lot. I would like to think that my work has had an impact on people's thoughts about the female sexual interest/arousal disorder (FSIAD) diagnosis, about why it's gendered and how it is problematic, but I think that there are real difficulties with speaking across disciplinary lines, especially to psychologists.

Part of the problem is that there is a political economy to all of this, too. There are huge amounts of money, which is never really discussed. There are psychologists who identify as feminists who are writing about responsive desire and doing studies of mindfulness with hundreds of women. They have *so* much funding and they have the media spotlight. And most problematically, some of these experimental psychologists and sexologists, they do a study and then they say "okay, this is the truth of people's desire." Or "we did this meta-analysis, we looked at all these different studies, and this is the truth."

But who conducted the studies? Who were the subjects? What is the role of social factors in the "facts" you discovered? They run these studies, and then two years later they run different studies and say "we discovered this instead. Now it is a little different." I want to say: "why are you constantly telling us what the truth of women is?" (Laughs) It's like, "clearly, you don't know."

Psychology is such a dominant discipline. Far more dominant than Sociology (or at least the kind of Sociology I do). And often it is so uncritical. I guess I just have to say that the interdisciplinarity has really been so tough. But I am so committed to it. It has been such a bummer to try so hard to engage interdisciplinarily with these people that think they are the most feminist people ever.

But in their discipline, maybe they *are* the most feminist people ever, right? Because they are dealing with these old white cis men psychologists who are actively transphobic! So they say "No, we're studying women, we're going to talk about mindfulness!" and they think it is the most radical thing ever. But within the lineage, it actually is a huge step.

I notice that your work dwells within, but also around, across and between, realms that are often treated as distinct: the mental and the bodily, the female and the male, the interpersonal/familial and the social-structural, etc. This is an unenviable task considering how difficult these lines are to trace in reality.

And in your interviews for Diagnosing Desire, you also bear witness to the deeply felt traumas and experiences of real people: traumas and experiences that might further defy any attempt to fit given conceptual templates. I get the sense that you strive to primarily allow your interview material to inform your theorizing (even as you must necessarily deal with existing language, frameworks and categories), rather than the other way around.

This makes me think about psychotherapeutic and psychiatric practice, which also entail a meeting between patient and expert, and thus between lived experience and interpretation. I am then reminded of the added challenges that come with a psychodynamic approach to revealing, unpacking, and attending to trauma, as such an approach posits internalizations of socially contingent power regimes as well as desires and motivations that may not be fully conscious. I therefore wonder if you are willing to speak to how you as a scholar find yourself approaching the task of listening to (and inevitably, to some degree, processing and interpreting) the trauma of others. What have you learned as you developed in this regard, and what are the biggest takeaways that your experiences as an interviewer have left you with?

I was so young when I did these interviews – or at least it feels that way, in retrospect! It was so great to do them, and I learned so much. I even learned about my own gender and sexuality, as I've said a few times now. It has been a really interesting journey for me, personally. At the time, I didn't realize how much I fit into the categories of the people I was studying, so there was an autoethnographic experience of doing those interviews, as well.

But even more than that, I came to realize what is at stake when it comes to how medical and therapeutic discourses are translated into lived experience. Or how they bear upon lived experience in a way that can be oppressive and harmful to people. These discourses produce a certain kind of femininity that can, at the very least, just lead to an undesirable way to have sex and experience pleasure (or *not* experience it), or an undesirable way to experience gender in relation to having sex. That is what was particularly relevant to me.

I do think that most of my participants really enjoyed the interviews. I only talked to a little over 30 people at the time; that was the most I could do. I am not a wealthy psychologist who is super well-funded. (Laughs) But they all just really appreciated it. I say somewhere in the book that someone described the interview as a "queer intake," and that it felt like I was doing a psychosexual history evaluation in a way that felt queer and feminist. So that was a really great aspect of it.

I will say that I wasn't prepared to hear some of the stories of trauma that I did hear. And fortunately, I don't think that anyone I spoke with was in an actively abusive situation. But there was a recounting of certain experiences that was difficult because, you know, I'm not a trained psychoanalyst. I don't have any therapeutic training.

So I think I would have benefited from having some training in those instances. That is actually one reason that I am really considering getting analytic training. I would also say, if I am being honest just about how much I have changed and grown in the last decade since this project, I wish I had talked more about race and cultural differences with these participants. I think that I end up producing a scathing critique of white, cis-hetero-femininity as it's produced in psychological spheres, and I outline its consequences, but I did not delve into race or culture with my interviewees, who were racially diverse.

What is true is that at the time, I felt conflicted as a white person about imposing a discussion of race upon a person color. I felt like I wanted the interviews to be organic and kind of go where the participants wanted them to go, so they were pretty open-ended. There were times where people would speak about race, ethnicity and cultural background, which I do mention throughout the work, but I think I could have structured it better.

To some degree that was a problem with being a novice. With being where I was in my intellectual development, to use kind of a strange term, at the time. But the psychological discourse I interrogate and critique is also really white-washed, and so race is integral to discuss when considering the white bourgeois nature of much contemporary psychology. However, I was thinking about gender in a way that I wish was more nuanced than it was at the time. I would do things differently now, including by looking to the work of Black feminist psychoanalysts and psychoanalytic thinkers such as Hortense Spillers (1987) (whose work I do cite in the book) but also Gail Lewis (2020), Dorothy Evans Holmes (1992), and so many others for guidance.

I just want to thank you for being so open and vulnerable and honest about that. One thing that I am beginning to understand is how, for white people and for people of color but perhaps in different ways, racism operates by making us play these mind games of whether or not to talk about race. We are made to feel that it is inappropriate.

Yeah, absolutely. I would love to talk with you more about that given your work on Fanon and your experiences with race and arts education. There is so much to unpack.

But the final thing I want to say on this question about my experience with the interviews. . . . One thing that is important to mention is another piece that is a little bit imprecise. I am imprecise with *trauma*. Some of that is just where I was in my life and in my theoretical lexicon: what I knew and what I didn't know.

Some of it, interestingly, also comes from how people spoke of trauma in the actual interviews. I was engaging with the ways that my interviewees were thinking and speaking about trauma, and perhaps their *idioms of trauma*, in the way that Christopher Bollas (1989) uses the term "idiom." There was almost a language of trauma that these folks were creating and utilizing.

All this is to say that, in the book, I am not talking about trauma with any kind of real precision. I am not drawing on any specific approach, but rather thinking about it more colloquially. But what I do want to do is separate it or hold a space for thinking about trauma as separate from *stress*. I know that seems weird given the fact that we often talk about "post-traumatic stress disorder." But I think the way that *trauma* is used and thought of and experienced, even colloquially, is different from *stress*.

This is important because one part of the contemporary psychological discourse of low female desire is the idea that women are "stressed out." Women are multitasking. The idea is that women are just too stressed out and they need to use mindfulness, for instance, to get in touch with their already-aroused bodies, which are presumed in this discourse to have objectively detectable, free-flowing physiological – yet often subjectively inaccessible – desire. That framing is a disservice to the violence that people who are feminized actually experience. And it is a disservice to the diversity of feminized people's experiences.

That's powerful.

Yeah.

The mindfulness example brings to mind some of the global political dimensions and questions inherent to your work. You illustrate not only how white supremacy and Eurocentric knowledge regimes enable psychiatric discourses that continue to traumatize, invisibilize, marginalize and alienate, but also how the feminized responsive desire framework persists even within alternative modalities, such as mindfulness therapy, and even outside of formally medical spaces, such as yoga, tantra, and feminine energy healing workshops.

One thing that strikes me here is how infused these alternative treatment options often are with Orientalist fantasies about the west's assumed opposite: "Eastern" medicine and practice.

When it comes to living out more liberatory, justice-seeking and caring models of sexual treatment and practice, is there a place for transformed conceptions of the "global," including of global cultural transmission or exchange? How might your research help to reimagine the "global" in the wake of Eurocentrism and/or the modern state?

Yeah, actually, the whole thing with the alternative or circular responsive feminine desire models and the kind of "Eastern-informed" treatment modalities with regard to enhancement and what I call *sexual carework* is that sexual carework becomes part of a neoliberal productivity regime. The idea here is that caring for the self sexually becomes a kind of mandate for women that is compulsory, but it also somehow feels like it's linked to reproducing the family and reproducing the cis male partner. There is a global neoliberal logic here, even in attempts to escape more conventional medical treatment modalities.

My critique would be a critique of the idea of "keeping it together," which I find to be very western and hyper-productive or capitalist. I actually have a book coming out in 2023 called *Decolonize Self-Care*, with co-author Zoë Meleo-Erwin, and it picks up on this very strand (Spurgas and Meleo-Erwin, 2023). Because I was so shocked at how much the mindfulness discourse has taken off. Now there is mindfulness *everywhere*. And mindfulness, when it comes to sex, is very feminized: it is most often women who are asked to be mindful or meditate to have better sex, not only for themselves but for their partners, or even for their own productivity or for their own *health*. There is this idea that women multitask too much, or they have too much going on, so they're stressed. And so they need to be more "mindful" to tune in to their free-flowing desire.

In this new book, I do touch on a lot of the political-economic ramifications of the mindfulness industry. It isn't just problematic because it's about telling feminized people to be women who have to organize their lives around satiating themselves and other people; it's also associated with an industry that, through its products and services, contributes economic and environmental harm. Zoë and I also go beyond just mindfulness and sexuality, although I take a couple of chapters to focus specifically on women and how the self-care industry is targeted to women, including through sexual health modalities. Zoë has a chapter on food and diet, and the political economy that surrounds all of that.

So maybe without giving too much away of the new publication, would you be willing to give a bit of a teaser on what a decolonized model of self-care might look like? And maybe how it relates to the idea of fracturing? Or is that too much for one interview? (Laughs)

I wish I had better answers for that. In the book we do some version of a manifesto where we advocate supporting local mutual aid collectives; we do actually name groups in New York that deliberately direct funds to allow Black folks and other people of color in the neighborhoods access to therapy or access to kinds of care that usually white people and gentrifiers reap the benefits of. We speak to different programs that we have seen happening in different ways that allow people to come together in support of one another. But we talk more in broad strokes and it is still pretty US-centric. Even though we do speak to global political and economic realities.

I do believe that a critique of whitewashed, cis-heteronormative, bourgeois, ableist, western or global north discourses is a vital component and a good start. We have to think about how these discourses travel and affect people in different ways around the world. But I am also cognizant of the fact that even though I have been primarily doing that kind of work, it is equally important to understand how individuals outside of the US and global north are providing care and writing about care work.

That's a thoughtful answer. I do think you offer a great deal that can fruitfully speak to, or at least be voiced alongside of, work that emerges from non-US contexts. In fact, other contributors for this volume are exploring the role that the modern state has played with regard to psychiatric knowledge, how it is constructed and how it is implemented in global contexts.

I personally cannot help but want to draw implications of this liberatory model of fracturing and falling apart for thinking about possibilities for "fracturing" the modern state or "fracturing" dominant regimes of psychiatric knowledge. There is so much there to explore.

Yeah. That's such a great way to put it. I wonder . . . were you kind of hoping that I was going to make an argument for fracturing the state? (Laughs)

(Laughs) Well, that question just came up for me now. But I think that it sort of speaks as a merit that you have trouble imagining or fully articulating a decolonized future for self-care. And yet I also see that you have these two strains in your work: a liberatory model of feminist care, and then an awareness of the oppressive logics of neoliberalism and the state. And I think that they speak to one another.

Yeah, absolutely. Absolutely. There is a kind of element of smashing the state for me. (Laughs) Yeah. Smash capitalism and fascism, for sure.

Conclusion (Alyson)

In early 2022, Elliott reached out to me to write a chapter for *Globalization, Displacement, and Psychiatry: Global Histories of Trauma*. This dialogue was borne out of a realization that, as the months went on, I was so overextended that I didn't feel I could contribute a brand new, full-length essay. I was very excited about the work. But by the time the summer and writing rolled around, two and a half years of the COVID-19 pandemic was taking its toll on me (like everyone else), and I was grappling with newly diagnosed autoimmune conditions and a variety of other physical and mental health concerns. So Elliott and I spoke on the phone and discussed what might be possible, if there were alternative formats we might employ so that I could still contribute. Together, we decided on an interview/dialogue format, wherein Elliott would propose questions to me, and we would record and transcribe the conversation.

Recording this dialogue with Elliott was incredibly rewarding; it felt therapeutic. In the same way that my interview participants described feeling like our interviews for my book *Diagnosing Desire* was a "queer intake" of sorts, I felt like this interview was a highly productive psychoanalytic exchange. Answering Elliott's provocative questions gave me a chance to think through my commitments and politics in relation to my work, and perhaps most importantly, to be vulnerable in this regard. I also got the chance to learn about Elliott and his brilliant work, and about the trials and tribulations of psychoanalytic training programs, and I valued this opportunity so much.

One exchange that didn't make it into this published version of our discussion was when Elliott asked me about my psychoanalytic influences and interlocutors:

> I notice that you consistently advocate for the inclusion of a figure of the unconscious mind while nonetheless avoiding delving too deeply into an analysis of its structure or nature (that is, beyond rebuffing a drive-theoretical model of unconscious motivations, or at least a reductionistic vision of unconscious drives). The theorist in me is curious to hear how you approach the ontological differences between the different psychoanalytic traditions that make their way (critically but often favorably) into your texts, including those stemming from Freud, Klein, Lacan, Laplanche and contemporary relationists. I am also curious if you make a conscious choice to keep from siding too explicitly with one given model over another, i.e., to keep ontological questions more open and bracketed, and how your intersectional and critical feminist or queer commitments inform your decision-making here.

I thought this was such a powerful question and I mulled it over for quite some time before our interview. I felt myself attempting to justify or rationalize why I didn't spell out a theory of the unconscious in my book. This was partly due to the fact that I have felt ill-equipped to properly articulate such a theory, as a sociologist, or like it isn't really under my purview, that it isn't my "place" to do so . . . but I have come to the conclusion that this omission was also in part due to a practical concern: my work, like Elliott's, is meant to be explicitly interdisciplinary, and thus I have felt reticent to get too bogged down in psychoanalytic theory as I feared this might distract from my larger critical project – which is meant to bridge gaps between sociology, psychology, and trauma studies, among others. After all, if most of the researchers I critique but also locute with eschew psychoanalytic explanations, how can I endeavor a conversation with them if I spend all of my time in the "muck" of (post-)Freudian theory? (This feeling, of course, also says a lot about how we, as a "culture," seem to feel about psychoanalysis, at least in this contemporary moment in the United States.)

However, at the end of the day, this explanation felt incomplete. The reality is also that: 1.) I often feel that I am not "expert" enough to speak on the subject of psychoanalysis, because there is always more to learn, and I have so much more learning to do, including perhaps through psychoanalytic training, *but* 2.) if I were forced to articulate my psychoanalytic commitments, I would say they are ultimately object relational and relational, but also broadly phantasmatic, concerned with counter/transference, and introjective. As Christopher Bollas has argued, and as I discuss earlier, trauma might be idiomatic, and in a similar vein, part of my project is about articulating a kind of on-the-ground, idiomatic *introjection*, in the sense that Nicholas Abraham and Maria Torok have described it, following Sandor Ferenczi and in line with Melanie Klein. Abraham and Torok simultaneously recuperate and put pressure on Freudian metapsychology, developing their own theory of phantoms, secrets, silence, and transgenerational haunting, via a detailed attention to introjection. Theirs is ultimately a theory of an unconscious that is fully embodied and always in flux; a theory that is firmly about reconstitution and reciprocity rather than normative development and psychopathology.

In an introductory note to a section in the first volume of *The Shell and the Kernel*, collection editor Nicholas Rand describes Abraham and Torok's introjection as "the idea that the psyche is in a constant process of acquisition, involving the active expansion of our potential to open onto our own emerging desires and feelings as well as the external world" (1994, p. 100).

Elucidating this idea in a 1968 essay entitled "The Illness of Mourning and the Fantasy of the Exquisite Corpse," Torok characterizes introjection as a gradual and reciprocal process, and one "that does not tend toward compensation, but growth" (p. 113). It is also inherently related to trauma. Further useful in this consideration is Laplanche (1976/1970), who explains the connection between embodied psychic "reminiscences" and "internal-external instances," linking it back to Freud: "Everything comes from without in Freudian theory, it might be maintained, but at the same time every effect – in its efficacy – comes from within, from an isolated and encysted interior" (pp. 42–43).

I am intimate with introjection. As it is a way of thinking about desire – and its proliferation, extension and vicissitudes – *it is a way of desiring*, and one that has everything to do with my study in *Diagnosing Desire*, particularly insofar as my participants and my research make clear the need to move away from restrictive evolutionary and developmental narratives, behavioristic notions of relationality and experience, and mindfulness as self-optimization, while simultaneously embracing nuanced and complex psychoanalytic thinking on gender, sexuality, trauma and embodiment. Introjectively is how I desire – sexually, sensually, erotically, intellectually, politically, materially, and in a way that collapses the boundaries among these distinctions. As a queer, a feminist and an anarchist, I desire toward disintegrating boundaries in a "self"-fashioning that is always also external, environmental and existing at different psychic strata.

In *Diagnosing Desire*, I end several of the chapters with a reversal or a displacement: feminine insurrection over female mind–body discordance or confusion; collective refusal and sabotage over sexual self-optimization and coercive carework; anarchism, agentic submission, and parasexual pleasure over naturalized female responsiveness; and finally, feminine fracturing and falling apart over sexually "functional" women "keeping it together." I want to end my conclusion to this dialogue in a similar fashion – with a reversal wherein an explicitly political call-to-arms, characterized by a rallying cry for queer feminist communitarianism, mutual aid and solidarity, displaces a psychological, psychiatric and/or sexological truism about "women" and their "responsive female desire." How might *introjection* be a radical reinvention of *receptivity*? Receptivity in this formulation pushes back against the naturalization of female passivity under regimes of cis-hetero-normative and violent "complementarity" (a masculine/feminine complementarity which is always a white supremacist, colonialist, anti-queer, and anti-trans fiction). It presents here instead as an ontogenetic form of encysting or growing-with, in a traumatizing and painful, yet connective and desire-inducing world.

References

Abraham, N. & Torok, M. (1994). *The Shell and the Kernel* (Volume 1). Chicago, IL: University of Chicago Press.

Bailey, M. (2010). They aren't talking about me. *Crunk Feminist Collective* 14.

Blatterer, H. (2016). Intimacy as freedom: friendship, gender and everyday life. *Thesis Eleven*, 132(1):62–76.

Bollas, C. (1989). *Forces of Destiny: Psychoanalysis and Human Idiom*. London: Free Association Books.

Chu, A.L. (2018). On liking women. *N+1*. www.nplusonemag.com/issue-30/essays/on-liking-women/.

Chu, A.L. (2019). *Females*. New York: Verso Books.

Gupta, K. (2015). Compulsory sexuality: evaluating an emerging concept. *Signs: Journal of Women in Culture and Society* 41:131–154.

Holmes, D.E. (1992). Race and transference in psychoanalysis and psychotherapy. *International Journal of Psychoanalysis* 73:1–11.

Laplanche, J. (1976). *Life and Death in Psychoanalysis.* Baltimore, MD: The Johns Hopkins University Press. (Original work published 1970).

Lewis, G. (2020). Once more with my sistren: Black feminism and the challenge of object use. *Feminist Review* 126.

Lewis, S. (2019). *Full Surrogacy Now: Feminism Against Family.* New York: Verso Books.

Rubin, G. (1975). The traffic in women: notes on the 'political economy' of sex. In R.R. Reiter (Ed.), *Toward an Anthropology of Women* (pp. 157–210). New York: Monthly Review Press.

Rubin, G. (1984). Thinking sex: notes for a radical theory of the politics of sexuality. In C.S. Vance (Ed.), *Pleasure and Danger: Exploring Female Sexuality* (pp. 267–319). Boston and London: Routledge & Kegan Paul.

Spillers, H. (1987). Mama's baby, papa's maybe: an American grammar book. *Diacritics* 17:64–81.

Spurgas, A. (2005). Body image and cultural background. *Sociological Inquiry* 75:297–316.

Spurgas, A. (2020). *Diagnosing Desire: Biopolitics and Femininity Into the Twenty-First Century.* Columbus, OH: Ohio State University Press.

Spurgas, A. (2021). Solidarity in falling apart: toward a crip, collectivist, and justice-seeking theory of feminine fracture. *Lateral* 10(1). https://csalateral.org/section/cripiste mologies-of-crisis/solidarity-falling-apart-toward-crip-collectivist-justice-theory-feminine-fracture-spurgas/.

Spurgas, A. & Meleo-Erwin, Z. (2023). *Decolonize Self-Care.* New York: OR Books.

8

REPRODUCTIVE VIOLENCE AND SETTLER STATECRAFT

*Elena Ruíz, Nora Berenstain
and Nerli Paredes-Ruvalcaba*

In April 2022, 26-year-old Lizelle Herrera was arrested after medical staff at the hospital where she sought treatment for an active miscarriage reported the case to local officials as a suspected case of self-induced abortion. Herrera was charged with murder and held in the Starr County jail in Texas on a $500,000 bail. A spokesperson for the Frontera Fund, a reproductive rights organization for the Rio Grande Valley, said of the case: "Low income people of color cannot walk into a hospital safely and know that they will be able to be honest with their medical providers and give them information that might save their life because they might go to jail" (Martinez, 2022). In the wake of the U.S. Supreme Court's June 2022 ruling in *Dobbs v. Jackson*, which ruled that there is no constitutional right to abortion, Herrera's case has risen to national attention as an illustration of the precarious legal and medical situations that pregnant people in the United States now face. We contend that the situation Herrera faced is not novel to the post-Dobbs era, nor an accidental feature of conservative policy that inflicts traumatic harm as a structural feature of gender-based violence. It is rather one moment in an evolving historical continuum of reproductive violence – the production of which adapts to meet the changing needs of white supremacist statecraft in settler colonial societies.

In 2018, two of us cautioned that the criminalization of women's adverse pregnancy outcomes and family planning choices was already a ubiquitous and predictable result of gender-based administrative violence in settler colonial societies (Ruíz and Berenstain, 2018). Critical to our argument was the well-documented trail of cases criminalizing suspected miscarriages of women of color and Indigenous women throughout North and South America, including in the United States. The view of reproductive violence we offered hinged on the structural

DOI: 10.4324/9781003311843-13

nature of gender-based violence as a system of regenerative and predictive inter-locking oppressions that dynamically change to align with the historical goals of settler colonial occupation, dispossession and settlement. That knowledge of these structures and their goals allows for predictions about the future patterns of harm they are likely to produce was a major contention of our 2018 paper. The rollback of reproductive rights under *Dobbs* is in line with our prediction that such reproductive violence would continue to escalate and expand its reach. If one is tracking the global order of settler colonial capital relations, which pro-duce social marginalization in relation to low-wage labor markets and adjacent institutions, state control of population-level reproduction should not come as a surprise. In a neoliberal economic context where the supply of low-wage labor is critically short in advanced industrial economies, and where women of color are disproportionately impacted by restrictions in provider access for reproductive health, the *Dobbs* decision marks an unsurprising moment in the colonial his-tory of reproducing reproductive violence to ensure market stabilization through investor confidence in a coming surge in low-wage workers. While all pregnant and pregnancy-capable people are adversely affected by the *Dobbs* decision, par-ticularly in emergency medicine and critical care scenarios, the disproportionate harm at the level of populations will predictably fall on low-income people of color and those who can least afford the travel expenses necessary to work around abortion provider scarcity. In short, our analysis provided a framework in which to understand Herrera's case as one of a continuing historical pattern of cases that highlight the complex infrastructure of gender-based administrative violence in settler colonial societies.

Here, we extend our analysis of gender-based administrative violence to the systems-level processes that ensure the historical continuity, global reach, and life-course exposure to reproductive and obstetric violence, particularly among youth of color. To do this, we frame our investigation of reproductive and obstetric vio-lence and structurally produced trauma through the lenses of (i) *historical continuity* and (ii) the *global architectures of neoliberal settler capitalism* that connect reproductive rights rollbacks in the United States with obstetric and reproductive violence across a world connected by colonial globalization. Not only do we reject the ubiquitous normative affect of *surprise* as a response to explicit state endorsement and promotion of reproductive violence – as in the U.S. Supreme Court's reversal of *Roe v. Wade* – we also reject the liberal narrative of the inevitability of *progress* (Seamster and Ray, 2018). To reject the inevitability-of-progress narrative does not mean we ascent to the violence done to us through state-sponsored pro-motion of reproductive harms. Our purpose, rather, is to identify the pathways through which violence continues to be reproduced, despite our historical resist-ance to it, in order to build structural interventions that take better aim at the configurations of power and supporting processes through which reproductive violence is sustained, generation after generation.

Constrictions of Reproductive Freedom, Expansions of Settler Governance

Our investigation begins from an understanding of settler colonialism as not merely a past historical event but an ongoing structure of domination (Said, 1994; Wolfe, 1998, 2006; Quijano, 2000; Gott, 2007; Speed, 2017; Goeman, 2017; Barker, 2017). The structure of settler colonialism has an expansive appetite for land, labor, resources, and capital, and is capable of maintaining itself over time by adapting its administrative systems to continue to meet its needs in the face of liberal social reform. This conception generates recognition that, because of the self-organizing and homeostatic features of settler colonial oppressions, not only do things not necessarily get substantively better after constitutionally afforded protections or laws are passed, they often invite a political backlash that can leave certain populations worse off than they were before (Anderson, 2016). For example, in the wake of the #MeToo movement, the Trump Administration initiated a series of Title IX rollbacks that significantly reduced the rights of survivors of sexual campus assault. The backlash included changes to the definition of sexual assault that made it harder to classify sexual assault as a crime and that gave institutions greater discretion over what burden-of-proof standards to apply in campus investigations of sexual assault cases and greater flexibility for the nonobservance of rape shield laws. This is one of many examples that reflect a reconsolidation of structural power to entrench and facilitate the right of certain populations to perpetrate sexual violence against others. This example also reflects the tendency of settler colonialism and the structural oppressions it licenses to re-entrench themselves in the face of political threats.

Promoting sexual violence has always been a strategy of settler statecraft, specifically against Indigenous women, children, and Two-Spirit people, whose lives and bodies vivify Indigenous political traditions via embodied webs of reciprocal relations rooted in mutual respect, non-coercion, autonomy and sovereignty (Simpson, 2017). In the United States, Indigenous Tribal Nations have historically been legally denied criminal jurisdiction over non-Native people who commit criminal acts on tribal lands, which prohibits Tribal Nations from pursuing accountability for non-Native perpetrators of sexual violence against Native women. In 1978, the U.S. Supreme Court ruled in *Oliphant v. Suquamish Indian Tribe* that tribal courts cannot exercise criminal jurisdiction over non-Indian defendants, as "Indian tribes do not have inherent jurisdiction to try and to punish non-Indians." This has had brutal and often deadly consequences for Native women. The vast majority of perpetrators of rape and sexual assault against Native women are non-Native men (Amnesty International, 2007). For decades, non-Native sexual predators, usually white men, have knowingly exploited this legal landscape in order to perpetrate sexual violence against Native women on reservations with impunity (Dunbar-Ortiz, 2015, p. 214).

That sexual and reproductive violence against Native women serves the project of settler statecraft is a guiding principle of the ongoing processes of colonization and colonial genocide that continue to underlie the existence of the United States. In line with this organizing principle of the settler colonial nation-state, Republican members of the United States Congress attempted to preserve this strategy in 2012, when Congress voted on reauthorization of the Violence Against Women Act (VAWA). In addition to reducing services to immigrants without legal status and opposing the extension of coverage to same-gender couples, the Republican-sponsored House version of the bill differed from the Senate version by specifically *not* including a provision that would repeal a part of *Oliphant* and allow for sovereign Tribal Nations to have jurisdiction over non-Native assailants who perpetrated sexual violence against Native women on tribal lands.[1] As Simpson (2017, p. 107) explains,

> A large part of the colonial project has been to control the political power of Indigenous women and queer people through the control of our sexual agency because this agency is a threat to heteropatriarchy. . . . Indigenous body sovereignty and sexuality sovereignty threaten colonial power.
>
> *(p. 107)*

The promotion of systemic sexual violence against Indigenous women, children, and Two-Spirit people is an essential mechanism to disrupt structures of governance grounded in mutual relationships among Indigenous peoples, lands, animal relatives and other Indigenous Nations – all of which pose a threat to settler governance structures.

Other forms of reproductive violence, such as the large-scale removal of Native children from their homes and nations, have long been cornerstones of settler colonial strategies of Indigenous genocide and spatial removal. The federal policy put in place to stanch the removal of Indigenous children from their communities – and with them the Indigenous futures they represent and make possible – is now being actively attacked in court by a white Texas family who is represented pro bono by the law firm Gibson Dunn, which is best known for representing the interests of oil and gas companies (Yona and Cremins, 2022). The 1978 Indian Child Welfare Act (ICWA), which is currently going before the Supreme Court in the case *Haaland vs. Brackeen*, established minimum standards for the adoption of Native children in the foster care system, the majority of whom had previously been placed both outside their extended families and outside of their Indigenous communities. The law's challengers argue that it enacts an unconstitutional racial preference (Totenberg, 2022), despite the fact that the United States' so-called "Indian Law" is not established on the basis of racial preference but on the recognition that the sovereignty of Native nations precedes the settler state. If the U.S. Supreme Court accepts the argument that the ICWA establishes an unconstitutional racial preference and rolls it back, much if not all of Indian Law will go with it. The rollback will leave Indigenous nations in the United States *much* worse off than before the ICWA was passed.

In this political moment surrounding abortion, in many ways, pregnancy-capable people in the United States have also been left worse off than we were before *Roe v. Wade* determined there was a constitutional right to abortion. In our current climate, there is significantly greater willingness to let women and pregnancy-capable people die because of life-threatening issues with their pregnancies, including with pregnancies that are inherently non-viable, like ectopic pregnancies. The State of Tennessee's 2020 abortion ban passed as a "trigger law," for instance, offers no exceptions for pregnancies threatening the life of the pregnant person. Instead, it offers only an "affirmative defense" for a doctor who performs a medically necessary abortion to save someone's life and is then charged with a Class C felony as the law categorizes any performed or attempted abortion (Human Life Protection Act SB 1257, 2019). The category of Class C felonies in Tennessee includes such crimes as aggravated assault and kidnapping and usually carries a prison sentence of 3–15 years and/or a maximum fine of $10,000. Predictably, the fact that the law places the burden on the doctor charged with a felony to prove that a life-saving abortion was medically necessary promotes fear among physicians in the state and severely limits the number willing to perform the procedure.

A *New York Times* article entitled " 'They're Just Going to Let Me Die?' One Woman's Abortion Odyssey" followed Madison Underwood's attempt to get an abortion in Tennessee (Bohra, 2022). After learning from physicians that her fetus had not formed a skull and would survive at most a few hours, if not minutes, after birth, Underwood was further told that the pregnancy was a threat to her own life, because the fetus' brain matter was leaking into the umbilical sac, which could cause sepsis and lead to critical illness or death. Though her doctors recommended she terminate the pregnancy for her own safety, she was unable to find anyone willing to perform the procedure in the state due to the confusing, threatening and quickly changing legal landscape – despite the fact that Tennessee's abortion ban had not yet gone into effect. We contend that it was a predictable and intended effect of the law to severely reduce the number of physicians willing to perform an abortion in the state, *including when the procedure is necessary for saving a pregnant person's life.* Pazzanese (2022) notes that, while "Even the staunchest abortion opponents once hedged when it came to saying the law should force a woman to continue a life-threatening pregnancy. But," she continues, "since the Supreme Court overturned Roe v. Wade last month, eliminating 'life of the mother' exceptions in abortion bans is no longer seen as politically unthinkable." Pazzanese cites a recent lawsuit by the Texas Attorney General against the Department of Health and Human Services, which challenges their reminder that doctors who perform a life-saving abortion are protected from prosecution under federal law, even in states that ban the procedure. These examples are indicative of the increased political desire of the forced birth movement to allow women and pregnant people to die when their pregnancies threaten their lives.

The fact that reproductive violence can produce seemingly inconsistent phenomena (such as the willingness to let pregnant people die but also to prevent the termination of pregnancies) becomes explainable when reproductive violence is understood as a structure of settler capitalism. As a structure, it produces differential outcomes that work to achieve the same systems-goal of generating profit and concentrated wealth for white settler polities. The administrative, military, and policy vehicles used to achieve this goal vary widely and adapt in ways that respond to the regional and global multi-sector interests of white polities (e.g., the investor class, the Religious Right, the political elite and donor class). For example, when weighing the risk of investing against expected rates of return, the investor class requires confidence that government policies and regulations will align with business environments that maximize profit. The investor class often intersects with religious conservatives and the Religious Right, as they do in Morgan Stanley's guide for "faith-based investing" or in the well-known New Covenant Growth Fund and Camco Investors Fund. They also intersect with the elite donor class, as in the Koch-led charitable foundations. Intersecting interests promulgate environments where those most likely to be harmed by policy have the least proximity to white settler wealth. In an inflationary downturn with low-wage worker scarcity, publicly traded companies look to the future for certainty about an incoming supply of workers. Consider the fact that, on the day the U.S. Supreme Court overturned *Roe v. Wade*, the stock market soared, breaking a month-long losing streak with an 800+ point gain and rallying for days afterward.[2] This is an unsurprising dynamic of settler capital market relations. Notice also that the settler capitalist labor-market goals of restricting abortion are not actually at odds with the escalating inclination to allow pregnant people to die as a result of preventable medical complications. Forced pregnancy as a mechanism of reproductive violence specifically harms cis women, non-binary people and trans men. It is a tool of cisheteropatriarchal control and domination that sends a message, especially to women, that they have value insofar as they are producing the next generation of either low-wage workers or white settler dynastic polities.[3] If they can't produce value, they are of little use to settler capitalist white supremacy and may as well be left to die while new targets for reproductive control are identified.

Two primary features of structures of oppression are their adaptive capacitates and their ability to elevate a system's capacity for exponential growth over time. These can be observed in the fact that there is a much greater appetite now to incarcerate people who *do* get abortions, as well as those who have miscarriages, and to publicize these arrests for conservative political gain. Before *Roe v. Wade*, it was not as common in the United States to see women prosecuted for homicide because of their pregnancy outcomes. Consider also that colonial courts in Latin America rarely saw prosecutions for the crime of abortion between the 17th and 19th centuries. However, this changed in later periods in response to greater gains in gender-based rights and reproductive care access (Jaffary, 2012). Similarly, in the United States, "under the common law, abortions were generally legal; it was not until the early nineteenth century that laws were passed prohibiting the procedure" (Butler, 1977). Prior to the *Dobbs* decision, homicide prosecutions of women for abortions and miscarriages were already becoming more routine in the United States, as we show in Ruíz and Berenstain (2018). And they are set to become even more common now, as the Right continues their efforts to entrench notions like "fetal personhood" and "fetal assault" in policies that pave the way for severely punishing those who lose their pregnancies and further depriving them of bodily autonomy through incarceration, forced medical procedures and forced institutionalization (Paltrow and Flavin, 2013).

These trends, while urgent and terrifying, are not new developments nor are they the result of increasingly contentious warring between political factions. Rather, they are the most recent iteration of a long-running legacy of repro- ductive violence that has formed a core branch of institutionalized population control, punishment and heteropatriarchal domination in the service of white supremacy and settler colonialism since Europeans first invaded, occupied and colonized the lands and peoples of the Americas (see e.g., Hartmann, 1999). To account for the half-millennium timescale of these trends, we tell a structural story that frames institutions and their outcomes as part of intentionally designed administrative systems whose functions are built around the goals of settler colo- nialism. We conceive administrative violence in terms of epistemic and institu- tional systems that structurally produce automated harm and death for certain populations, non-accidentally and by design. Specifically, our analysis considers how administrative systems in settler societies provide the gearwork for enforcing and maintaining forms of oppression, which are themselves oriented toward and structured by the goals of settler colonial white supremacy. Capitalism, ableism, and cisheteropatriarchy are foundational organizing principles of settler admin- istrative systems. They perform essential organizational functions to further the goals of settler colonialism. And, because of the functions of these structures, the violence they produce is predictable and observable, though it also tends to be intentionally excluded from what, in settler societies, is considered "real" vio- lence. And this is not an accident, as Elena Ruíz (2019, 2020, 2022) and Anishi- naabe scholar Leanne Betasamosake Simpson (2007, 2014, 2017) have pointed out. As Simpson notes, these systems are designed to ensure that the violence they produce is unnameable and even unidentifiable.

The increasingly explicit state endorsement and expansion of obstetric vio- lence and the structural production of reproductive trauma would not be possible without pervasive, organized structural gaslighting (Berenstain, 2020; Ruíz, 2020;

Davis and Ernst, 2019) aimed at those who have long been sounding the alarm about these empirically demonstrable trends of increasing policy and prosecutorial efforts toward reproductive violence. We call attention to this pattern of structural gaslighting and expand more fully on the concept later in this paper. Scholars such as Shannon Speed (2017, 2019), Sarah Deer (2015), Angela Davis (1983, 2005), Dorothy Roberts (1997, 2010) and Aida Hernandez-Castillo (2016) have all been warning us for quite some time about the power of systems of oppression to regroup, reorganize and morph into other forms to escape notice and continue producing structural violence. Their work not only influences the picture that we outline in the section "Structural Gaslighting and Reproductive Violence," but it also has clear implications for what is to come.

Efforts to roll back reproductive rights are not without historical precedent. Two significant backlashes to *Roe v. Wade* (1973) should be noted. The *Hyde Amendment* (1976) directly responded to the liberalized abortion laws established in *Roe* by cutting off federal funding for abortion. Title XIX of the 1965 Social Securities Act established the Medicaid program that provides federal assistance for medical treatment of indigent or financially in need persons, including for abortion care. As Davis writes, following the passage of the Hyde Amendment, "Black, Puerto Rican, Chicana and Native American Indian women, together with their impoverished white sisters, were thus effectively divested of the legal right to abortions" (Davis, 1983, p. 206). Prior to the Hyde Amendment, "most state Medicaid programs nominally appear to have reimbursed abortion like any other medical procedure" (National Research Council Committee on Population, 1998). The Hyde amendment prohibited the use of federal funds to pay for abortions through Medicaid. The Amendment passed without exceptions to save the mother's life, or for incest or rape (later versions restored these exceptions). In 1980, the U.S. Supreme Court upheld Hyde's Amendments restrictions in *Harris v. McRae*, leaving it to States to pass legislation to work around the Amendment's provisions.

Less familiar to most is the *Helms Amendment*, a 1973 amendment to the Foreign Assistance Act of 1961 (22 U.S.C. 2151b(f)(1)) that prohibits the use of federal funds to pay for abortions or to "motivate or coerce any person to practice abortions" by nongovernmental organizations (NGOs) that receive Federal funds. In 1984, Reagan expanded its reach (through what was known as 'the Mexico City Policy') to include any NGO that uses *non-Federal* funds to perform or disseminate information on, or to promote increased access to abortion. Trump significantly expanded on Reagan's expansion to further include organizations, businesses, or subcontractors that do business with any USAID-funded agency.

In the aftermath of *Roe*, the immediate rollback to abortion rights took place through global infrastructures of foreign aid that govern family planning services. Today, the United States is the world's largest provider of foreign aid for such services, rendering domestic policy de facto international policy in the 80% of the world where US foreign aid applies to family-planning provider infrastructures

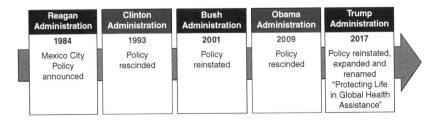

Reagan Administration	Clinton Administration	Bush Administration	Obama Administration	Trump Administration
1984	1993	2001	2009	2017
Mexico City Policy announced	Policy rescinded	Policy reinstated	Policy rescinded	Policy reinstated, expanded and renamed "Protecting Life in Global Health Assistance"

FIGURE 8.1 A timeline of the Helms Amendment

(Kumar, 2022). More than half of the global total of annual abortions occur in countries that receive US family planning aid and where abortion has been decriminalized in at least some circumstances (Kumar, 2022). Consider that today, although Ethiopia has liberalized abortion laws, half of the clinics will not provide one due to US foreign aid restrictions (Ibid.). In a 2019 study published in *The Lancet*, "Findings suggest that curbing US assistance to family planning organizations, especially those that consider abortion as a method of family planning, increases abortion prevalence in sub-Saharan African countries most affected by the policy" (Brooks et al., 2019). The global reach of US policy is critical to consider in the production of reproductive violence. Also critical are the systems-level features that allow such violence to persist throughout the ping-pong reinstatement and rescinding and policy marathon surrounding reproductive violence. Although US President Biden rescinded the Mexico City Policy in January 2021, the Dobbs decision puts that decision in peril.

Traditional policy narratives frame the back-and-forth policy fight over reproductive rights and abortion access as standard operating procedure in two-party representative governance. The most dominant narrative for explaining the increasing severity of policies through time is through narratives of social "polarization" in the political climate of "culture," sometimes cashed out in racist overtones of "tribalism." In contrast to these narratives, we frame this ping-pong policy pattern through the historical continuity of the global architectures of neoliberal settler capitalism.

Consider the structural relationship of the Helms Amendment to the 35 million unsafe abortions that occur annually across the globe (Kumar, 2022). Kumar notes that these are "among the world's most significant and most easily preventable public health tragedies." She further argues that restrictions on abortion access, particularly in places where it is difficult to access high-quality healthcare, predictably lead pregnant people to seek out unsafe abortions. She writes,

> In countries that currently accept U.S. family planning aid and where abortion is now legal under some circumstances, more than 19 million unsafe abortions occur annually – more than half of the global total.

These unsafe abortions result in complications requiring medical treatment — ranging from minor bleeding to shock and sepsis — for more than 11.8 million women and girls in those countries every year. And every year, more than 16,000 of the women and girls who have received these unsafe abortions die from more serious complications. Repealing Helms would no doubt save some women from this fate.

(Kumar, 2022)

The effects of the Helms Amendment leading to a greater number of unsafe abortions and the deaths that these cause are both predictable and known. Thus, we contend that they are also *non-accidental*, both in the sense of being caused in part by Helms, and in the sense of being a deliberately intended effect of Helms — just as the recent move in the United States toward letting people with life-threatening pregnancies die is non-accidental. These also represent the ability of settler colonial governance to reproduce itself not just diachronically but synchronically in an exponential expansion of settler statecraft. Thus, the gender-based administrative violence mandated by settler colonialism displaces and replaces other governance practices worldwide that not only demonstrate greater respect for women and pregnancy-capable people but lead to lower levels of structural violence and death. This colonial expansion of reproductive violence and control is facilitated by a policy that masquerades as "foreign aid." This structural gaslighting narrative fits into the long pattern of portraying practices of colonization, including forms of reproductive coercion, as beneficial to those targeted by them (Million, 2013).

The Structural Character of Reproductive Violence in Settler Statecraft

Gender-based administrative violence, including the forms of reproductive violence exemplified here, are, on our account, the result of intentionally designed systems organized to enact structured violence through the production of the colonial system of gender (Lugones, 2007). For instance, settler colonial forms of heteropatriarchy were introduced in the Americas as a strategy for displacing Indigenous peoples from their lands so that white settlers could acquire them and replace Indigenous lifeways with settler lifeways (Simpson, 2017). This is a complex process that requires sophisticated infrastructures to carry out. The institution of heterosexual marriage, for instance, enforces the heteropatriarchal ideal of the nuclear family as the most morally privileged kinship unit and living situation (Collins, 2000). Its purpose was to regulate kinship and reproduction in such a way that would disrupt the many varied Indigenous communal living practices so that a system of land privatization governed by the notion of "private property" could be enforced (Meissner and Whyte, 2017; Rifkin, 2010). It was necessary for settler administrative systems to impose a domination-based relationship of ownership to land so that Indigenous land, which encompasses webs of reciprocal relationships far more varied and less violent than the ownership relation that characterizes colonial notions of private property, could be transferred to settlers under a framework of legalized theft. This one example of how gender is used as a tool of administrative violence is part of a repeated pattern from the settler colonial playbook that has been deployed across a range of contexts.

Reproductive and obstetric violence are mechanisms of gender-based administrative violence oriented toward accomplishing settler colonial goals through the establishment of white supremacist heteropatriarchal capitalism. The use of the term "obstetric violence" originated in Latin America by activists wanting to tell a structural story of the patterns of mistreatment, abuse, and non-consensual interventions faced by birthing and pregnancy-capable people at all stages of reproduction (van der Waal et al., 2022). Central to their story was a recognition of the structurally racist and misogynistic dimensions of these patterns, as well as the fact that applying the sometimes-contentious term *violence* to these patterns was necessary to capture the serious and intentional physical, emotional and sexual harms that were being committed against, especially, populations of Black, Brown and Indigenous women.

But obstetric violence is by no means unique to Latin America, as reproductive coercion is a central arm of imperialist white supremacist capitalist patriarchy and settler statecraft. As we emphasized in Ruíz and Berenstain (2018), settler colonial systems of administrative violence are not hemmed in by the boundaries of settler nation-states, since the flow of colonial power strategies preceded settler colonial borders. Ongoing patterns of reproductive violence against Latin American women are thus structurally connected to historical and contemporary efforts in the United States and Canada to exert coercive reproductive control over Black women, Brown women and Indigenous women "to sustain cultures of gender-based violence in support of settler colonial configurations of power." An early example of an intentionally designed system of reproductive violence in the colonies and early United States is the legal doctrine of *partus sequitur ventrum*, which defined the status of a child as free or enslaved depending on the status of their mother. It meant that any child born to an enslaved woman would legally be considered enslaved. This doctrine formed a legal foundation for reifying the intersecting effects of white supremacy, patriarchy, and capitalism on Black women's bodies (Collins, 2000). Under slavery, white enslavers systematically used sexual violence against enslaved Black women as a form of control and domination (Davis, 1983, p. 175), but this legal doctrine also encouraged their use of rape against enslaved Black women by economically incentivizing sexual violence as a tool of white wealth production (Collins, 2000). Thus, white enslavers not only treated Black people as property, they treated Black women's bodies as units of capital capable of producing additional units of capital. This form of gender-based administrative violence rooted in settler colonial white supremacist capitalist patriarchy created a lasting legacy of white supremacist and state-sponsored coercive control over Black women's fertility and reproduction (Roberts, 1997) that continues to affect Black women's structural vulnerability to sexual, reproductive and obstetric violence today. The crisis of Black maternal mortality in the United States is but one gruesome yet preventable culmination of these intersecting systems of violence.

On our view, all forms of gender-based administrative violence in settler societies are inextricable from the goals of settler colonial white supremacy. When theorizing colonial violence, it is of paramount importance to recognize that colonialism is an ongoing process, not a past historical event (Arvin et al., 2013; Wolfe, 2006). Indigenous feminist theorists have been at the forefront of the promotion of this understanding of colonialism and its relation to gender-based violence (Maracle, 2015; Denetdale, 2017; Goeman, 2017; Barker, 2017; Speed, 2019). In her book *Incarcerated Stories* (2019), Chickasaw scholar Shannon Speed lays out how the socially organized character of violence against incarcerated Indigenous migrant women today is part of a longer continuum of colonial violence rather than just a consequence of the immediate economic interests of local townships and for-profit policing. A structural understanding of colonialism as a set of intergenerational, self-transformational practices that automate inequality irrespective of who is in power is what we mean by a *historically continuous* view of colonial violence.

When we refer to reproductive violence being endorsed and promoted by "the state," we are not referring to specific state entities or emissaries – for example, to the many dedicated people in civil service and even in elected public office who know this history of systemic oppression and how it continues to impact their constituents who desperately need the affordable healthcare, civil rights protections, and critical infrastructure goods that are systematically denied to them. Rather, we are talking about *systems-level properties of settler colonial white supremacy* that make such a task exceedingly difficult as effective and long-lasting measures for social change as something other than a rollback in the making.

Consider the relationship between reproductive violence and "the state" in the Latin American context, which is characterized by the settler nationhood configuration for ancestral and occupied territories of Indigenous people from Turtle Island and Abya Yala. In this context, the question of state interests in reproductive violence is not how are the two related, but how are they *not*? Matters of reproductive violence are deeply and essentially interwoven with state interests and methods of state-sponsored terrorism. There is always economic interest in subjugating domestic populations in settler societies, and that interest is often tied to foreign economic interests as well. In the South of Mexico, for instance, paramilitary and state-sponsored militarization of Indigenous zones protect extractivist interests and pave the way for private mining megaprojects. Because Mexico has (among other resources) the raw materials needed to build semiconductors and batteries to solve supply chain woes in the United States, state-sponsored militarization of sexual violence enjoys widespread impunity, and very few resources exist to address it. Neither are there resources to address the structural conditions currently driving a huge spike in early and teen marriages, sexual and domestic abuse, and increasingly restrictive access to teen obstetric care – and this is by design. This is why state terror and sexual violence in all its forms are theorized as part of a reproductive justice platform in the region.

A structural conception of these interrelated forces forms a core part of the massive "Green Wave" (Marea Verde) feminist movement – where women have marched in the millions for reproductive justice and access to safe and legal abortions while also calling for anti-neoliberal reform and pushing back against normalized gaslighting about state accountability.[4] A critical component of Green Wave feminism is the fight against compulsory motherhood for children and for access to safe abortions for all pregnancy-capable youth. In 2012, pregnant 16-year-old Rosaura Almonte Hernández died from leukemia after doctors in the Dominican Republic denied her life-saving chemotherapy so as to avoid causing a miscarriage (Oppenheim, 2021). She could not request an abortion, because the procedure was illegal without exceptions. High-profile cases such as hers helped center the plight of minors and young adults in organized resistance to reproductive violence throughout the region (Amnesty International, 2016)

Children and youth are particularly vulnerable to the harms of medical decision-making guided by conservative social policy. In many cases, the policies in place either ignore or criminalize the underage victim while also closing off accountability pathways for the abuser, leaving many children worse off than before the abuse was brought to the attention of providers through clinical encounters. Consider the case of Paulina del Carmen Ramírez Jacinto, which was brought before The Inter-American Commission on Human Rights in 2002 (Report No. 2107, Petition 161–02). In 1999, when Paulina was just 14 years old, she was raped by an intruder in her home in Mexico. Paulina and her mother reported the rape, yet she was not given any medical attention. Health officials specifically withheld information from her regarding the availability of emergency oral contraceptives. After learning she was pregnant as a result of her rape, she asked for an abortion under a Mexican law that, at the time, decriminalized abortion in cases of rape "if the incident was duly reported" to the prosecutor's office. Despite having reported the rape and asked for an abortion, she was coerced by public health officials into a forced birth. Paulina's case illustrates the wide range of mechanisms that (i) generate work-arounds to health equity and reproductive rights in settler colonial societies, (ii) the broad reach of reproductive violence across the lifespan, and (iii) the role of health interventions in actively producing non-accidental failure of care for members of marginalized populations. We explore these structural mechanisms below via a discussion of recent

(2022) semi-structured interviews conducted with mother–child dyads and health professionals in Veracruz, Mexico.

In Mexico, the high incidence of gender-based violence includes high rates of maternal mortality. As such, an increasing number of policies purportedly aiming to prevent maternal mortality have been implemented. However, such policies primarily mandate data collection through questionnaires administered during healthcare appointments about whether pregnant people are facing situations of violence, without providing any additional resources when reporting occurs, thus impugning their purported goal of prevention. This practice of data collection without intervention is further employed in cases in which the pregnant patient is a minor child and her partner or husband is an adult man. This indicates the primary value of such data collection is to enact a form of surveillance by the settler state, as it endorses structural reproductive violence by condoning through tacit approval the institution of child marriage and the corresponding practice of child rape.

Below is an excerpt from an interview with a physician explaining what they have to do to detect if one of their pregnant patients if facing violence:

All minor patients who have a partner who is someone of legal age, are reported to the public ministry, due to everything that is happening right now with violence and femicides. Well, a notice is given to the health jurisdiction, and if a problem arises, then they [public ministry] come. We have had two or three cases of pregnant women in situations like this. This has to be handled with a lot of discretion, with a lot of privacy, to give her confidence. Because, for example, we have cases in which there are 14-year-old girls with 40-year-old men who don't like to denounce, so they are supposedly fine but in reality they are not. In fact, from the age difference in the couple, it already sounds like something [bad] is happening. So all these things are talked about during the intake consultation. We have to detect and prevent, for example, in the case of violence, more violence during the pregnancy.

(Fieldnotes, October 2022)

When asked if they were able to detect cases of violence regularly, they responded:

Well . . . not too many, but sometimes it's a little alarming, because, I think no woman, particularly no pregnant women, deserves to experience violence. Because sometimes it is not just physical violence, but also psychological, economic. Or for example, when a girl sees a person as a way out and they imagine a better world and then it is not like that and she is disappointed. So we have to detect all of that because we have had patients whose couples infected them with HIV, cases of beatings, cases of alcoholism, cases of sexual abuse.

But you cannot intervene there. You simply use the tool [the questionnaire] and give notice [to the health jurisdiction].

(Ibid.)

These responses suggest that the purpose of the information gathered from the questionnaire is for healthcare institutions to detect the violence. But it appears that they do not offer any resources to the people experiencing violence. When asked about what happens when violence is detected, the physician responded:

A document is added to their medical file. In the event that she [pregnant person] does not want to file a complaint, we already gave notice [to the health jurisdiction], so if something were to happen to the patient we can say, "well, here it is, I did detect it, I did give notice." But the patient keeps the right to report or not.

All these issues are very delicate. We have to be very careful. Because right now there are some norms [to prevent] obstetric violence, there are many things that are protecting them [pregnant people], but still sometimes they don't want to report it and we can't judge why they make that decision.

It appears that public healthcare institutions are committed to detecting violence as a way to protect themselves from liability in the case that further violence, such as femicide, is perpetrated against their pregnant patient. Telling a patient that what they are reporting qualifies as violence, without offering them further resources may also lead to people underreporting violence if they sense that it will create additional problems and vulnerabilities for them. Thus, this tool allegedly implemented to *detect* violence may actually be a tool to *reproduce* violence through a form of surveillance that is both complicit with and encouraging of child sexual abuse through the reinforcement of structural impunity. The data collection without intervention practices can also be understood in the genealogy of state-sponsored surveillance tactics used to coerce Indigenous mothers to parent their babies in ways dictated by the settler state (Smith-Oka, 2013).

These cases reveal the wide range of phenomena that constitute reproductive violence in settler societies and the myriad ways the state colludes in their perpetration. Decades ago, Angela Davis (1983) laid out the case for why a state would be interested in enacting administrative violence targeted at women's reproduction in the US context. Davis argued that the structures of reproductive violence are formed not just in response to economic and political interests, but to the intimate interrelations between the two. As we show here, these interests also play out at the global scale in ways that reflect their cultural roots in colonialism. In the next section, we consider the narrative mythologies that are invoked to obscure the structural factors producing policies, practices, and self-organizing systems of reproductive violence under settler colonialism.

Structural Gaslighting and Reproductive Violence

Structural gaslighting is defined as any conceptual work that functions to obscure the productive relationship of structures of oppression to the individual and population-level harms they bring about (Berenstain, 2020). All settler colonial structures of oppression require narratives that perform the function of structural gaslighting to justify their systems-level harms and deflect from their root causes. We examine some of the structural gaslighting narratives deployed to obscure the oppression causes of reproductive violence against targeted populations.

To fully understand the ways that settler colonialism invokes myriad forms of supremacy in furtherance of its goals, it is essential to recognize the centrality of ableism and eugenicist policies to settler systems of reproductive violence and intergenerational trauma. Eugenics is at the very center of the story of reproductive violence. In addition to gender oppression, it involves the nexus of ableism, racism and white supremacy, capitalism, xenophobia and colonialism. Between 1930 and 1970, for instance, more than one-third of Puerto Rican women were forcibly sterilized. US colonialism dispossessed the vast majority of the Puerto Rican population, leaving people landless and in poverty. US eugenicists blamed the resulting poverty on overpopulation and seized the opportunity to enact reproductive violence as a matter of policy on Puerto Rican women (Briggs, 2002). This included not just sterilization but medical experimentation. Clarence Gamble, of Procter & Gamble was one of the main proponents of eugenics as a solution to poverty in Puerto Rico (Briggs, 2002). He also argued that reducing the African American birth rate in the United States was necessary to address poverty in the American South, which motivated him to fund Margaret Sanger's 1939 "Negro Project" to reduce Southern Black birth rates (Schuller, 2018). This is part of a long history of using controlling images about Black women's mothering and reproduction as a cause of Black poverty to produce structural gaslighting narratives that deflect from the political and economic mechanisms that maintain white supremacy and the capitalist transfer of wealth from Black communities to white ones (e.g., Seamster, 2016; DOJ, 2015; Coates, 2014). While racism, capitalist exploitation, and colonialism are all essential to understanding the history and presence of coercive control over reproduction in the Americas, it is those targeted by the violence of these systems who are portrayed as causing their own oppression.

Today, there are laws in 31 states and Washington DC that explicitly allow for the forced sterilization of disabled people (NWLC, 2022). Women with intellectual disabilities are sterilized more frequently than non-disabled women, and they are sterilized at a younger age than nondisabled women. Disabled Black women are sterilized at higher rates than disabled white women. Narratives about reproductive rights that focus solely on gender not only miss these essential structural factors, but in our view, actually function to entrench and reinforce them by hiding them from view. Shelley Tremain (2017) has incisively shown how white feminists and white feminist philosophers traffic in structural gaslighting narratives that not only ignore but actually collude with the systems that enable these forms of racist, ableist reproductive violence and the extermination of disabled people more generally.

Those seeking to entrench reproductive violence against targeted populations use similar narrative tactics of structural gaslighting. Because they not only leave out but actively obscure structural factors, we argue that it is a mistake to take their arguments at face value. This is especially true when it comes to the main reasons that opponents of abortion offer for why they want to ban abortion. If abortion opponents were primarily concerned with the so-called loss of fetal life, they would be equally concerned with preventing miscarriages as with preventing abortions. This is because somewhere between 10 and 20 percent of pregnancies end in miscarriage. An important part of reducing the high rate of "loss of fetal life" that comes from miscarriages involves preventing unwanted pregnancy, and the best way to do that is to make birth control free and accessible to everyone who wants it. Of course, that is not something we see the anti-abortion movement working toward; in fact, we see just the opposite. Many in the anti-abortion movement are committed to *limiting* the accessibility and affordability of birth control.[5] If they sincerely cared first and foremost about reducing preventable loss of fetal life, they would advocate as ferociously for free and accessible birth control as they do for banning abortion.

Another way to determine that abortion opposition has little to do with anything regarding the "sanctity of life" is by looking at how anti-abortion institutions treat life in other cases. Consider the Catholic Church, for instance, which has been a major opponent of abortion because of its purported commitment to the sanctity of human life. Yet the Church's commitment to the sanctity of human life was nowhere to be found in 1493 when Pope Alexander VI issued papal bulls articulating the Doctrine of Discovery, allowing Europeans to commit genocide against the Indigenous peoples of the Americas to exterminate them from the lands to which the Church legitimized Christian claims of sovereignty (Reid, 2010). Nor from the 1880s to the 1900s when it continued its genocides by removing Indigenous children from their homes and shipping them off to residential schools, which were institutions not only of forced assimilation, but of systematic physical, sexual, emotional and spiritual abuse with the goal of producing intergenerational trauma (Austen, 2022). The Catholic Church killed thousands of Indigenous children in these carceral institutions. Residential schools are only one of the genocidal tactics the Catholic Church has used in its enactment of settler colonial violence across the Americas. While genocide is incompatible with a commitment to the sanctity of human life, it has been central to the history of the Catholic Church in the Americas. Similar foundational inconsistencies can be found in much religious anti-abortion strategy and rhetoric. It is imperative to not only remain skeptical about the sincerity of the professed values that abortion opponents offer for violating the bodily autonomy of pregnancy-capable people but push back against the terms of the debate they set, as the public acceptances of such terms is essential to abortion opponents' ability to successfully perform structural gaslighting.

This is not to say that religious concerns do not play a role in the political motivations for forced pregnancy and forced birth via abortion restrictions. But it is important to be specific about *whose* religious concerns we are talking about and *what it is* they are concerned with. Some of the most relevant religious concerns that should be attended to are the concerns of the white Christian Right with maintaining and preserving the social order. Anthea Butler's (2021) work demonstrates how white supremacy and heteropatriarchy have long been among the core political commitments of white evangelicals in the United States. The manifestations of these commitments have included using the Bible to justify slavery, oppose desegregation and preserve the freedom to racially discriminate, and to promote a gender ideology that upholds cultures of rape and abuse by requiring women's unquestioning subservience to their husbands as both their heads of household and their spiritual leaders. Certain strains of white evangelical Christianity have thus been deeply and lastingly invested in upholding extraordinarily violent forms of social order and domination.

It is important to recognize the close relationship between Christianity and settler colonialism in the United States. Consider, for instance, the writings of Horatio Robinson Storer, a white Christian physician who, in the mid-19th century, mobilized a group of white male doctors to begin pushing for the criminalization of abortion across the United States. In his anti-abortion opus, he plainly expresses the settler colonial underpinnings of his project. In addition to clearly stating that abortion jeopardizes women's ability to carry out their essential duties as wives and mothers, he also admonishes that abortion jeopardizes the future of white settler dominance. At the very end of his book, he references the newly depopulated western "frontiers" and he asks whether these areas shall "be filled by our own children or by those of aliens? This is a question that our own women must answer; upon their loins depends the future destiny of the nation" (1868). The suggestion that cisgender white women are responsible for maintaining the strength of the white settler population – against encroachment by immigrants of color – remains in circulation today. In June 2022, the head of The Conservative Political Action Committee (CPAC), Matt Schlapp, suggested that banning abortion would be an effective strategy to solve the problem of the so-called "great replacement" – a white supremacist conspiracy theory that alleges that immigrants of color are being brought into the United States to "replace" the white population and upset white political power. Schlapp remarked, "If you say there is a population problem in a country, but you're killing millions of your own people every year through legalized abortion every year, if that were to be reduced, some of that problem is solved" (Weinberg, 2022). He went on to admonish, "Start with allowing our own people to live." By "our own people" Schlapp obviously means *white* people. It is not necessarily a mistake to think that banning abortion and criminalizing pregnancy are motivated by religious concerns. Rather, the mistake lies in separating the category of "religious concerns" from the commitments of settler colonialism, white supremacy, and heteropatriarchy. Because, for an increasingly politically powerful minority in the United States, these *are* some of their core religious concerns (Butler, 2021; Martí, 2020; Kobes du Mez, 2020).

In the Latin American context, these goals and policy agendas are similarly interwoven and ultimately inseparable from the goals of settler colonialism and specifically, neoliberal formations of settler capitalism. The Evangelical movement in Latin America not only has deep roots in anti-abortion policy; it also has a history of partnering with free-market enterprise and the neoliberal push of the "Washington Consensus" to make foreign economies friendlier to private investment and extractivism. They have been incredibly successful in blurring the lines between these agendas over the last 20 years. Consider the influential work of Capitol Ministries, whose mission is "Making Disciples of Jesus Christ in the Political Area Throughout the World." It is certainly in concert with the Republican push to pack the courts with judges who will restrict or ban abortion. But what is significant is that, since 1996, they have targeted state legislatures *all over the world*, not only in the United States, to pursue their economic interests and promote policies of reproductive violence. They use Bible study groups to recruit members of Congress and other political officials to do this work, and they are very effective. They currently hold "discipleship ministries" in over 40 foreign federal capitols (Capitol Ministries Annual Report, 2021). The World Congress of Families is another example of an organization pushing a similar strategic agenda across Eastern Europe, Africa and Australia, specifically promoting extremist anti-LGBTQ policies under the guise of protecting the "natural" family. This pattern offers ample evidence of where things are headed based on the *infrastructure* alone that these organizations have been successful in building. And it gives enormous reason for concern. Katherine Stewart's (2020) book *The Power Worshippers* has received a great deal of attention, because it lays out these goals in terms of Christian Nationalism. The larger structural issues of white supremacy, racialized misogyny, dispossession, and rape culture behind religious motivations in the political arena are just as central, however, and require the same amount of critical analysis and attention.

Concluding Remarks

The picture offered here points us toward a politics that takes this adaptive design of colonial violence into account through strategy for policy, action, and resistance – because the architecture of colonial violence seeks to construct a world in which you think you have no options or reasons to keep resisting. That is a message that we explicitly reject. We take our framework to offer serious warnings about the trajectory of increasing levels of administrative violence against intentionally marginalized and subordinated populations. We also emphasize the need to envision and preempt the ways that settler states and their self-organizing systems of reproductive coercion promote, extend and evolve new and different pathways to create harm and hyper-vulnerability for groups such as youth of color.

Our picture also directs attention to the problematic approach of delinking an understanding of the production of trauma from structural violence. As Ruíz makes clear in her forthcoming book, such an approach, which is characteristic of western mental healthcare systems, obscures and upholds settler colonialism by compounding the harms it produces for targeted populations such as Indigenous women, women of color and populations of color more generally. Trauma, rather than being an inevitable risk of human existence that is "built into the very fabric of being in a gambled tradeoff for living self-determined lives" must be understood as an intentionally produced tactic of settler colonial violence aimed at certain populations by design. Medical and mental health professionals who lose sight of this risk colluding in the structural harms of settler colonial white supremacy for targeted populations.

The possibility of ending these forms of violence requires rejecting the narrative of an inexorable march toward progress or justice. This is why we have focused on, and urged the reader to focus on the inevitability of continuing settler colonial reinventions and reincarnations of reproductive violence. We do this not to promote fatalism about these forms of settler colonial violence but rather to promote a commitment to their fatality.

Notes

1 Subsequent to *Oliphant*, Congress restored Tribal Nations' criminal jurisdiction over non-Indians who abuse Native people on tribal lands in their 2013 reauthorization of VAWA (Violence Against Women Reauthorization Act of 2013 Section 904, U.S.C 1304 (2018). In 2020, *McGirt v Oklahoma* ruled that since Congress had never disestablished the Creek reservation, the State of Oklahoma did not have jurisdiction to prosecute crimes by Native Americans on that land; only tribal courts and the Federal Government did. The ruling did not affect land ownership, and no land changed hands. However, in 2022, the Supreme Court limited the scope of its earlier *McGirt* ruling in *Oklahoma v. Castro-Huerta*, thereby threatening the ability of Tribal Nations to actually use the tribal criminal jurisdiction restored by Congress in VAWA. The majority opinion, penned by Brett Kavananaugh, stated that "Indian tribes lack criminal jurisdiction to prosecute crimes committed by non-Indians such as Castro-Huerta, even when non-Indians commit crimes against Indians in Indian country" (*Oklahoma v. Castro-Huerta*). To support this interpretation, the Court cited *Oliphant* as precedent.
2 For an economic analysis of this dynamic, see Card and Kreuger (1994).
3 See Ruíz (forthcoming) for an analysis of the intergenerational material and epistemic benefits that accrue to white settler populations in terms of white dynastic formations.

4 This complex conception of the state's role in sexual and reproductive violence is reflected in a popular song, "Un violador en tu camino," which means "there's a rapist in your path." So many women and girls know this song that it has been performed all over the world during mass protest events, including in packed stadiums (Pais, 2019). Part of the chorus says "the rapist is you. It's the police, it's the judicial system, it's the state, it's the president, the oppressive state is a macho rapist!"

5 The 2014 U.S. Supreme Court decision in *Burwell vs. Hobby Lobby*, for instance, ruled that the contraceptive mandate of the Affordable Care Act violated corporations' right to religious freedom. The decision, which effectively limits the affordability and accessibility of birth control for workers whose employers no longer cover its costs, was a win for the Religious Right. The decision also may have been leaked to conservative Evangelical leader Rob Schenck by Justice Alito after the former spent months ingratiating himself with court officials and engaging in outreach efforts with conservative Justices Alito, Thomas and Scalia (Kantor and Becker, 2022).

References

Amnesty International. (2007). *Maze of Injustice: The Failure to Protect Indigenous Women From Sexual Violence in the USA.* www.amnestyusa.org/reports/maze-of-injustice/.

Amnesty International. (2016, March). 'They Never Saw Me as a Person, They Saw Me as an Incubator': How the State Promotes Violence Against Women – Sexual and Reproductive Health in Latin America and the Caribbean. www.amnesty.org/en/wp-content/uploads/2021/05/AMR0141402016ENGLISH.pdf.

Anderson, C. (2016). *White Rage: The Unspoken Truth of Our Racial Divide.* New York: Bloomsbury.

Arvin, M., Tuck, E. & Morrill, A. (2013). Decolonizing feminism: challenging connections between settler colonialism and heteropatriarchy. *Feminist Formations* 25(1):8–34.

Austen, I. (2022, July 25). Canada's residential schools were a system of 'cultural genocide,' a commission found. *The New York Times.* www.nytimes.com/2022/07/25/world/canada/canada-school-system-pope.html.

Barker, J. (2017). Introduction: critically sovereign. In J. Barker (Ed.), *Critically Sovereign: Indigenous Gender, Sexuality, and Feminist Studies* (pp. 1–44). Durham: Duke University Press.

Berenstain, N. (2020). White feminist gaslighting. *Hypatia* 35(4):733–758.

Biden, J. (2021, January 28). Memorandum on protecting women's health at home and abroad. *The White House.* www.whitehouse.gov/briefing-room/presidential-actions/2021/01/28/memorandum-on-protecting-womens-health-at-home-and-abroad/.

Bohra, N. (2022, August 1). 'They're just going to let me die?' One woman's abortion odyssey. *New York Times.*

Briggs, L. (2002). *Reproducing Empire: Race, Sex, Science, and U.S. Imperialism in Puerto Rico.* Berkeley and Los Angeles: University of California Press.

Brooks, N., Bendavid, E. & Miller, G. (2019). USA aid policy and induced abortion in sub-Saharan Africa: an analysis of the Mexico City policy. *Lancet Global Health* 7(8):e1046–e1053.

Butler, A. (2021). *White Evangelical Racism: The Politics of Morality in America.* Chapel Hill: University of North Carolina Press.

Butler, P. (1977). The right to Medicaid payment for abortion. *Hastings Law Journal* 28(4):931–977.

Capitol Ministries Annual Report. (2021). www.e-digitaleditions.com/i/1485747-2021-capitol-ministries-annual-report/31?.

Card, D. & Kreuger, A. (1994). *The Effect of the Minimum Wage on Shareholder Wealth.* Working Paper 337. https://davidcard.berkeley.edu/papers/minwage-shareholder.pdf.

Coates, T. (2014, June). The case for reparations. *The Atlantic.*

Collins, P.H. (2000). *Black Feminist Thought: Knowledge, Consciousness, and the Politics of Empowerment.* New York: Routledge.

Davis, A. (1983). *Women, Race, and Class.* New York: Random House.

Davis, A. (2005). *Abolition Democracy: Beyond Empire, Prisons, and Torture.* New York: Seven Stories Press.

Davis, A. & Ernst, R. (2019). Racial gaslighting. *Politics, Groups, and Identities* 7(9):761–774.

Deer, S. (2015). *The Beginning and End of Rape: Confronting Sexual Violence in Native America.* Minneapolis: University of Minnesota Press.

Denetdale, J.N. (2017). Return to 'the uprising at beautiful mountain in 1913': marriage and sexuality in the making of the modern Navajo nation. In J. Barker (Ed.), *Critically Sovereign: Indigenous Gender, Sexuality, and Feminist Studies* (pp. 69–97). Durham: Duke University Press.

Department of Justice. (2015). *Investigation of the Ferguson Police Department.* www.justice.gov/sites/default/files/opa/press-releases/attachments/2015/03/04/ferguson_police_department_report.pdf.

Dunbar-Ortiz, R. (2015). *An Indigenous Peoples' History of the United States.* Boston: Beacon Press.

Goeman, M. (2017). Ongoing storms and struggles: gendered violence and resource exploitation. In J. Barker (Ed.), *Critically Sovereign: Indigenous Gender, Sexuality, and Feminist Studies* (pp. 99–126). Durham: Duke University Press.

Gott, R. (2007). Latin America as white settler society. *Bulletin of Latin American Research* 26(2):269–289.

Hartmann, B. (1999). *Reproductive Rights and Wrongs: The Global Politics of Population Control* (Revised Edition). Cambridge, MA: South End Press.

Hernandez-Castillo, A. (2016). *Multiple Injustices: Indigenous Women, Law, and Political Struggle in Latin America.* Ruscon: University of Arizona Press.

Human Life Protection Act. (2019). *Tennessee Laws Pub. Ch. 351 (S.B. 1257).* www.tn.gov/content/dam/tn/attorneygeneral/documents/pr/2022/pr22-21-human-life-protection-act.pdf.

Jaffary, N.E. (2012). Reconceiving motherhood: infanticide and abortion in colonial Mexico. *Journal of Family History* 37(1):3–22.

Kantor, J. & Becker, J. (2022, November 19). Former anti-abortion leader alleges another Supreme Court breach. *The New York Times.*

Kobes du Mez, K. (2020). *Jesus and John Wayne: How White Evangelicals Corrupted a Faith and Fractured a Nation.* New York: Liveright.

Kumar, A. (2022, October 18). Abortions are legal in Ethiopia: but half of these clinics won't provide one. *The New York Times.*

Lugones, M. (2007). Heterosexualism and the colonial/modern gender system. *Hypatia* 22(1):186–219.

Maracle, L. (2015). *Memory Serves: Oratories.* Edmonton: NeWest Press.

Martí, G. (2020). *American Blindspot: Race, Class, Religion, and the Trump Presidency.* Lanham: Rowman & Littlefield.

Martinez, F. (2022, April 14). Latinx files: the troubling care of Lizelle Herrera. *The Los Angeles Times*. www.latimes.com/world-nation/newsletter/2022-04-14/latinx-files-lizelle-herrera-release-latinx-files.

Meissner, S.N. & Whyte, K. (2017). Theorizing indigeneity, gender, and settler colonialism. In P.C. Taylor, L.M. Alcoff & L. Anderson (Eds.), *The Routledge Companion to the Philosophy of Race*. London: Routledge.

Million, D. (2013). *Therapeutic Nations: Healing in an Age of Indigenous Human Rights*. Tucson: University of Arizona Press.

National Research Council Committee on Population. (1998). *In Welfare, the Family, and Reproductive Behavior: Research Perspectives* (R.A. Moffitt, Ed.). Washington, DC: National Academies Press. www.ncbi.nlm.nih.gov/books/NBK230343/.

National Women's Law Center (NWLC). (2022, January 24). *Forced Sterilization of Disabled People in the United States*. https://nwlc.org/resource/forced-sterilization-of-disabled-people-in-the-united-states/.

Oklahoma v. Castro-Huerta 597 U.S. (2022). www.supremecourt.gov/opinions/21pdf/21-429_8o6a.pdf.

Oppenheim, M. (2021, February 18). Dominican Republic could follow Argentina's lead and overhaul 'cruel' total abortion ban. *The Independent*. www.independent.co.uk/news/world/americas/dominican-republic-abortion-ban-legislation-argentina-b1804109.html.

Pais, Ana. (2019, December 6). Las Tesis sobre 'un violador en tu camino': 'se nos escapó de las manos y lo hermoso es que fue apropiado por otras'. *BBC News Mundo*. https://www.bbc.com/mundo/noticias-america-latina-50690475.

Paltrow, L. & Flavin, J. (2013). Arrests of and forced interventions on pregnant women in the United States, 1973–2005: implications for women's legal status and public health. *Journal of Health Politics, Policy, and Law* 38(2):299–343.

Pazzanese, C. (2022, July 19). 'Life of the mother' is suddenly vulnerable. *The Harvard Gazette*.

Quijano, A. (2000). Coloniality of power, Eurocentrism, and Latin America. *Nepantla: Views from South* 1(3):533–580.

Reid, J. (2010). The doctrine of discovery and Canadian law. *The Canadian Journal of Native Studies* XXX(2):335–359.

Rifkin, M. (2010). *When Did Indians Become Straight?: Kinship, the History of Sexuality, and Native Sovereignty*. Oxford: Oxford University Press.

Roberts, D. (1997). *Killing the Black Body*. New York: Random House.

Roberts, D. (2010). Privatization and punishment in the new age of reprogenetics. In M.A. Fineman (Ed.), *Transcending the Boundaries of Law: Generations of Feminism and Legal Theory*. Abingdon: Routledge.

Ruíz, E.F. (2019). Between hermeneutic violence and alphabets of survival. In A. Pitts, M. Ortega & J. Medina (Eds.), *Theories of the Flesh: Latinx and Latin American Feminisms, Transformation, and Resistance*. Oxford: Oxford University Press.

Ruíz, E.F. (2020). Cultural gaslighting. *Hypatia* 35(4):687–713.

Ruíz, E.F. (2022). Women of color structural feminisms. In S.A. Tate & E.G. Rodríguez (Eds.), *The Palgrave Handbook of Critical Race and Gender*. Cham: Palgrave Macmillan.

Ruíz, E.F. (Forthcoming). *Structural Violence: White Dynastic Formations and the Making of Settler Colonial Impunity*. Oxford: Oxford University Press.

Ruíz, E. & Berenstain, N. (2018). Gender-based administrative violence as colonial strat egy. *Philosophical Topics* 46:209–227.

Said, E. (1994). *Culture and Imperialism.* New York: Vintage.

Schuller, K. (2018). *The Biopolitics of Feeling: Race, Sex, and Science in the Nineteenth Century.* Durham: Duke University Press.

Seamster, L. (2016). *Race, Power and Economic Extraction in Benton Harbor, MI.* Doctoral Dissertation. Durham: Duke University.

Seamster, L. & Ray, V. (2018). Against teleology in the study of race: toward the abolition of the progress paradigm. *Sociological Theory* 36(4):315–342.

Simpson, A. (2007). On ethnographic refusal: indigeneity, 'voice' and colonial citizenship. *Junctures* 9.

Simpson, A. (2014). *Mohawk Interruptus: Political Life Across the Borders of Settler States.* Durham: Duke University Press.

Simpson, L.B. (2017). *As We Have Always Done.* Minneapolis: University of Minnesota Press.

Smith-Oka, V. (2013). *Shaping the Motherhood of Indigenous Mexico.* Nashville: Vanderbilt University Press.

Speed, S. (2017). Structures of settler capitalism in Abya Yala. *American Quarterly* 69(4):783–790.

Speed, S. (2019). *Incarcerated Stories: Indigenous Women Migrants and Violence in the Settler Capitalist State.* Chapel Hill: University of North Carolina Press.

Stewart, K. (2020). *The Power Worshippers: Inside the Dangerous Rise of Religious Nationalism.* New York: Bloomsbury.

Storer, H.R. (1868). *Why Not? A Book for Every Woman.* Boston: Lee and Shepard.

Totenberg, N. (2022, November 8). Supreme Court considers fate of landmark Indian adoption law [Radio broadcast]. *National Public Radio.* https://www.npr.org/2022/11/08/1134668931/supreme-court-icwa.

Tremain, S. (2017). *Foucault and Feminist Philosophy of Disability.* Ann Arbor: University of Michigan Press.

van der Waal, R., Mayra, K., Horn, A. & Chadwick, R. (2022). Obstetric violence: an intersectional refraction through abolition feminism. *Feminist Anthropology.* https://anthrosource.onlinelibrary.wiley.com/doi/full/10.1002/fea2.12097.

Violence against women reauthorization act. (2013). *Section 904, U.S.C 1304.* www.govinfo.gov/content/pkg/PLAW-113publ4/pdf/PLAW-113publ4.pdf.

Weinberg, A. (2022, May 20). At CPAC, 'the great replacement' theory meets anti-abortion. *Mother Jones.* www.motherjones.com/politics/2022/05/cpac-abortion-matt-schlapp-great-replacement/.

Wolfe, P. (1998). *Settler Colonialism and the Transformation of Anthropology.* New York: Continuum Publishing.

Wolfe, P. (2006). Settler colonialism and the elimination of the native. *Journal of Genocide Research* 8(4):387–409.

Yona, L. & Cremins, D. (2022). It's time to hold law firms accountable for their role in climate change. *The Nation.* www.thenation.com/article/activism/law-firms-climate-change/.

9

ASIAN AMERICANS AND PACIFIC ISLANDERS (AAPI)

Cases/Experiences of Trauma and Healing

Crystal Han and Shinnyi Chou

Introduction

The term "Asian American" evokes an array of associations and emotions. To study the group identified as Asian American and Pacific Islanders (AAPI), given the complexity of its heterogeneous cultures with unique histories, is too much for one chapter; we must start by acknowledging that this chapter can only scratch the surface. AAPI are "born in the United States and born in Asia; of exclusively Asian parents and of mixed race; urban and rural; refugee and non-refugee; communist-identified and anticommunist; fluent in English and non-English speaking; educated and working class" (Lowe, 1991).

Partly given the western oversimplification and aggregation of the diaspora into a monolith, AAPI represents the fastest-growing race in the United States between 2000 and 2019 at 82% growth (United States Census Bureau, 2021), yet issues such as colorism, classism, and inequity plagues this population. For example, AAPI represents the ethnicity with the widest wealth gap among its sub-groups, with an average poverty rate below 5% for Japanese but greater than 15% among Hmong, Nepalese, and Burmese communities (AAPI Data Quick Stats, 2022). In addition, the National Center for Health Statistics reported in 2016 that attempts to disaggregate AAPI data revealed a significantly higher percentage of Vietnamese adults to be in fair to poor health compared to Chinese, Filipino, Asian Indian or Japanese adults (Bloom and Black, 2016), and a similar study noted that while within-city AAPI racial segregation was not significant when AAPI was examined as an aggregate, subgroup analysis identified greater racial segregation within neighborhoods for cities with significant Chinese or Vietnamese populations (Spoer et al., 2021).

DOI: 10.4324/9781003311843-14

The complexity is furthered by other social factors such as the timing and context of cultural interface, inter-minority conflicts, and the growth of multiracial families. Yet this historical confluence affecting AAPI identity development is often either erased or manipulated by the dominant cultural narrative.

As an example, the earliest AAPI migrants to the United States – Chinese – were first praised by capitalists for their hardworking attributes in the mines and on the railroads (Kiang et al., 2016). When white laborers sounded alarms of economic competition and casted them as the "Yellow Peril" that threatened the sanctity of US superiority, however, the establishment of the 1882 Chinese Exclusion Act swiftly shifted the internal lives of US Chinese from one of hope to inferiority. Over subsequent decades, US Chinese faced various iterations of assault upon their worth, notwithstanding the repeal of the Exclusion Act in 1943. The rise of the "Model Minority Myth" in the 1960s, which portrayed Chinese and AAPI collectively as self-lifting (despite being driven by a selective 1965 Immigration Act that allowed only the wealthy and educated to immigrate), fueled inter-minority hostilities by portraying the African American Civil Rights leaders as guilty of self-perpetuated disenfranchisement. Through it all, Chinese and AAPI communities have faced a silent epidemic of identity confusion and cultural trauma (Yi and Todd, 2021).

Berry's Orthogonal Theory of Acculturation (Berry, 1997) champions environments and opportunities where minorities can explore and develop both socially dominant and ancestral cultural identities, which are directly associated with positive mental health outcomes (Tikhonov et al., 2019). Berry demonstrates how the rejection of one or both cultures hinders belonging and self-identity integration (Kohut, 1977), which can in turn predict mental health decline (Allen et al., 2021; S. Lee et al., 2009).

Unsuccessful acculturation may at times be attributable to familial cultural conflicts (Chang et al., 2013; Juang et al., 2007). However, we argue that it is also, and likely more frequently or saliently, the result of coloniality (the worldviews, social structures, knowledge regimes and patterns of power emanating from colonialism), manifesting as western projections of orientalist fantasies and disavowals of complex migration histories. This is poignantly expressed by the title of a recent qualitative study on AAPI racial socialization: "Race was something we didn't talk about" (Young et al., 2021). Continuing legacies of AAPI xenophobia in the 1800s and the Model Minority Myth during the mid to late 20th Century, the perpetual foreigner stereotype (famously embodied in the "Where are you really from?" exchange) (Cheryan and Monin, 2005), hypersexualization and gendered emasculation (Tran, 2021), lack of AAPI representation in the media, and the disproportionately low number of AAPI individuals in leadership positions across all industries (Gündemir et al., 2019) all perpetuate racism toward this population. This is evidenced by reviewing the recent first quarter data between

2020 and 2021, indicating an increase of 169% in AAPI hate crimes across major US cities (Levin, 2021).

Importantly, these forces culminate in *internalized* racism, defined as "the individual inculcation of the racist stereotypes, values, images, and ideologies perpetuated by the white dominant society about one's racial group, leading to feelings of self-doubt, disgust, and disrespect for one's race and/or oneself" (Pyke, 2010). More recently, research confirmed a significant positive association between the intensity of internalized racism and the severity of depressive symptoms in AAPI (Choi et al., 2017). This complements extant literature establishing the link between the trauma of navigating race-based systemic oppression and the precipitation and perpetuation of psychiatric conditions including depression, anxiety, hypervigilance, avoidance and somatic symptoms (Carter, 2016; Gee et al., 2009; O'Keefe et al., 2015).

Despite the prevalence of mental health concerns, AAPI communities are less likely to seek psychiatric services (Kisch et al., 2005). Among the many hypothesized explanations for this trend include language barriers, where non-English-speaking AAPI access mental health treatments at a significantly lower rate than English-speaking AAPI (Kim et al., 2011; Sentell et al., 2007). Others have noted differential beliefs and attitudes about illness, wherein AAPI report medical complaints such as pain or poor memory as predominant concerns when presenting with depressive symptoms, and many in fact do not view their conditions as psychiatric in nature (Chen et al., 2015). Even when AAPI individuals do acknowledge psychiatric suffering, many have suggested that the low prioritization of mental health within their cultural values, as well as perceived shame and stigma within AAPI communities, deter service utilization (Kwok, 2013; S. Lee et al., 2009; Park et al., 2015; Yang et al., 2008). Most importantly, however, even when AAPI individuals actively desire and seek mental health services, many are disheartened to find their emotional subtleties lost amid culturally divergent communication styles (Naito et al., 2020), as well as the lack of access to culturally aware and competent mental health professionals who appreciate stigmas and challenges unique to their communities (Augsberger et al., 2015).

In the following section, we present a series of individual cases drawn from real-life experiences to illustrate the nuances and complexities embodied within the discussion above. We revisit the concepts of acculturation, stereotyping, cultural erasure, divergent illness conceptualizations, healthcare mistrusts and ways of healing in more detail. We begin with a case where Berry's Orthogonal Theory of Acculturation proves to be an effective model for thinking about minority care, and then build from this basis in the following cases to successively demonstrate how the global political dimension of AAPI trauma presents additional complexities and challenges that are often unaccounted for in treatment.

Keeping in mind that the full scope of AAPI mental health journeys cannot be distilled into six simple stories, the overarching objective of this chapter is to encourage readers to begin actively dismantling internalized cultural biases, reflecting upon the failures and successes of AAPI mental health experiences, and appreciating why a monolithic approach to addressing the complexity of AAPI mental health needs is severely inadequate. We thereby also encourage readers to contemplate and advocate for nontraditional approaches to engage and embrace this population and conclude by advancing a table of practical, guiding strategies and questions to aid in doing so.

Case Samples

The Tiger Mom and the Daughter

A is a 12-year-old biracial female of Nigerian and Chinese descent who came to the psychiatry clinic with her mother for struggles with academics and depression. Her mother is originally from China and her father, who was from Nigeria, passed away on a business trip abroad a few months prior to initial evaluation. A's mother reported concern about A's worsening grades, hygiene and appetite decrease. A disagreed with many of her mother's complaints but conceded that her grades have dropped from As to Cs. A is more concerned about feeling sad the past couple of years, a sadness that has worsened from feeling overly criticized by her mother and 14-year-old brother.

A did feel that her father's passing had an impact on the family but struggled to elaborate how. Her mother felt that because none of them had a close relationship with the father, his passing was not particularly impactful for A. Their father passed away while in Nigeria on a business trip. It was never clarified how he died. His body could not be sent to the United States due to the COVID-19 pandemic. A's family did not have a memorial service for their father and were merely sent photos from his burial in Nigeria. This has left A without a sense of closure and feeling confused.

A's mother emigrated from China to the United States in her thirties to complete her master's degree. She works as a property manager. Her maternal family remains in China. She expressed strongly held values regarding academic success and hard work. She shared that she came to the United States with poor English skills but took extra classes and got two degrees to set an example for her children. A's mother stated that she believed hardships in life are inevitable and that "what doesn't kill you makes you stronger." She saw explicit verbal support as "spoiling" children. The mother felt her role as a mother was to prepare her children to navigate a world that is harsh and difficult. She maintained Confucian values such as parental love, including providing for all of their children's physical and financial needs, as well as guidance and instruction. In return, she believed in filial piety, as she expected children to respect their parents' advice, and to work hard in their academics to build a stable future.

A demonstrated fast progress in exploring and processing her emotions and experiences. She continued to work on identifying the layers of grief and persecution she felt due to her father's death, her brother's mistreatment of her, and her mother's emotional distance. She verbalized examples of how her cultural values conflict with those of her mother: such as her mother's emphasis on academic achievement and her mother's justification of her brother's intrusive attitudes due to his good grades. She was able to work through these experiences, grieve her father's death, and find other avenues of support through peers. Ultimately her grades, mood, and relationship with her mother improved.

Her mother attended monthly parent guidance sessions where she explored her own cultural values and wishes for her daughter. She was able to consider alternative ways of communicating with A in order to achieve their mutual goals. She was receptive to building skills such as reflective listening and mirroring. She was able to start setting parental boundaries with the brother to better meet A's need for emotional protection.

With a focus on parent–child acculturation gaps, communication styles and cultural experiences, the culturally humble psychotherapeutic approach initiated the process of allowing the patient and mother to align cultural values, personal priorities, and repairing the parent–child relationship.

In Berry's Orthogonal Theory of Acculturation, receiving-culture acquisition and heritage-culture retention are cast as independent dimensions (Berry, 1997). Within this model, these two dimensions intersect to create four acculturation categories – assimilation, separation, integration and marginalization. A appears to be more assimilated, identifying more with western cultural values such as autonomy, individual identity, and increased verbal emotional expression. Her mother aligns herself more with Chinese traditional cultural values including obeying older family members, emotional restraint (to maintain group harmony), and self-cultivation through experiences of hardships (Hamilton, 1990). The division caused by the differing prioritizations of values and identity was the primary source of dysfunctional family dynamics, including the strained mother–child relationship, and was a major factor in the development of depressive symptoms in the identified patient.

The Adopted Korean

M has a complicated psychiatric history which includes behavioral issues and aggression starting from age 4, when he was diagnosed with ADHD and started stimulant treatment. From age 5, he started expressing suicidal ideation such as asking his mother to shoot him with a gun. Trials of antidepressants were started at that time. He holds diagnoses of ADHD (combined type), generalized anxiety disorder, major depressive disorder and disruptive mood dysregulation disorder.

M was born to a teenage mother in South Korea that was unable to care for him and took him to the hospital shortly after birth, at which point he was placed in foster care until 8 months of age when his adoptive family adopted him. He has two older adoptive siblings, both white, who live across the country and are in their 30s.

M's parents describe him as having "social issues" and few friends at school and being very defiant and oppositional with parents at home. He has had multiple individualized treatments and occupational therapy at school with unclear benefit.

On interview, initially M stated he was admitted for his "anger" which was triggered when he does not get his way. He reported a long history of anger and irritability, which he struggles to control. On initial interview, he and parents denied any history of physical, emotional or sexual trauma. A few days into the hospitalization, he stated that he becomes violent when "people bully him, especially about being Asian." He shared that at school people would make comments about his "slanty eyes," call him "ch★nk" or "Asian b★tch." He would verbally defend himself but also slammed one of his peers into a locker. He admitted that it is difficult to be the only Asian person in his family, and one of the few Asian kids at school, and this leads to him feeling angry and suicidal. He also shared that he sometimes thinks about his biological mother and wonders about his biological family and if they think of him. He stated he had never told this to any of his previous providers or his family as he did not think they could understand, but he felt comfortable sharing with us (the psychiatric trainee, the first author of this chapter and her attending psychiatrist) because we are both Asian.

By discharge, M's mood was more stable, and multiple family sessions were held to work on better communication. In one family meeting, M shared with his parents his experiences with racism at school, his struggles with his racial identity and with feeling alone. Medication management and individual therapy were recommended after discharge at an outpatient clinic, which would include exploring M's racial and cultural identity and his experiences with racism at school along with his family. His parents also agreed to seek support from a community of other families with Korean adoptive children.

M's experiences at school can be understood, in part, as a function of his falling victim to the "perpetual foreigner" stereotype. This stereotype ascribes American identity to white Americans alone, resulting in an othering of ethnic minorities and foreclosing the capacity for them to be acknowledged and embraced as American (even if they are raised by American parents). Consciously or not, this construct enables microaggressions that question national citizenship, questions English proficiency, and convey messages of exclusion and inferiority. In one study, awareness of the perpetual foreigner stereotype was a significant predictor of identity conflict, lower sense of belonging to the American culture, lower hope and decreased life satisfaction for AAPIs (Huynh et al., 2011).

AAPI transracial adoptees are underrepresented in psychiatric studies, and their experiences are not generally well understood in the United States. Small studies attempting to fill this knowledge gap have found discrepancies in cultural self-identification between South Korean adoptees, US-born and immigrated

Korean/Korean Americans (R. Lee et al., 2010), that Asian adoptees struggle with processing the surge of Anti-Asian hate during the COVID-19 pandemic due to feeling that they do not fully belong in either the AAPI community or white America, and that "colorblind" parenting contributes to children internalizing the lack of importance of racial and cultural identity (McDermott, 2021; Westerman, 2021).

The Khmer Rouge Psychosis

R is a 74-year-old Cambodian refugee with diabetes, long-standing schizophrenia and more recent major neurocognitive disorder who was presented involuntarily to an inpatient geriatric psychiatric unit for aggression toward the care staff at the nursing home where he resided, as well as a decline with respect to the activities of his daily life such as hygiene and self-care. On arrival, it became quickly evident that R had limited English-speaking abilities, and an in-person Cambodian translator was unavailable in the area, so his care was largely conducted through phone interpreter assistance. However, given the disorganization in R's thoughts, the interpreters were at times unable to fully decipher his (Cambodian language) responses to our questions, presenting communication difficulties during the first few weeks of his treatment.

Through the piecemeal information the treatment team gathered, a picture emerged of a man who, through unclear motivations, became gradually less trusting of his nursing home care staff and hesitant to take his daily medications, leading to a precipitous decline and relapse of his psychiatric symptoms.

During the first few weeks of his hospitalization, R adamantly refused medication and attacked staff whenever he was approached. In particular, he refused any care related to his hygiene and spent weeks without showering or changing out of the clothing he was presented with. In order to appear overheated and discomforted, he wore all-black items from head to toe, including multiple layers of black tops (shirts, sweatshirts) as well as three pairs of black pants. Every time the staff attempted to discuss his clothing, he simply repeated "all black, black black black . . . must wear black . . . black safe."

Due to concerns of his diabetes status and ongoing aggression toward others limiting his ability for recovery, the treatment team eventually solicited a second opinion and began involuntary medical and psychiatric treatment for his uncontrolled diabetes and psychosis. Initially, R continued to refuse medication, and restraints were required to administer nightly injections. Over time, R became more linear in his thought processes and conversations, with brighter affect and decreased agitation, and became more willing to actively engage with hospital staff and participate in his own hygiene care, though he continued to be very protective of his belongings and refused to switch his wardrobe despite its tattered condition.

After much effort, the team was finally able to contact a family member: R's daughter. She explained that R expressed paranoid delusions to her prior to admission, which she elaborated, developed from past political trauma. Specifically, R shared with his daughter that a white hospital staff had stolen his money as part of his persecutory paranoia (the nursing facility clarified that the staff member placed R's money along with his other belongings in a locked room for safekeeping, in accordance with facility policy, which had been explained to R). His daughter also shared that he said, "medicine make me die . . . medicine from Chinese I know . . . Chinese make Cambodia not good."

As treatment progressed into well over one month, R gradually shared his past with his providers. He began spontaneously telling stories regarding his journey to America, noting that he had many stories to share. He explained that he was sent to the United States after Phnom Penh fell, and felt that the white people he met had not been kind to him since his arrival and that he instead preferred the company of Black people and Asians. R mentioned that white people changed his name and that he preferred his old name, that he was assigned to work in a diamond mine, and that he was jailed years ago for unclear charges. He worried that there were still individuals that may want to harm him, despite acknowledging that many of them were incarcerated.

This case illustrated the complexity of AAPI mental health engagement on multiple fronts. Most practically, language barriers significantly impeded his care. Though the team was able to find a phone translator service, given the lack of physical proximity, the communication remained poor. It may have been possible to look to local communities for visitation support, or reach out to national refugee organizations to seek guidance. Communication with R was especially challenging in the context of his psychotic thought disorganization, demonstrating how a combination of cultural and psychiatric barriers requires highly attuned, individualized plans.

Additionally, R's entire treatment team was initially ignorant of his political trauma in the clinical formulation. This is partly a function, we argue, of a widespread neglect (including often erasure) of global political history from the perspective of marginalized populations. The ignorance of R's providers about the specifics of Cambodian political history, and the fact that seeking out this knowledge was not an immediate strategy for treatment, potentially led to the less-than-ideal treatment option of involuntary injections.

As Phnom Penh fell in 1975 after five years of civil war, the victory of the Khmer Rouge and Pol Pot's ideal of a societal revolution (backed, importantly, by a Chinese regime led by Mao Zedong) meant not only the purging of the former Cambodian culture but also of many people who participated in shaping its history, leading to the infamous "Killing Fields" (Chhun, n.d.). The new regime mandated clothing that consisted of black pajama-like shirts and pants (along with a red scarf). Although R had no access to the scarf, he was afraid of shedding his black clothing, and he wore a piece of black shirt as a scarf at all times, claiming "must wear black . . . black safe." Had R's providers been actively focused upon working to understand the unique political dimensions of their patient's trauma, they may have been better able to establish a safe environment, affirm the importance of his culturally driven delusions (despite their bizarre appearance) (Campbell et al., 2017; Stompe et al., 1999), and take more equal responsibility for comprehending the fuller context of R's journey.

The Devout Catatonic

D is a 37-year-old Korean American male with schizophrenia with catatonia who was presented involuntarily to an inpatient psychiatric unit for jumping in front of traffic, poor self-care and disorganized behavior. On arrival, D was mostly non-verbal, had significant speech latency and periods of mutism. Medications at the time were aripiprazole 30 mg by mouth every evening, lorazepam 1 mg by mouth twice daily and lorazepam 1 mg every 4 hours as needed. Parents reported inconsistent compliance because "some days he is fine and doesn't need them, some days he just needs to go to church"

Examinations and collateral information from parents suggested a decompensation of psychotic illness with catatonia. He recently exposed himself to children and also touched female staff on the unit to prove to others "I am not homosexual like they all think." He reported memories and recent experiences of voices talking about him, calling him derogatory names, and telling him to kill himself. He exhibited multiple catatonic symptoms including mutism, stupor and staring, echopraxis, and compulsive disrobing.

He has been hospitalized multiple times in lifetime, including more than 10 times in the few years prior to admission. Past medication trials included multiple antipsychotics including clozapine, as well as lithium, multiple benzodiazepines, diphenhydramine and trazodone. Trials of SSRIs were conducted for compulsive psychogenic polydipsia.

Born in South Korea, D and his parents emigrated to the United States when he was 16 years old. He is single and unemployed; he last held a job working in the financial aid office at age 20 in college. He lives with parents who are highly involved in his care and who are devout Christians. He had lived in group homes before, though had persecutory thoughts that others thought he was homosexual. In order to prove them wrong, he started touching females and was discharged.

His family history includes depression in both his mother and father, and schizophrenia in his older brother who lost his life to suicide one year prior.

Upon admission, due to mutism, stupor and immobility, D required assistance for all activities of daily living (ADLs) including eating, using the toilet and bathing. Lorazepam was titrated up to 20 mg a day divided into four doses with minimal improvement in catatonia. Multiple family meetings were held with parents (using a Korean language translator) but they consistently declined recommended medication trials including clozapine as well as electroconvulsive therapy (ECT). D's parents consistently voiced a preference to discontinue all medications, discharge their son and accompany him every day to church to utilize prayer and the comfort of home and community for healing. D's inpatient team consisted entirely of white providers who struggled to find compromise between their treatment plan based primarily on pharmacological and neuromodulation interventions, and the family's prioritization of spiritual intervention.

Due to D's inability to eat, drink, or function due to catatonia, as well as his parents' ongoing reluctance to consent to ECT, court-appointed guardianship was ultimately applied for and granted. D was started on thrice weekly ECT and improved, eventually requiring no physical or verbal prompts to eat, drink, perform ADLs. After 28 ECT treatments, D had full affect, improved speech fluency, no more compulsive incidents of disrobing or groping others. He was discharged on Lorazepam 4 mg orally three times a day and olanzapine 5 mg twice daily with outpatient maintenance ECT weekly.

Parents continued to visit daily, were very involved in his care and accepted a disposition plan to a group home with nursing near their home and church.

ECT is one of the most effective and rapid treatments for catatonia but is underutilized by many demographic groups. There are significant differences in ECT usage based on ethnicities. Among studies from Asia, the majority of patients and families reported they had not received adequate information about ECT and its risks and adverse effects, citing this as a main factor in declining it. However, a majority were satisfied after getting the treatment and maintained a positive attitude toward its use. When conflicts arise between providers and families, they are often related to differing views on "good care," where provider views are grounded on western biomedical care models and families' explanatory models of illness may be different and possibly inspired by a more holistic care approach. Strategies helpful in navigating conflicts include finding common values, investing in the provider-family relationship through cultural humility, and a willingness to navigate disagreement.

One helpful approach centers on a "best interest standard" based on community norms, compelling a focus on cultural values and social and familial contingencies (as well as the individual personalities) behind every patient's admission. In the case of D, given his family's emphasis on spiritual healing, alternative adjuncts to treatment intervention could have included by consulting the hospital's spiritual services or involving a trusted church leader in family meetings and treatment planning.

The White Therapist

L is an adolescent AAPI female who started seeing Dr. A, a white female therapist, in individual psychotherapy for depression, anxiety and academic struggles.

Much of the therapy focused on L's ambivalence and conflicting feelings toward her critical and sometimes cruel mother. L also brought up frustration at being in a predominately white school with white friends who seemed to pity or not understand her experience. She admitted that speaking to a white therapist felt uncomfortable at times and was encouraged by Dr. A to let her know when these feelings arise.

Six months into treatment, Dr. A unexpectedly got a request that L wanted to transfer to a therapist of color. L shares that she feels "a difference of understanding" and feels like a therapist of color would not judge, would understand the way she grew up, and she wouldn't have to explain herself. She was scared of being "othered" by Dr. A and would feel more welcomed with a person of color (POC). With Dr. A, L worried about painting her mom in a bad light, or for Dr. A to see her family as "weird."

Dr. A's immediate reaction was her own feelings of sadness/abandonment. She had felt warm, maternal feelings toward L and thought they were doing good work together. She initially assumed she must have said something insensitive or offensive and wondered, "am I racist? Am I a bad therapist?" Dr. A had read a number of books about race and wished she had these books on display in the office to demonstrate that she is doing her part to understand her patient's experience.

Even taking cultural differences into account, her mother often said many hurtful things to L. Dr. A had been validating L's occasional feelings of anger toward mom, affirming that these feelings were natural and "okay" even if her mom was doing her best. Dr. A wondered if this felt too threatening or if L assumed that Dr. A looked down on her mom/family for not following western norms. L did have a history of fleeing relationships when there was friction, which often occurred regardless of race. Dr. A wondered: to what degree are L's personal struggles a function of her concerns about being misunderstood based on her racial identity and experience, versus more universal, familial relationship patterns that are explicable or explorable without recourse to racial differences?

Regardless of the acceptance that Dr. A felt toward her patient, in a society premised upon (and continually perpetuating) racialized difference, how possible would it be for L to feel comfortable with Dr. A? Dr. A wondered if L could only be herself and feel safe without filtering/censoring around people of color. Similarly, maybe L would be better able to take in what was offered by a therapist of color. The same exact ideas that Dr. A expressed may be experienced much differently by L from a therapist of color, due to the effects of racialization upon the psyches of non-white subjects. In the context of a racist society, which upholds whiteness as powerful, as the ideal and norm, people of color (POC) evaluate themselves against a "white gaze," which cannot but permeate the therapeutic dyad. Given this reality, it is likely that Dr. A's discussion of L's mother will be interpreted by L as rejecting and judgmental even if not intended in that way.

Dr. A expressed a lot of curiosity and openness to talking about racial difference and how it manifests between the two of them, acknowledged that she has likely missed the point at times and expressed hope that L would let her know when it happened again in the future. At the same time, Dr. A referred L to a number of clinical and community resources involving providers of color as well as an AAPI affinity group. Ultimately, L did not pursue those referrals and opted to stay in treatment with Dr. A.

Dr. A embodied an important, but often overlooked, aspect of providing treatment and care to patients of color for white therapists. To more genuinely reach the psychic realities of these patients, it is integral for white providers to "put in the work" of reading and learning from materials outside of those conventionally associated with psychiatric training (which remains pervasively Eurocentric and conceptually limited), and to understand the political and historical underpinnings of racism, specific to patients' experiences. It is also important for white therapists to recognize, acknowledge and validate racial trauma, especially given that cognitively reframing, "analyzing" or "interpreting" these experiences in a colorblind way only serves to "gaslight" and further perpetuate racism and trauma for patients of color. It was integral for Dr. A to respect L's wishes and put in the effort to refer her to other sources of community and healing that she requested, rather than assuming that their dyadic therapy, that is, working through this together, was the best way forward. The reality is: white therapists *cannot fully empathize with* the feeling of otherness many POC feel, the burden of their existing under a white gaze, and the burden of perpetually being asked to explain "what it's like." When L requested healing that she felt she could only find from a therapist of color, Dr. A showed respect and granted her agency by working to help her find providers of color as well as other community supports, while still staying invested and engaged in the relationship.

The Group

Over the course of October 2020 through May 2022, a local AAPI affinity group was held monthly at a major university in the Eastern part of the United States. These groups were meant to address the community needs of lack of safe affinity spaces, stigma against discussing mental health, and creating AAPI community and solidarity. The mission was creating a safe community for Asian and Asian Americans of all ethnic backgrounds to explore the impact of their culture, heritage, race and identities on mental health and wellness. Participants included high school, undergraduate, graduate and postgraduate students with 5–10 participants a group. The following are some themes discussed in the groups.

Relationship to Black Lives Matter (BLM) Movement

There was a pervasive fear of "stepping on the toes" of BLM or "stealing their thunder" when giving voice to anti-Asian racism and the AAPI experience – some people wondered "is our pain valid?" The concept of "Oppression Olympics" was discussed, and the idea of marginalized groups being in a competition of who has it worse. Many AAPI experienced being told that we "don't have it as bad," leading to feelings of guilt for taking up space, and feelings that our suffering matters less. Groups were able to process the counterproductivity of this practice, to affirm and validate our suffering and to acknowledge that no one group's trauma takes away from any other's. The history of racial tension between AAPI and Black communities – anti-Black sentiments in AAPI communities and vice versa – was discussed frequently; this process included a collective learning about the 1990 LA riots and ways our communities have often been pitted against one another (toward white supremacist ends). We discussed how to move forward from those tensions and how to strive for solidarity and allyship.

COVID-19

Many participants experienced a hyperawareness of their AAPI ethnicity, including feelings of being "othered" and "looked at," during the pandemic and amidst the anti-Asian violence that came with it. Group members commonly expressed fear their own physical safety and for their families' due to anti-Asian attacks and anti-Asian racism, and expressed resentment about its limited news coverage, especially before the 2021 Atlanta spa shootings. Many underwent a painful reckoning of the conditionality of our acceptance in society and how quickly the discourse goes from "model minority" back to yellow peril.

Microaggressions

Participants reported an increase in racially and culturally based microaggressions in professional workplaces and in their personal lives (on the street, in grocery stores, etc.). Subsequent to these interactions, participants reported commonly telling themselves to not "make it a big deal" or "overreact," or even heard these phrases from others. Participants discussed this using the language of "gaslighting," realizing that in the face of microaggressions relating to their AAPI identity, they would often "gaslight themselves." The group processed how this phenomenon may represent a survival tactic and/or a manifestation of internalized racism. There was a universal experience of shame and guilt in not knowing the "right" way to respond in such situations, wondering "does our silence send the message of acceptance of unacceptable behavior?" Participations also asked: "Are we obligated to educate perpetrators of microaggressions?" A sense of healing came from a collective forgiveness that emerged for the times that we do not speak or respond. The group processed ways of thinking about how a more *conscious* passivity can represent AAPI advocacy by acknowledging and affirming the importance of our individual sense of safety in these moments.

Model Minority Myth (MMM)

The group discussed the difficulties of challenging deeply internalized traits, often expected of AAPI subjects, of being quiet, obedient, and not "rocking the boat." Participants shared expectations of humility and deferring to authority, and expressed difficulties in speaking up and advocating for themselves in situations with family, at work, or at school. We discussed how coming from countries and societies where political violence was pervasive has made our communities generally fearful of political activism. We struggled with how to reconcile these legacies with our need for empowerment and activism in the US context.

Many participants described feeling boxed up in stereotypes, only valued and rewarded for things related to the MMM, and continuing to feel that their unique experiences and voices were ignored. Participants insightfully identified that if the belief is that AAPI are "doing well," the impression will be that they should not be suffering from mental health issues. The group discussed how this conflict, which often plays out internally, may become compounded by a fear that white providers may not understand the complexity of AAPI experiences, risking inadequate care or even re-traumatization.

Finding Identity

Many participants voiced a struggle with defining their personal identities due to a lack of knowledge taught and shared about family history, family migration history, their home countries' histories, and Asian American history. This lack of sense of self is compounded by a lack of accurate representation, and oftentimes erasure, of AAPI voices, experiences, and contributions in school settings, media and politics. Participants described feeling lost and unseen, and many discussed this lack or confusion of self-identity in relation to internalized racism and self-hatred. Many participants described being called "twinkie" or "banana" (yellow on the outside and white on the inside), embodying a proximity to whiteness that will nevertheless never be completely accepted. The group often marveled at the seemingly infinite variations of experiences within the AAPI community that are nonetheless often collapsed, erased or kept invisible at the expense of AAPI sense of self.

Culture Clash

The group discussed value clashes between "western" and "Eastern" worlds, and how AAPI are left to negotiate tensions between American values of autonomy, individual freedom, and "pursuing dreams" and more collectivist values of social harmony, filial piety, emotional restraint and humility. We questioned how to set boundaries and limits when the definition of appropriate boundaries varies between these worlds. Many participants expressed longing for the aspects of a collectivist social ethos that include emotional warmth, social generosity and large family ties, aspects that can be difficult to replicate in the United States where nuclear families and individual partners are seen as "normal" family units. We also processed thinking about "tiger parenting" as a trauma response and survival mechanism given many Asian countries' politically violent histories (and meritocratic histories of rigorous school examinations, as well), rather than an inherent or essentialistic cultural trait.

Communication with Family

Many participants conceptualized care in AAPI communities in terms of "love languages," identifying "acts of service" and questions about physical wellness ("did you eat yet?") as characteristic of AAPI family care, rather than the open verbal communication characteristic of western affection.

Filial piety, a duty and obligation to family members, was felt to be a core value of participants' upbringings. Given that voicing disagreement with parents often was seen as disrespectful, we processed how to honor cultural values while finding and maintaining our individual voices. It became helpful to bring the political dimension into group discussion. We processed how traumas and feelings may be difficult for AAPI family members to share because of family histories wherein family members had neither the luxury nor access to channels for processing trauma or identifying issues of mental health. It became healing for group participants to collectively acknowledge and grieve for legacies of family trauma, and to feel admiration for their strength together.

Conclusion

We affirm that mental health service providers can continue to play an important role in advancing recent efforts to identify and address the psychic experiences of AAPI subjects, especially within a social context of continued racial oppression (Doàn et al., 2019; Hall and Yee, 2012; Kanaya et al., 2022). As we hope to have demonstrated through these many case examples, and through their complexity, the global political dimensions of AAPI trauma necessitate treatment strategies that are attentively as complex and contingent as AAPI experiences themselves. Believing that this begins[9] first and foremost with sustained, mindful and informed self-reflection, we encourage providers to seek resources and texts about colonial oppression, migration history and AAPI identity beyond those conventionally offered by psychiatric and psychotherapeutic education. This

TABLE 9.1 Guiding Questions and Strategies for Better AAPI Care

Promoting racial healing	Questions to help address disparities in AAPI mental healthcare	Questions to help increase AAPI representation
Naming, acknowledging and validating experiences including discrimination, microaggressions, examples of systemic racism and oppression, and racial socialization	How does my work environment foster understanding and acceptance of cultural differences?	Do program leaders value ethnoracial equity and model a shared commitment to dismantling anti-AAPI racism?
Preparation for racism and racist experiences	How do patient materials accurately represent the histories, experiences and contributions of various cultural groups?	In teaching and learning, is the curriculum being used to challenge racial inequity and strive for cultural humility?
Promoting social support, empowering individuals, families and communities, encouraging sense of agency	How do my assessment methods reflect the diversity of patient experiences, languages and cultures?	Do AAPI students, staff and faculty feel valued, safe and respected?
Promoting cultural, racial and ethnic pride	How does my work tap into patients' families, languages and cultures as foundations for healing?	Are AAPI trainees, students and faculty well-being being seen as a priority and are there supportive spaces and mentorship that exist for AAPI in the program?
Facilitating cross-racial relationships, coalitions and solidarity	Beyond just fostering coping skills, what are providers and institutions doing to make racial healing and coping safe, normative, accessible and health promoting?	
Giving permission to pause and rest		
Healing beyond just coping including encouraging development of efficacy and agency, collective and authentic spaces, creativity and dreaming, and self-determination		

begins a process that can extend toward validation, acknowledgment and cultural humility to promote healing. To aid the process of mindful reflection and treatment, and to suggest guiding questions and strategies for providing better AAPI care, we provide Table 9.1 for practical use by treatment providers in their work with AAPI patients and we encourage practitioners to consult it often.

References

AAPI Data Quick Stats. (2022, April 1). *Poverty by Detailed Group (National)*. https://aapidata.com/.

Allen, K.A., Arslan, G., Craig, H., Arefi, S., Yaghoobzadeh, A. & Sharif Nia, H. (2021). The psychometric evaluation of the sense of belonging instrument (SOBI) with Iranian older adults. *BMC Geriatrics* 21(1).

Augsberger, A., Yeung, A., Dougher, M. & Hahm, H.C. (2015). Factors influencing the underutilization of mental health services among Asian American women with a history of depression and suicide. *BMC Health Services Research* 15(1).

Berry, J.W. (1997). Immigration, acculturation, and adaptation. *Applied Psychology: An International Review* 46(1):5–34.

Bloom, B. & Black, L. (2016). *Health of Non-Hispanic Asian Adults: United States, 2010–2014*. NCHS Data Brief 247. https://www.cdc.gov/nchs/data/databriefs/db247.pdf.

Campbell, M.M., Sibeko, G., Mall, S., Baldinger, A., Nagdee, M., Susser, E. & Stein, D.J. (2017). The content of delusions in a sample of South African Xhosa people with schizophrenia. *BMC Psychiatry* 17(1).

Carter, R.T. (2016). Racism and psychological and emotional injury: recognizing and assessing race-based traumatic stress. *The Counseling Psychologist* 35(1):13–105.

Chang, J., Natsuaki, M.N. & Chen, C.N. (2013). The importance of family factors and generation status: mental health service use among Latino and Asian Americans. *Cultural Diversity & Ethnic Minority Psychology* 19(3):236–247.

Chen, J.A., Hung, G.C.L., Parkin, S., Fava, M. & Yeung, A.S. (2015). Illness beliefs of Chinese American immigrants with major depressive disorder in a primary care setting. *Asian Journal of Psychiatry* 13:16–22.

Cheryan, S. & Monin, B. (2005). 'Where are you really from?': Asian Americans and identity denial. *Journal of Personality and Social Psychology* 89(5):717–730.

Chhun, S. (n.d.). *RSR*. Retrieved June 30, 2022, from https://redscarfrevolution.com/#red-scarf-revolution.

Choi, A.Y., Israel, T. & Maeda, H. (2017). Development and evaluation of the internalized racism in Asian Americans scale (IRAAS). *Journal of Counseling Psychology* 64(1):52–64.

Doàn, L.N., Takata, Y., Sakuma, K.L.K. & Irvin, V.L. (2019). Trends in clinical research including Asian American, Native Hawaiian, and Pacific Islander participants funded by the US National Institutes of Health, 1992 to 2018. *JAMA Network Open* 2(7).

Gee, G.C., Ro, A., Shariff-Marco, S. & Chae, D. (2009). Racial discrimination and health among Asian Americans: evidence, assessment, and directions for future research. *Epidemiologic Reviews* 31(1):130–151.

Gündemir, S., Carton, A.M. & Homan, A.C. (2019). The impact of organizational performance on the emergence of Asian American leaders. *The Journal of Applied Psychology* 104(1):107–122.

Hall, G.C.N. & Yee, A.H. (2012). U.S. mental health policy: addressing the neglect of Asian Americans. *Asian American Journal of Psychology* 3(3):181.

Hamilton, G.G. (1990). *Zhongguo Shehui Yu Jingji (The Economy and Society of China)* (W. Chang, J. Chen & B. Zhai, Eds.). Taipei: Lianjing.

Huynh, Q.L., Devos, T. & Smalarz, L. (2011). Perpetual foreigner in one's own land: potential implications for identity and psychological adjustment. *Journal of Social and Clinical Psychology* 30(2):133.

Juang, L.P., Syed, M. & Takagi, M. (2007). Intergenerational discrepancies of parental control among Chinese American families: links to family conflict and adolescent depressive symptoms. *Journal of Adolescence* 30(6):965–975.

Kanaya, A.M., Hsing, A.W., Panapasa, S.V., Kandula, N.R., Araneta, M.R.G., Shimbo, D., Wang, P., Gomez, S.L., Lee, J., Venkat Narayan, K.M., Mala Mau, M.K.L., Bose, S., Daviglus, M.L., Hu, F.B., Islam, N., Jackson, C.L., Kataoka-Yahiro, M., Kauwe, J.S.K., Liu, S. . . . Hong, Y. (2022). Knowledge gaps, challenges, and opportunities in health and prevention research for Asian Americans, Native Hawaiians, and Pacific Islanders: a report from the 2021 national institutes of health workshop. *Annals of Internal Medicine* 175(4):574–589.

Kiang, L., Tseng, V. & Yip, T. (2016). Placing Asian American child development within historical context. *Child Development* 87(4):995–1013.

Kim, G., Worley, C.B., Allen, R.S., Vinson, L., Crowther, M.R., Parmelee, P. & Chiriboga, D.A. (2011). Vulnerability of older Latino and Asian immigrants with limited English proficiency. *Journal of the American Geriatrics Society* 59(7):1246–1252.

Kisch, J., Leino, E.V. & Silverman, M.M. (2005). Aspects of suicidal behavior, depression, and treatment in college students: results from the Spring 2000 national college health assessment survey. *Suicide & Life-Threatening Behavior* 35(1):3–13.

Kohut, H. (1977). *The Restoration of the Self.* New York: International Universities Press.

Kwok, J. (2013). Factors that influence the diagnoses of Asian Americans in mental health: an exploration. *Perspectives in Psychiatric Care* 49(4):288–292.

Lee, R.M., Yun, A.B., Yoo, H.C. & Nelson, K.P. (2010). Comparing the ethnic identity and well-being of adopted Korean Americans with immigrant/U.S.-Born Korean Americans and Korean international students. *Adoption Quarterly* 13(1):2.

Lee, S., Juon, H.S., Martinez, G., Hsu, C.E., Robinson, E.S., Bawa, J. & Ma, G.X. (2009). Model minority at risk: expressed needs of mental health by Asian American young adults. *Journal of Community Health* 34(2):144–152.

Levin, B. (2021). *Report to the Nation: Anti-Asian Prejudice & Hate Crime.* San Bernadino: Center for the Study of Hate & Extremism, California State University.

Lowe, L. (1991). Heterogeneity, hybridity, multiplicity: marking Asian American differences. *Diaspora: A Journal of Transnational Studies* 1:24–44.

McDermott, F. (2021). *Understanding the Lived Experiences of Asian American Transracial Adoptees in College.* Honors Program Theses 452. Cedar Falls: University of Northern Iowa. https://scholarworks.uni.edu/hpt/452.

Naito, T., Chin, J., Kim, T.U., Veera, S., Jeannette, M. & Lomiguen, C.M. (2020). Further reduction in help-seeking behaviors amidst additional barriers to mental health treatment in Asian populations: a contemporary review. *Cureus* 12(11).

O'Keefe, V.M., Wingate, L.R., Cole, A.B., Hollingsworth, D.W. & Tucker, R.P. (2015). Seemingly harmless racial communications are not so harmless: racial microaggressions lead to suicidal ideation by way of depression symptoms. *Suicide & Life-Threatening Behavior* 45(5):567–576.

Park, J.E., Cho, S.J., Lee, J.Y., Sohn, J.H., Seong, S.J., Suk, H.W. & Cho, M.J. (2015). Impact of stigma on use of mental health services by elderly Koreans. *Social Psychiatry and Psychiatric Epidemiology* 50(5):757–766.

Pyke, K.D. (2010). What is internalized racial oppression and why don't we study it? Acknowledging racism's hidden injuries. *Sociological Perspectives* 53(4):551–572.

Sentell, T., Shumway, M. & Snowden, L. (2007). Access to mental health treatment by English language proficiency and race/ethnicity. *Journal of General Internal Medicine* 22(Supplement 2):289–293.

Spoer, B.R., Juul, F., Hsieh, P.Y., Thorpe, L.E., Gourevitch, M.N. & Yi, S. (2021). Neighborhood-level Asian American populations, social determinants of health, and health outcomes in 500 US cities. *Ethnicity & Disease* 31(3):433–444.

Stompe, T., Friedman, A., Ortwein, G., Strobl, R., Chaudhry, H.R., Najam, N. & Chaudhry, M.R. (1999). Comparison of delusions among schizophrenics in Austria and in Pakistan. *Psychopathology* 32(5):225–234.

Tikhonov, A.A., Espinosa, A., Huynh, Q.L. & Anglin, D.M. (2019). Bicultural identity harmony and American identity are associated with positive mental health in U.S. racial and ethnic minority immigrants. *Cultural Diversity & Ethnic Minority Psychology* 25(4):494–504.

Tran, A.G.T.T. (2021). In or out of the game? Counter-stereotype paradoxes and Asian-identified student-athlete mental health. *Cultural Diversity & Ethnic Minority Psychology* 27(4):579–592.

United States Census Bureau. (2021, April 19). *A More Diverse Nation*. Webpage. www.census.gov/library/visualizations/2021/comm/a-more-diverse-nation.html.

Westerman, A. (2021, March 27). *'Am I Asian Enough?' Adoptees Struggle to Make Sense of Spike in Anti-Asian Violence*. National Public Radio. www.npr.org/2021/03/27/981269559/am-i-asian-enough-adoptees-struggle-to-make-sense-of-spike-in-anti-asian-violence.

Yang, L.H., Phelan, J.C. & Link, B.G. (2008). Stigma and beliefs of efficacy towards traditional Chinese medicine and western psychiatric treatment among Chinese-Americans. *Cultural Diversity & Ethnic Minority Psychology* 14(1):10–18.

Yi, J. & Todd, N.R. (2021). Internalized model minority myth among Asian Americans: links to anti-Black attitudes and opposition to affirmative action. *Cultural Diversity & Ethnic Minority Psychology* 27(4):569–578.

Young, J.L., Kim, H.D. & Golojuch, L. (2021). 'Race was something we didn't talk about': racial socialization in Asian American families. *Family Relations* 70(4):1027.

INDEX

Note: Page numbers in **bold** indicate a table and page numbers in *italics* indicate a figure on the corresponding page.